SQL Database for Beginners

SQL Database for Beginners

SQL Database for Beginners

Martin Holzke
with Tom Stachowitz

LearnToProgram, Inc.
Vernon, Connecticut

LearnToProgram.tv, Incorporated
27 Hartford Turnpike Suite 206
Vernon, CT 06066
contact@learntoprogram.tv
(860) 840-7090

ISBN-13: 978-0-9904020-7-7
ISBN-10: 099040207X

Mark Lassoff, Publisher
Martin Holzke, Author
Tom Stachowitz, Technical Writer
Kevin Hernandez, VP/ Production
Alison Downs, Copy Editor
Alexandria O'Brien, Book Layout

Dedication:

To all our students. Whether you're trying to further your career, broaden your horizons, or just learn a new skill for fun—this book is for you.

Courses Available from LearnToProgram, Inc.

3D Fundamentals with iOS
Advanced Javascript Development
AJAX Development
Android Development for Beginners
Become a Certified Web Developer (Level 1)
Become a Certified Web Developer (Level 2)
C++ for Beginners
C Programming for Beginners
Creating a PHP Login Script
Creating an MP3 Player with HTML5
CSS Development (with CSS3!)
Design for Coders
Game Development with Python
Game Development Fundamentals with Python
GitHub Fundamentals
HTML and CSS for Beginners (with HTML5)
HTML5 Mobile App Development with PhoneGap
Introduction to Web Development
iOS Development Code Camp
iOS Development for Beginners Featuring iOS6/7
Java Programming for Beginners
Javascript for Beginners
Joomla for Beginners
jQuery for Beginners
Mobile Game Development with iOS
Node.js for Beginners
Objective C for Beginners
Photoshop for Coders
PHP & MySQL for Beginners
Programming for Absolute Beginners
Project Management with Microsoft Project
Python for Beginners
Ruby on Rails for Beginners
SQL Database for Beginners
Swift Language Fundamentals
User Experience Design

Books from LearnToProgram, Inc.

Create Your Own MP3 Player with HTML5
CSS Development (with CSS3!)
HTML and CSS for Beginners
Javascript for Beginners
PHP and MySQL for Beginners
Programming for Absolute Beginners
Python for Beginners
Swift Fundamentals: The Language of iOS Development

TABLE OF CONTENTS

About the Author:

Martin Holzke

While studying Physics at Philips in the late 1980s, Martin Holzke accepted an offer to learn to program, and the rest was history! Once graduated, Martin started his own business developing applications and systems as a freelance IT Consultant, which he still does to this day. His journey continues to take him through a vast array of technologies, methodologies and languages like OOP, UML, C++, .NET, ADF, PHP, Zend, Oracle, and SQL to name just a few.

About the Technical Writer:

Tom Stachowitz

Tom Stachowitz was born in Florida but spent his childhood in northwestern Connecticut. He had always been interested in writing and technology but didn't begin programming until high school. Tom studied Journalism at the University of Indianapolis' overseas campus in Athens, Greece and, after living in England, Greece, New York, Arizona, Colorado, Washington DC, and Virginia and then serving in the Army, he returned to Connecticut to focus on writing and technology.

In his spare time Tom enjoys hiking, games, and spending time with his beautiful wife, Krista, and their two cats.

CHAPTER 1

RELATIONAL DATABASES

CHAPTER OBJECTIVES

- You will understand what databases are, as well as their structural elements.
- You will understand the fundamental structure of a table.
- You will learn the data types and constraints that are applied to the fields of a table and when to apply them.
- You will learn about primary and foreign keys, relationships, and referential integrity.
- You will use MySQL Workbench to create an entity-relationship diagram and the corresponding database.

1.1 WHAT ARE DATABASES?

A **database** is an organized collection of data stored in a safe and secure location. A database can be physically located on the hard drive of your home computer, the RAID (redundant array of independent drives) on your office server, or on the multiple servers of data centers where users or clients from anywhere in the world can access it.

A **database management system (DBMS)** is a set of software tools that lets authorized administrators and users define, manipulate, retrieve, and manage the data in a database. It is the DBMS itself that adds, modifies, and deletes not only the data in the database but also the data formats, the row and column names, the table structures and everything else about the database. It also defines and maintains the rules that validate the integrity of the database's data. If it were not for the DBMS, then the authorized administrators and users would have to code the routines the handle all the tasks we just mentioned that the DBMS customarily carries out.

> **database**

> **DBMS**
> Database
> Management
> System

There are basically three types of databases:

> **Relational:** This is the most widely used type of database. Data is organized as logically independent tables and relationships among tables are shown through shared data.

➤ **Hierarchical:** In this rare type of database, data is organized into a tree-like structure and governed using parent/child relationships. Two widely used examples are IMS (Information Management System) by IBM and the Windows Registry by Microsoft.

➤ **Object-Oriented:** In this type of database, data is organized along the lines of object-oriented programming (OOP) concepts. There was a time when industry observers predicted that object-oriented databases would replace relational databases. That never happened. Instead, object-oriented features have been slowly added to relational databases. Still, object-oriented databases are popular with artificial intelligence and CAD/CAM applications, as well as hospital patient care tracking systems.

In this introductory book on SQL, we will discuss only relational databases or, more specifically, relational database management systems, also known as RDBMS or DBMS.

In a DBMS, data is organized into **tables** and within the tables data is organized into **rows** and **columns**.

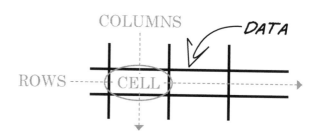

Here is a diagram of a table called *person*.

id	lastname	firstname	dob
1	Baker	Susan	
2	Briggs	Joe	1975-02-07
3	James	Jenny	11-1970-11-03

Diagram 1.1: The table *persons* in a relational DBMS.

This table has three rows and four columns of data. (The first row gives the names of the columns as a pictorial aid and is not part of the table.) Two important things about tables are:

1. Each row of data must be unique. For example, in our table *person*, there cannot be two records of Joe Briggs with identical data, as shown in the following diagram.

id	lastname	firstname	dob
1	Baker	Susan	
2	Briggs	Joe	1975-02-07
2	Briggs	Joe	1975-02-07
3	James	Jenny	11-1970-11-03

Diagram 1.2: This table is invalid because a set of row values should be unique.

You could have two Joe Briggs who have the same date of birth, but they should be assigned different *id* values as shown in the following diagram.

id	lastname	firstname	dob
1	Baker	Susan	
2	Briggs	Joe	1975-02-07
4	Briggs	Joe	1975-02-07
3	James	Jenny	11-1970-11-03

Diagram 1.3: This is a valid table. There are no duplicate rows.

2. Column names must be unique. Again, for example, in our table *person,* you cannot have two columns named *firstname,* whether either column holds data or not, as shown in the following diagram.

Id	lastname	firstname	firstname	dob
1	Baker	Susan		
2	Briggs	Joe		1975-02-07
3	James	Jenny		11-1970-11-03

Diagram 1.4: This is an invalid table *Persons*. No two columns should have the same name.

While tables are the most common structural element in a DBMS, they are not the only ones. There are also indexes, views, schemas, catalogs, clusters, and others.

In all the chapters of this book, our main example will be a very simple Project Monitoring System we will call *projmon.*

These are the real-life specifics of our Project Monitoring System, *projmon*.

1. A company has several employees, who we refer to as persons.
2. A company has several ongoing projects.
3. A person can be assigned to several projects.
4. When a person is assigned to a project, they are also assigned a role in that project.
5. A company has various means of contacting its employees, such as a mobile phone, an email address, an instant messenger username, a postal address, and so on.
6. A person can have several means of being contacted

In designing database applications for real-life situations, a very popular and effective tool used is the **entity-relationship diagram, ERD**. This is a representation of the overall logical plan of a database. As its name suggests, this diagram models entities and their relationships to each other. The term for the logical plan of a database is **schema**. The schema is the database structure described in a formal language and is made up of entities, attributes, and relationships.

> ## ERD
> Entity-Relationship Diagram

> ## Schema

> ## MySQL Workbench

The following is an ERD of our simplified Project Monitoring System, *projmon*. This diagram was generated by a software tool called **MySQL Workbench,** which you will work with as you go through the chapters of this book.

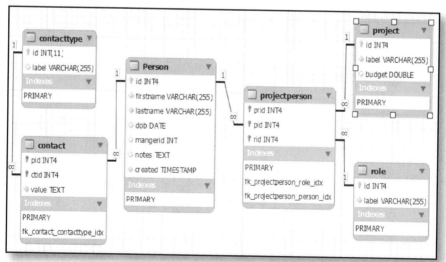

Figure 1-1: E-R Diagram for a Project Monitoring System

NOTE: The data type INT(11) is the same as INT4.

Each entity is represented by a box with the name of the entity listed at the top of the box. The attributes of an entity are listed within the white portion of the box. The relationships between entities are represented by lines between the boxes.

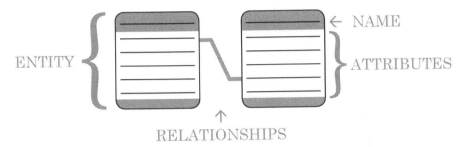

Now, let's define and clarify those terms entity, attributes, and relationships and use examples from *projmon* to illustrate those terms.

An **entity** is a real-life object or concept. It can be a person, a customer, an object, an invoice, a job description, or a report. We can store data about entities - that data is known as attributes. The entities in our *projmon* are *person, role, project,* and *contact type.*

What about *contact* and *projectperson?* Well, they are not really entities because there are no equivalent real world entities for *contact* and *projectperson.* Instead, *contact* and *projectperson* are **composite entities**. Their purpose is to represent a **many-to-many** relationship between two other entities.

The data that we store for an entity are its features or attributes, which uniquely describe and identify that entity. The attributes of an entity are listed top-to-bottom within the rectangle, as shown in figure 1-2.

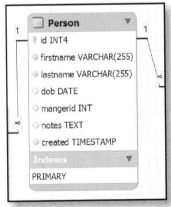

Figure 1-2: The rectangle for the entity *person.*

As we can see from the rectangle for the *person* entity, its attributes are *id, firstname, lastname, dob, managerid, notes,* and *created.*

Attributes are assigned a **data type**. The data types follow the attribute name. For example, INT4 or INT11, VARCHAR(255), DATE, INT, TEXT and TIMESTAMP.

Attributes are also assigned one or more **constraints**. This is a rule or combined set of rules imposed on the possible values of an attribute. These constraints are represented by icons which come before the attribute name, such as these:

data type

constraints

Now, take a look at the portion of our *projmon* ERD which shows the three tables: *contacttype, contact,* and *person.*

Focus on the line joining *person* and *contact.*

This line represents the relationship between those two entities. The end of the line, at the *person* entity, has the number 1 just above it, while the other end, at the *contact* entity, has the symbol infinity ∞ just above it.

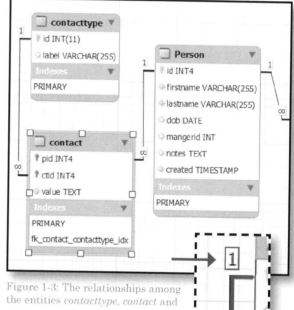

Figure 1-3: The relationships among the entities *contacttype, contact* and *person.*

This means that a **one-to-many** relationship exists between *person* and *contact.* Stated in practical terms, this type of relationship means that one person can be contacted many ways—through their mobile phone, email, postal address, IM account and so on.

You can also note that ends of both lines are positioned exactly on an attribute. On the *person* entity, the

one-to-many

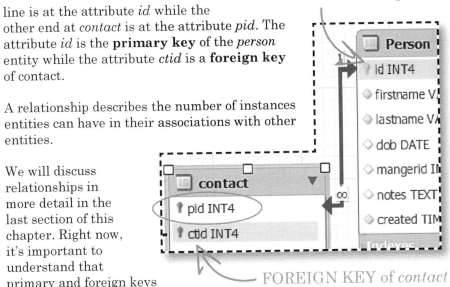

PRIMARY KEY of *person*

line is at the attribute *id* while the other end at *contact* is at the attribute *pid*. The attribute *id* is the **primary key** of the *person* entity while the attribute *ctid* is a **foreign key** of contact.

A relationship describes the number of instances entities can have in their associations with other entities.

We will discuss relationships in more detail in the last section of this chapter. Right now, it's important to understand that primary and foreign keys are the structural elements that a DBMS uses to implement relationships.

FOREIGN KEY of *contact*

Now that we have explained how to understand and interpret entity-relationship diagrams, we will introduce a powerful and very popular tool used by database developers: MySQL Workbench. MySQL Workbench is a visual database design tool that integrates SQL database development, administration, design, creation, and maintenance into a single integrated development environment for the MySQL database system.

Using MySQL Workbench, database application developers can complete all the necessary details of the entity-relationship diagrams and then let Workbench convert this ERD into an actual database system ready to accept live data.

However, for beginners we will not use this feature. Instead, we will construct the database using the MySQL data definition language in order to practice the commands and syntax required in all database tasks.

In the next chapter we will not only install MySQL Workbench but also use it to create our sample database *projmon* and enter test data into *projmon*. We will be using *projmon* and its test data in all the succeeding chapters of this introductory book on SQL.

1. What is the set of software tools called that lets authorized administrators and users define, manipulate, retrieve, and manage the data in a database?
   a. Entity relationship system.
   b. Database application system.
   c. Database management system.
   d. Project monitoring system.

2. What are the structures used in organizing the data in a table of a relational database?
   a. Primary and foreign attributes.
   b. Entities and relationships.
   c. Clusters and views.
   d. Indexes and foreign keys.

3. What are the three structural elements of an entity-relationship diagram?
   a. data, entities, keys.
   b. objects, boxes, lines.
   c. entities, attributes, relationships.
   d. constraints, rows, columns.

4. Which of the following is the most numerous object in a database?
   a. Entities.
   b. Tables.
   c. Relationships.
   d. Views.

LAB ACTIVITY

Consider the scenario of a simple library Borrowers and Books System. The real-life scenario for this system is:

1. The library has thousands of books and hundreds of borrowers.
2. The library is open every day of the year, except for Christmas and New Year's Day.
3. A borrower can borrow a maximum of three books at any one time.
4. A book has to be returned seven days after it was taken out.
5. A book has a title and a unique ISBN.
6. A book can have more than one author.
7. An author can write more than one book.

As a budding database application developer, you are tasked with conceptualizing an entity-relationship diagram for the system prior to actually creating a database application to handle this simple Borrowers and Books System.

For now, you will just have to use pen and paper to accomplish this.

After you have completed your initial ERD, please answer the following questions:

1. What would be the main or true entities in your ERD?
2. What table structure would let you know what books a borrower currently has?
3. How would you know who is (are) the author(s) of a book?
4. What attributes would you need to monitor overdue books?
5. What entity would you use to find out what books are with a borrower?
6. What entity would you use to find out what books an author has authored or co-authored?

LAB SOLUTION

1. *borrowers, books, authors*
2. A composite entity, named *booksborrowed* whose attributes are a *book's* primary key and a *borrower's* primary key.
3. We have to create another composite entity, named *booksauthors* whose attributes are a *book's* primary key and an *author's* primary key.
4. In the *booksborrowed* composite entity, you would include the following date attributes: *dateborrowed, datedue, datereturned.*
5. *booksborrowed.*
6. *booksauthor.*

1.2 SETTING UP THE DEVELOPMENT ENVIRONMENT

Before we continue, there are two software packages that we need to install:

→ WampServer
(www.wampserver.com/en)

→ MySQL Workbench
(http://dev.mysql.com/downloads/workbench/)

WampServer is actually a package of software, namely Apache, PHP, MySQL and phpMyAdmin.

> **TIP:** WAMP is an acronym for **W**indows (OS), **A**pache (web-server), **M**ySQL (database), **P**HP (language). **M**ampServer is a version of Wampserver for the **M**ac operating system, while **L**ampServer is a version for **L**inux.

Instead of installing just the MySQL database software, we install WampServer because it already includes the MySQL software and phpMyAdmin, which is software similar to MySQL Workbench. You are encouraged to study phpMyAdmin's features and capabilities and many developers actually prefer it over Workbench.

> **TIP:** Note that phpMyAdmin is not stand-alone client software like Workbench, but a web-based software.

We have to install WampServer first and then MySQL Workbench. When we install MYSQL Workbench, it will automatically search for any existing MySQL databases and configure itself accordingly. By installing WampServer first and then Workbench afterwards, we save ourselves the effort of carrying out some Workbench configuration tasks.

For Mac users, a version of WampServer for the Mac, MampServer, can be downloaded from http://www.mamp.info/en/. For Linux users, it is recommended to use instead Xampp which includes Perl. Versions of Xampp for Windows, Mac and Linux can be downloaded from https:// www.apachefriends.org/download.html.

TIP: If you have gone through our introductory course on PHP programming, you should already have WampServer installed.

This is the opening screen of www.wampserver.com/en.

Figure 1-4: WampServer's opening installation screen.

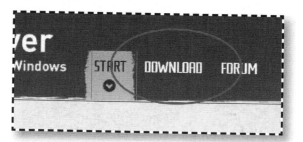

Clicking on "Download" in the upper portion of the screen will bring you to the following screen.

Figure 1-5: WampServer provides 32-bit and 64-bit versions for Windows.

Once you select either the 32-bit or 64-bit version of WampServer, you will see this screen (which is for the 64-bit version).

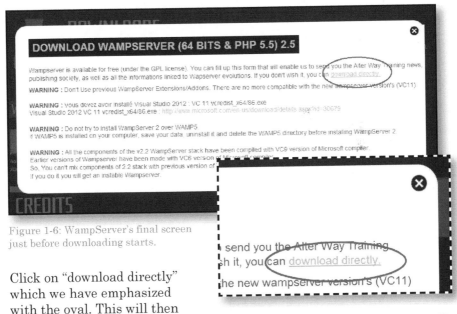

Figure 1-6: WampServer's final screen just before downloading starts.

Click on "download directly" which we have emphasized with the oval. This will then bring you to a screen similar to the following screenshot. Your screen will have some differences, but the screen should show a message that the download will start in a few seconds or has already begun.

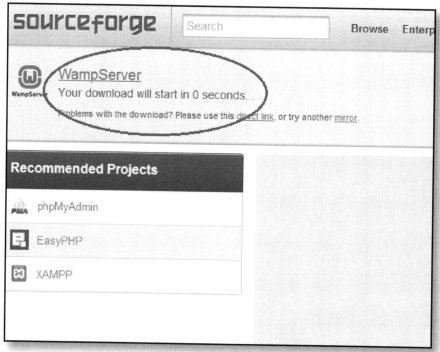

Figure 1-7: WampServer's notification that it is downloading.

You will end up with an .exe file of about 30mb with a name similar to the following:

```
wampserver2.2e-php5.3.13-httpd2.2.22-mysql5.5.24-x64.exe
```

The filename you get may have numbers greater in value than in our example, indicating a more recent version. Just run this file and it will install WampServer.

Once WampServer is installed, it should appear as one of the choices in your Start Menu as shown in the following screenshot.

START

Figure 1-8: WampServer's icon in the Windows Start Menu.

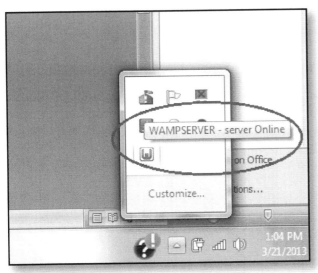

When you click on "start WampServer," it will appear as one of the icons (a fancy "W" in green) in Window's hidden icon tray as shown in this screenshot.

Clicking on the WampServer icon will bring up WampServer's main menu as shown in this screenshot.

Figure 1-9: WampServer's icon in the hidden icon tray.

You can clearly see the "phpMyAdmin" and "MySQL" menu options. The last menu choice, "Put Offline," indicates that WampServer is up and running. If this were not the case, then the last menu choice would read "Put Online."

To further test that WampServer is online, start your browser and in the URL window, type "localhost". You should get the following screenshot which indicates that WampServer is running properly.

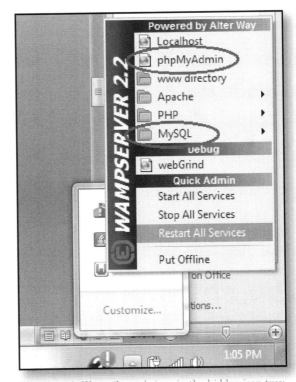

Figure 1-10: WampServer's icon in the hidden icon tray.

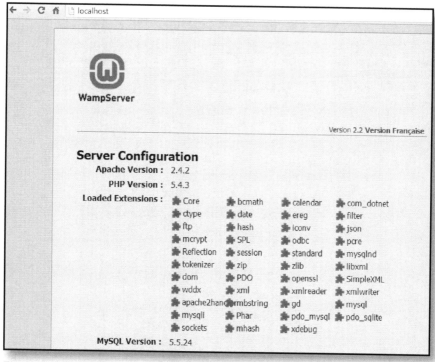

Figure 1-11: WampServer's opening page.

If you do not see this screen when you navigate to localhost then something has gone wrong with your WampServer installation. One common problem is incorrect or missing .DLL files in your Windows installation. There are solutions to many common issues on the WampServer website in their forum section, located at http://forum.wampserver.com.

Now, let's download and install MySQL Workbench. This is the opening page of its download site.

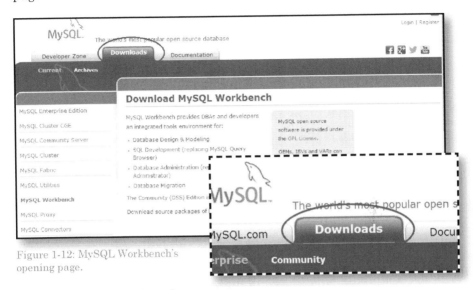

Figure 1-12: MySQL Workbench's opening page.

Clicking "Downloads" at the top of the screen will bring you the following page.

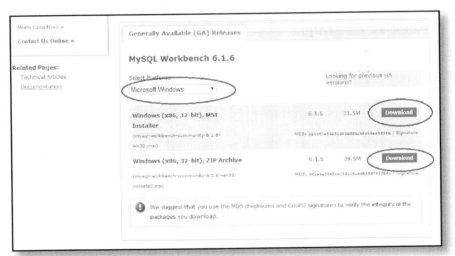

Figure 1-13: MySQL Workbench's download page.

We suggest downloading the MSI version, whose filename is shown below, as it is smaller (31.5mb) and requires just a click to install, while downloading the Zip archive (39.5mb) will require a utility to decompress it and the creation of several levels of folders where it will be installed.

The filenames for both 32-bit and 64-bit versions are:

```
mysql-workbench-community-6.1.6-win32.msi
mysql-workbench-community-6.1.6-win64.msi
```

Once MySQL Workbench is installed, it will appear in the Windows Start Menu as shown in this screenshot. CE means community edition, as there are commercial versions of Workbench available for purchase.

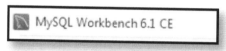

Figure 1-14: Workbench's Start Menu option.

Clicking on Workbench's Start Menu option will bring up its opening screen.

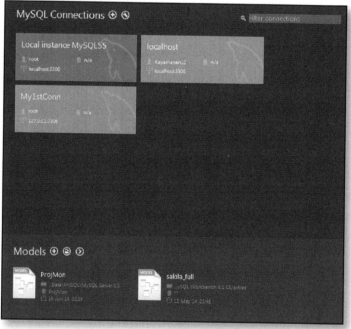

Figure 1-15: MySQL Workbench's Opening Screen.

In this opening screen of MySQL Workbench, there are three grey rectangles, representing connections, in the upper portion of the screen, labelled:

Your opening screen may have one or only two grey boxes representing either or both of the first two connections listed above.

A **connection** is the means by which a database server and its client software communicate with each other. The client software uses the connection to send commands to and receive replies from the server. The client software and the server are in physically separate locations.

connection

In our situation, both the client software (MySQL Workbench), and the database server (WampServer on localhost) with the MySQL DBMS software, reside in the same computer. But we still need a connection between the client software and server, even though they are physically in the same computer.

We will now go through the steps of creating a connection which we will name "My1stConn."

First, on the Workbench's opening screen, click the ⊕ icon near the "MySQL Connections" label. This will open the MySQL Workbench "Setup New Connection" wizard as shown in figure 1-16.

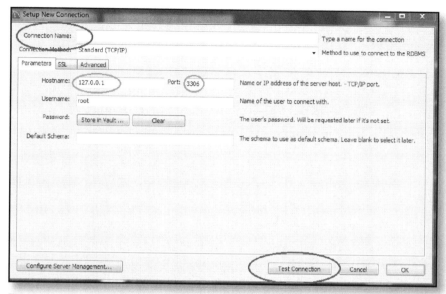

Figure 1-16: MySQL Workbench's Wizard for new connections.

Enter "My1stConn" in the "Connection Name:" field (or some other name you prefer).

Workbench will fill in the "Hostname:" and "Port:" fields. You can test these values by clicking the "Test Connection" button. DO NOT click the "OK" button.

Figure 1-17 indicates that the connection parameters are valid. You may get a different IP address and port number.

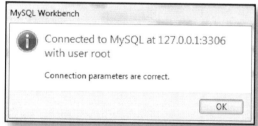

Figure 1-17: Connection parameters are valid.

Clicking on "OK" will close this window, bringing you back to the Workbench Wizard screen. Now, you can click "OK" on this screen and it will bring you to the opening screen of MySQL Workbench where you will see your new connection as a grey rectangle, as shown in figure 1-18.

Figure 1-18: Connection parameters are valid.

Now click on this grey box and you will be presented with Workbench's SQL Editor. The following screenshot shows only the left portion of the entire screen of Workbench's SQL Editor, as the right portion is mostly empty space.

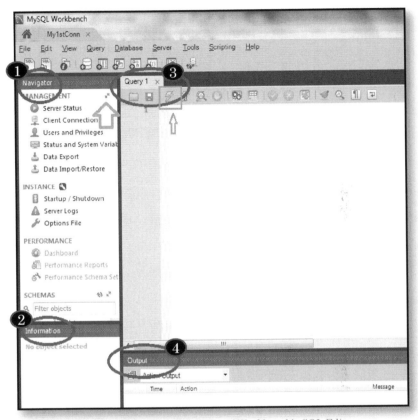

Figure 1-19: The opening screen of Workbench's SQL Editor.

We can see four panels in the previous screenshot as highlighted by the ovals, namely:

1. Navigator
2. Information
3. Query
4. Output

"Query1" or the "Query" panel is where we type our SQL commands or scripts, and the panel labeled "Output" is where status and error messages on the execution of our SQL commands or scripts are displayed.

Now, take a look at the icon within the square and pointed to by the arrow on the right. (The square and arrow have been added as visual aids and are not part of the SQL editor screen.) This icon of a mustard-colored lightning bolt , is the execute SQL command or script icon.

After typing your script and making sure it is free of syntax errors, you click this 'Run Script' icon to execute your script. In fact, if you position your cursor over this icon, you will get this pop-up message:

```
Execute the selected portion of the script or
everything, if there is no selection.
```

The "Navigator" panel has two windows within it: the "Management" window and the "Schema" window.

The "Schema" window will show all the databases (and all the objects within each database) that we will create.

As for the "Management" window, we will temporarily hide it from the screen display, as we will hardly use it.

So, click that small icon of two arrows pointing to each other . (The arrow on the left is aimed at that icon.) This icon will close the "Management" window of the "Navigator" panel and display the "Schema" window entirely in the "Navigator" panel. Your Workbench SQL editor screen should now look like this:

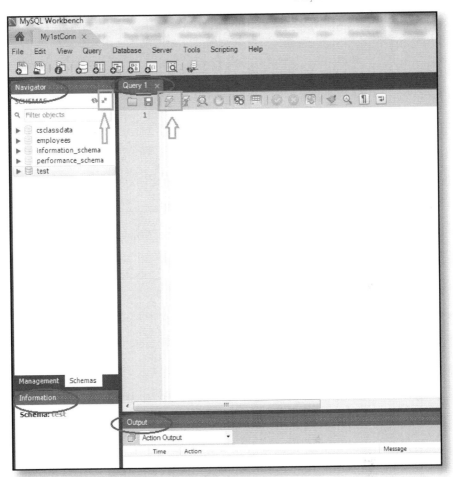

Figure 1-20: The "Navigator" panel has a less cluttered look.

Now, our "Navigator" panel looks less cluttered and the "Schema" window is fully displayed.

Our first task is to create our Project Monitoring database, *projmon*. In the "Query" panel, type:

```
CREATE DATABASE projmon;
```

(The case you use makes no difference, but uppercase is often used for language commands in order to improve clarity.)

Then press the "Run Script" icon ![icon].

Next, take a look at the "Output" panel near the bottom of the following screenshot. It has one row of various text displayed. The important thing is the icon of a white check mark on a green background ![icon]. This icon means that the SQL script or command was successfully executed.

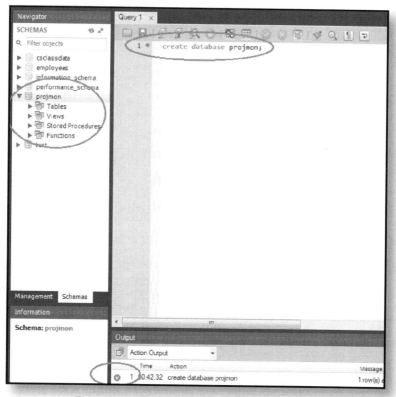

Figure 1-21: The newly created *projmon* database.

In the following screenshot, we have enlarged the portion of the "Output" panel showing the icon of a white arrow on a green background.

In contrast to the icon of a white arrow on a green background, the following screenshot of the "Output"

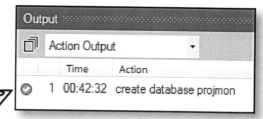

Figure 1-22: The enlarged icon of a white check mark on a green background.

panel shows an icon of a white X on a red background. This signifies a fatal error in your script in that the particular line indicated failed to execute because of some error.

Ideally, you shouldn't see this fatal error icon at all, but you will. When you do, examine the error messages as they provide enough detail for you to determine what error to correct in the SQL script.

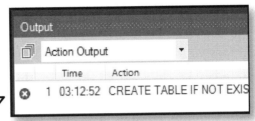

Figure 1-23: The enlarged icon of an X on a white background.

Now, in the "Navigator" panel, you should see the name *projmon* appear. If it isn't there, right-click on any object in the "Navigator" panel and select "Refresh All."

Click on the triangle to the left of *projmon* to expand it and see "Tables," "Views," "Stored Procedures," and "Functions" listed under *projmon*.

We have to create the six tables of *projmon*, namely: *person, contacttype, project, role, contact,* and *projectperson,* and input test data in them. Actually, we will not only be creating the tables and their columns or fields but also their primary and foreign key indexes. These indexes will define the relationships of the tables with one another.

First, we create the tables *person, contacttype, project* and *role,* and enter their data. We can create these four tables in any order.

Then, after creating the previous four tables, we create either *contact* or *projectperson* and enter their data.

We will go into detail about the mechanics of table creation later in the book. For now, follow the examples precisely, as *projmon* is the basis for the exercises we will use to learn how to interact with databases.

Now, in the navigator panel, *projmon* should be displayed in bold font indicating that it is the default schema or database. If *projmon* is not displayed in bold, right-click it and select "Set as Default Schema."

We will start with the *person* table. Enter the following SQL script into an empty query window of Workbench.

TIP: In all the scripts that we will ask you to enter in Workbench's SQL editor, it is important that you do not make any changes at all to the script. In particular, do not rearrange the lines. The primary key values will be automatically generated by MySQL and it is important that the primary keys automatically generated by MySQL on your system matches the primary keys that will be displayed in the succeeding screenshots in the various chapters of this book.

CODE LISTING:
CREATES THE *PERSON* TABLE AND ITS INDEX

```
CREATE TABLE IF NOT EXISTS person (
  id int(11) NOT NULL AUTO_INCREMENT,
  firstname varchar(255) NOT NULL,
  lastname varchar(255) NOT NULL,
  dob date DEFAULT NULL,
  managerid int(11) DEFAULT NULL,
  notes text,
  created timestamp NOT NULL DEFAULT
CURRENT_TIMESTAMP ON UPDATE CURRENT_
TIMESTAMP,
  PRIMARY KEY (id)
) ENGINE=InnoDB DEFAULT CHARSET=utf8;
```

This is a screenshot of your script in the "Query" panel. Now click the "Run Script" icon 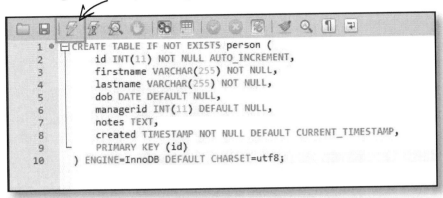 (in the square).

```sql
 1 ● ⊟CREATE TABLE IF NOT EXISTS person (
 2         id INT(11) NOT NULL AUTO_INCREMENT,
 3         firstname VARCHAR(255) NOT NULL,
 4         lastname VARCHAR(255) NOT NULL,
 5         dob DATE DEFAULT NULL,
 6         managerid INT(11) DEFAULT NULL,
 7         notes TEXT,
 8         created TIMESTAMP NOT NULL DEFAULT CURRENT_TIMESTAMP,
 9         PRIMARY KEY (id)
10     ) ENGINE=InnoDB DEFAULT CHARSET=utf8;
```

Figure 1-24: SQL script to create the table Person and its primary index.

Now, right-click any object under "Schemas" in the "navigator" panel and select "Refresh All." You should see the table *person* appear, as shown in the following screenshot.

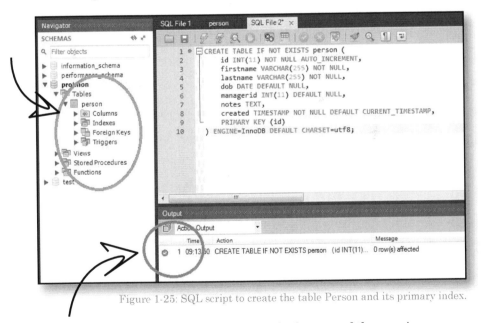

Figure 1-25: SQL script to create the table Person and its primary index.

Now, if you look at the "Output" panel at the bottom of the previous screenshot, you will see our icon of a white check mark on a green background. Success! The table *person* has been created with all its columns or fields and its primary index.

Now, we will create test data for *person*. Enter the following SQL script into the query window of Workbench, overwriting the previous script.

```
INSERT INTO person (lastname, firstname,
dob) VALUES ('Briggs', 'Joe', '1975-02-
07');
INSERT INTO person (lastname, firstname,
dob) VALUES ('Miller', 'Paul', '1980-08-
20');
INSERT INTO person (lastname, firstname,
dob) VALUES ('Palmer', 'Jenny', '1990-04-
29');
INSERT INTO person (lastname, firstname,
dob) VALUES ('James', 'Jenny', '1970-11-
03');
INSERT INTO person (lastname, firstname,
dob, managerid, notes) VALUES ('Walker',
'Rick', '1960-10-10', 0, 'Rick Walker is
the CEO of web.com');
INSERT INTO person (lastname, firstname,
dob, managerid, notes ) VALUES ('Baker',
'Susan', 0,0, "RickWalker's assistant, no
project involvement");
```

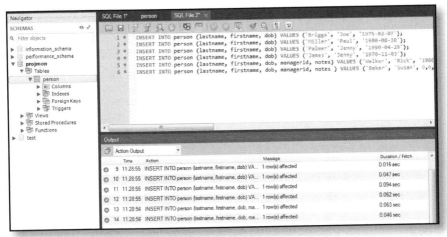

Figure 1-26: SQL script to create test data for the table Person.

Make sure that *projmon* is the default database. Click on the "Run Script" icon to execute the script.

Now, right-click on the table *person* in the "Navigator" Panel and choose "Select Rows – Limit 1000." A "Result Grid" will appear just below the "Query" panel. This is the screenshot of the query grid that shows the six rows we created for the table *person*.

```
1 •  SELECT * FROM person
```

id	firstname	lastname	dob	manager	notes	created
1	Joe	Briggs	1975-02-07	5	NULL	2014-09-17 09:01:13
2	Paul	Miller	1980-08-20	5	NULL	2014-10-15 15:01:01
3	Jenny	Palmer	1990-04-29	5	NULL	2014-09-17 09:01:13
4	Jenny	James	1970-11-03	5	NULL	2014-09-17 09:01:13
5	Rick	Walker	1960-10-10	NULL	Rick Walker is the CE...	2014-09-17 09:01:13
6	Susan	Baker	0000-00-00	5	Rick Walker's assista...	2014-09-29 11:06:25
* NULL	NULL	NULL	NULL	NULL	NULL	NULL

Figure 1-27: The six rows of the table *Person*.

If the data you generate does not match the data in figure 1-27, particularly the values of the primary key field id, then you have to redo the process of creating the table and entering its data.

First, right-click on the table name in the "Navigator" panel and select "Drop Table." This will remove or delete the table entirely. Then, enter the script into the "Query" window and go through the process again.

We now move on to the next table *contacttype* and create it and its test data in one script. Enter the following SQL script into an empty query window of Workbench:

CODE LISTING:
CREATES TABLE CONTACTTYPE AND ITS TEST DATA.

```sql
CREATE TABLE IF NOT EXISTS contacttype (
   id int(11) NOT NULL AUTO_INCREMENT,
   label varchar(255) DEFAULT NULL,
   PRIMARY KEY ('id')
) ENGINE=InnoDB DEFAULT CHARSET=utf8;

INSERT INTO contacttype (label) VALUES
('email');
INSERT INTO contacttype (label) VALUES
('phone');
INSERT INTO contacttype (label) VALUES
('address');
INSERT INTO contacttype (label) VALUES
('IM');
```

```
1  ● ⊟CREATE TABLE IF NOT EXISTS PROJMON.contacttype (
2         id int(11) NOT NULL AUTO_INCREMENT,
3         label varchar(255) DEFAULT NULL,
4         PRIMARY KEY (id)
5    └ ) ENGINE=InnoDB DEFAULT CHARSET=utf8;
6
7  ●    INSERT INTO contacttype (label) VALUES ('email');
8  ●    INSERT INTO contacttype (label) VALUES ('phone');
9  ●    INSERT INTO contacttype (label) VALUES ('address');
10 ●    INSERT INTO contacttype (label) VALUES ('IM');
```

Figure 1-28: Creating the table *contacttype* and its test data.

Make sure that "**projmon**" is the default database. Click on the "Run Script" icon to execute the script. The "Output" panel should show icons of a white check mark on a green background, as in the following screenshot.

	Time	Action	Message
⊘ 31	15:23:35	CREATE TABLE IF NOT EXISTS contacttype (id INT(11) NOT NULL AU...	0 row(s) affected
⊘ 32	15:23:35	INSERT INTO contacttype (label) VALUES ('email')	1 row(s) affected
⊘ 33	15:23:36	INSERT INTO contacttype (label) VALUES ('phone')	1 row(s) affected
⊘ 34	15:23:36	INSERT INTO contacttype (label) VALUES ('address')	1 row(s) affected
⊘ 35	15:23:36	INSERT INTO contacttype (label) VALUES ('IM')	1 row(s) affected

Action Output

Figure 1-29: The six rows of the table *person*.

Now, right-click on "Tables" under "projmon" (or any object under "Schemas") and select "Refresh All." The table *contacttype* should appear under "Tables" of "projmon."

Now, right-click on the table *contacttype* in the "Navigator" Panel and choose "Select Rows – Limit 1000." A "Result Grid" will appear just below the

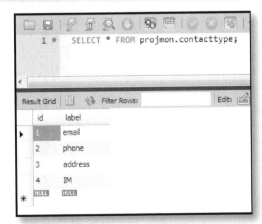

Figure 1-30: The four rows of table *contacttype*.

"Query" panel as shown in figure 1-30. The grid will show the four rows we created for the table *contacttype*.

At this point, we have created two tables, *person* and *contacttype,* and populated them with test data. The steps we carried out for both tables were:

1. Make sure that *projmon* is the default database. (Right-click *projmon* in the "Navigator" panel and select "Set as Default Schema.")
2. Enter the SQL script into the "Query" window and execute it.
3. Check the "Output" panel for any error messages.
4. Right-click any object in the "Navigator" panel and left-click "Refresh All" to see the newly created table.
5. Right-click the newly created table and click "Select Rows – Limit 1000" to see its test data.

Now, carry out the previous five steps in creating the table *project* and its test data. Here is the script to use:

CODE LISTING:
CREATES TABLE *PROJECT* AND ITS TEST DATA.

```
CREATE TABLE IF NOT EXISTS project (
  id int(11) NOT NULL AUTO_INCREMENT,
  label varchar(255) NOT NULL,
  budget double DEFAULT NULL,
  PRIMARY KEY (id)
) ENGINE=InnoDB DEFAULT CHARSET=utf8;

INSERT INTO project (label, budget) VALUES
('Website', '2000');
INSERT INTO project (label, budget) VALUES
('Facebook App', '999.95');
INSERT INTO project (label, budget) VALUES
('Google+', '250');
```

After executing this script, figure 1-31 should show the data in your *Project* table.

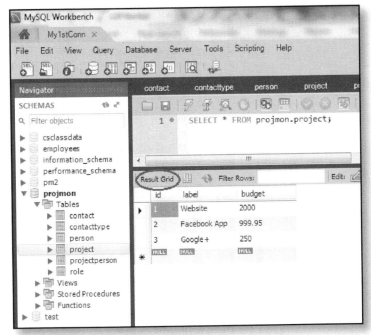

Figure 1-31: The three rows of table *project*.

Now, do the five steps again for the table *role*. Here is the script to use.

CODE LISTING:
CREATES TABLE *ROLE* AND ITS TEST DATA.

```
CREATE TABLE IF NOT EXISTS role (
  id int(11) NOT NULL AUTO_INCREMENT,
  label varchar(255) NOT NULL,
  PRIMARY KEY (id)
) ENGINE=InnoDB DEFAULT CHARSET=utf8;

INSERT INTO role (label) VALUES ('Product
Manager');
INSERT INTO role (label) VALUES ('Project
Manager');
INSERT INTO role (label) VALUES
('Developer');
INSERT INTO role (label) VALUES ('Tester');
```

After executing this script, this is the data that should be in your *Role* table:

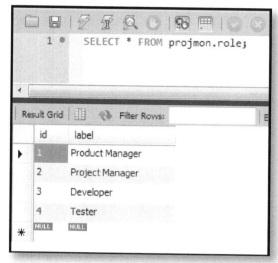

Figure 1-32: The four rows of table *Role*.

At this time, we have executed six queries and we will be executing four more. The top of your "Query" window will look something like the following screenshot, which shows seven queries that have been created and probably executed. To save some memory and screen clutter, you can start closing these queries beginning with the rightmost query (as shown by the oval in figure 1-33) by clicking on the "X" until only the "SQL File 1" tab is left.

Figure 1-33: Existing queries in the "Query" panel of Workbench.

Now, we come to the last two tables of our *projmon* database: *contact* and *projectperson*. These are the two tables with foreign keys. When we discuss foreign keys in the next section, you will understand why we had to first create the four tables *person, contacttype, project,1* and *role* and their data before creating *contacts* and *projectperson* and their data.

Here is the script for the table *contact*.

CODE LISTING:
CREATES TABLE *CONTACT* AND ITS TEST DATA.

```
CREATE TABLE IF NOT EXISTS contact (
  pid int(11) NOT NULL,
  ctid int(11) NOT NULL,
  value text NOT NULL,
  PRIMARY KEY (pid,ctid),
  KEY fk_contact_contacttype_idx (ctid),
  CONSTRAINT fk_contact_contacttype FOREIGN
KEY (ctid) REFERENCES contacttype (id) ON
DELETE CASCADE ON UPDATE CASCADE,
  CONSTRAINT fk_contact_person FOREIGN KEY
(pid) REFERENCES person (id) ON DELETE
CASCADE ON UPDATE CASCADE
) ENGINE=InnoDB DEFAULT CHARSET=utf8;

INSERT INTO contact (pid, ctid, value)
VALUES ('1', '1', 'jbriggs@web.com');
INSERT INTO contact (pid, ctid, value)
VALUES ('1', '2', '+1 800 121 2222');
INSERT INTO contact (pid, ctid, value)
VALUES ('2', '1', 'gener@yah.co.uk');
INSERT INTO contact (pid, ctid, value)
VALUES ('2', '2', '+44 7777 123 657');
INSERT INTO contact (pid, ctid, value)
VALUES ('2', '3', '10 Wee Lane Newtown AX10
5BG UK');
INSERT INTO contact (pid, ctid, value)
VALUES ('3', '1', 'jpalmer@web.com');
INSERT INTO contact (pid, ctid, value)
VALUES ('3', '2', '+1 800 121 2255');
INSERT INTO contact (pid, ctid, value)
VALUES ('4', '1', 'jjames@facebook.com');
INSERT INTO contact (pid, ctid, value)
```

```
VALUES ('4', '2', '+49 89 3324 44 0');
INSERT INTO contact (pid, ctid, value)
VALUES ('5', '1', 'rwalker@web.com');

INSERT INTO contact (pid, ctid, value)
VALUES ('5', '2', '+1 800 121 2200');
INSERT INTO contact (pid, ctid, value)
VALUES ('5', '3', 'Web.com 425 Rodeo Av San
Francisco CA 94437');
INSERT INTO contact (pid, ctid, value)
VALUES ('6', '1', 'sbaker@web.com');
INSERT INTO contact (pid, ctid, value)
VALUES ('6', '2', '+1 800 121 2201 ');
```

This is the test data for *contact*.

pid	ctid	value
1	1	jbriggs@web.com
1	2	+1 800 121 2222
2	1	gener@yah.co.uk
2	2	+44 7777 123 657
2	3	10 Wee Lane Newtown AX10 5BG UK
3	1	jpalmer@web.com
3	2	+1 800 121 2255
4	1	jjames@facebook.com
4	2	+49 89 3324 44 0
5	1	rwalker@web.com
5	2	+1 800 121 2200
5	3	Web.com 425 Rodeo Av San Francisco CA 94437
6	1	sbaker@web.com
6	2	+1 800 121 2201
NULL	NULL	NULL

Figure 1-34: The rows of table *Contact*.

Finally, here is the script for table *projectperson* and its test data.

CODE LISTING:
CREATES TABLE *PROJECTPERSON* AND ITS TEST DATA.

```
CREATE TABLE IF NOT EXISTS projectperson (
  prid int(11) NOT NULL,
  pid int(11) NOT NULL,
  rid int(11) NOT NULL,
  PRIMARY KEY (prid,pid,rid),
  KEY fk_projectperson_role_idx (rid),
  KEY fk_projectperson_person_idx (pid),
  CONSTRAINT fk_projectperson_person
FOREIGN KEY (pid) REFERENCES person (id) ON
DELETE CASCADE ON UPDATE CASCADE,
  CONSTRAINT fk_projectperson_project
FOREIGN KEY (prid) REFERENCES project (id)
ON DELETE CASCADE ON UPDATE CASCADE,
  CONSTRAINT fk_projectperson_role FOREIGN
KEY (rid) REFERENCES role (id) ON DELETE
CASCADE ON UPDATE CASCADE
) ENGINE=InnoDB DEFAULT CHARSET=utf8;
INSERT INTO projectperson (prid, pid, rid)
VALUES ('1', '1', '3');
INSERT INTO projectperson (prid, pid, rid)
VALUES ('2', '2', '3');
INSERT INTO projectperson (prid, pid, rid)
VALUES ('2', '2', '4');
INSERT INTO projectperson (prid, pid, rid)
VALUES ('1', '3', '4');
INSERT INTO projectperson (prid, pid, rid)
VALUES ('2', '4', '2');
INSERT INTO projectperson (prid, pid, rid)
VALUES ('2', '4', '4');
INSERT INTO projectperson (prid, pid, rid)
VALUES ('1', '5', '1');
INSERT INTO projectperson (prid, pid, rid)
VALUES ('1', '5', '2');
```

```
INSERT INTO projectperson (prid, pid, rid)
VALUES ('2', '5', '1');
```

This is a screenshot of *projectperson's* test data.

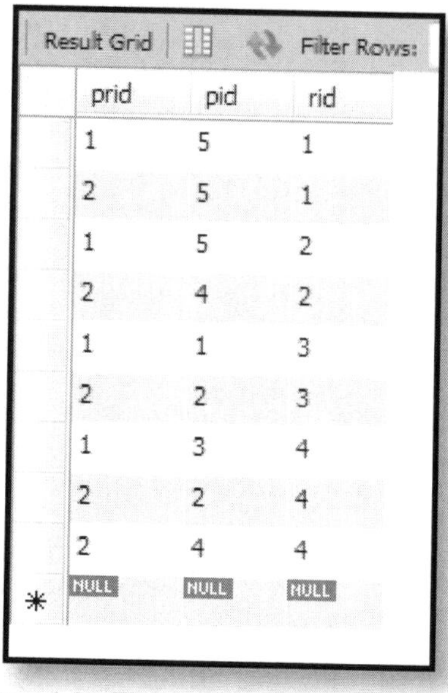

Result Grid | Filter Rows:

prid	pid	rid
1	5	1
2	5	1
1	5	2
2	4	2
1	1	3
2	2	3
1	3	4
2	2	4
2	4	4
NULL	NULL	NULL

Figure 1-35: The rows of table *projectperson*.

Congratulations! You have just completed creating the database *projmon* and its six tables as well as entering test data into those six tables.

QUESTIONS FOR REVIEW

1. Why is it helpful to install WAMP before you install MySQL Workbench?
   a. It is good practice to install programs in reverse alphabetical order.
   b. WAMP contains the database server that MySQL Workbench will connect to.
   c. It is not helpful to install WAMP first.
   d. WAMP contains .DLL files that MySQL Workbench requires.

2. MySQL Workbench is required to work with MySQL.
   a. True.
   b. False.

3. What is the purpose of the yellow lightning bolt icon in MySQL Workbench?
   a. It is the "Run Script" icon.
   b. It is the "Delete Script" icon.
   c. It is the "Smite My Foes" icon.
   d. It has no purpose.

4. MySQL commands must be entered in uppercase.
   a. True.
   b. False.

LAB ACTIVITY

Use MySQL Workbench to create an ERD for *projmon*. Utilize the available MySQL literature to complete this task in order to familiarize yourself with the software and its support materials. We will walk you through the process in the lab solution.

Load MySQL Workbench and open *projmon*. Once it's open, go to "File" and select "New Model."

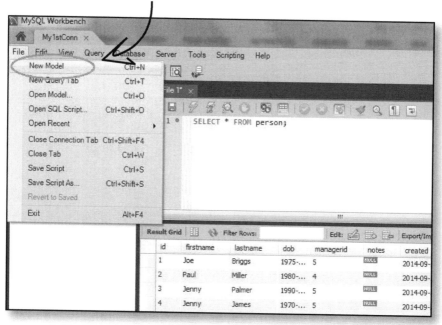

A model tab will launch with options for a database model. You do not have to worry about the details.

"MySQL Model"

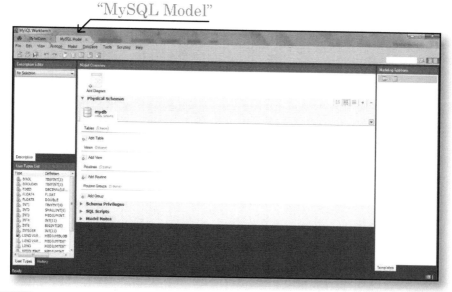

Ensuring that you have the model tab selected, choose the "Database" menu and select "Reverse Engineer." This will allow you to build an ERD from *projmon*.

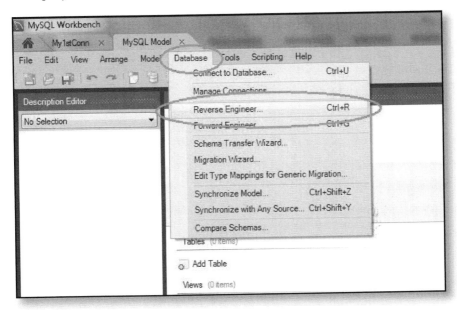

The "Reverse Engineer" wizard will guide you through the process. You first need to connect to your database using the connection name from earlier.

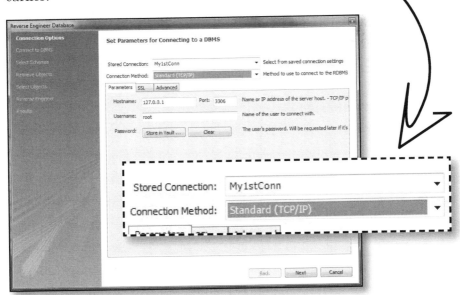

Once the database is connected, select the *projmon* schema.

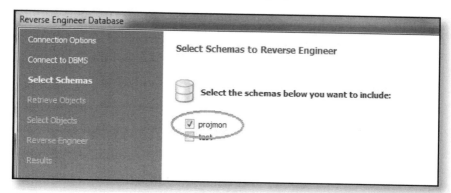

After *projmon* loads, choose to import all database objects.

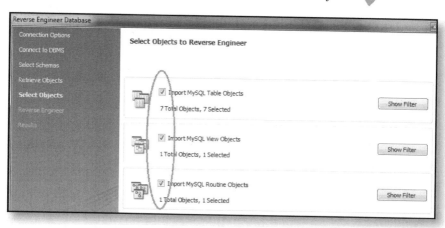

Use the defaults for the remaining steps of the wizard and you will have a new tab with an ERD of *projmon* available for you to use or refer to as needed!

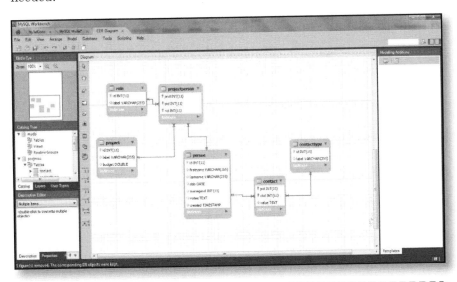

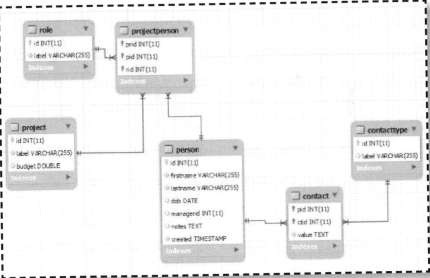

1.3 ATTRIBUTE DATA TYPES AND CONSTRAINTS

In this section, we examine in detail the columns or fields of a table. For each column of a table, we assign a data type and we impose any number of constraints. First, we tackle the columns of a table.

Figure 1-36 shows the box for the table *person*. Within the box are listed the column names of *person* (*id, firstname, lastname,* and so on). Before each column name is one of three types of icons: a yellow key, a hollow rhombus and a blue-shaded or blue-filled rhombus. These icons represent a constraint or a set of constraints. After each column name are the data types of each column. We now explain what these data types and constraints are.

The following table shows the same information that is represented inside the box of the table *person*.

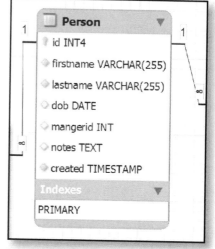

Figure 1-36: Entity diagram of *person* with its attributes

CONSTRAINTS	Column or Field Name (Attributes)	Data Type
Yellow key	id	int(11)
blue rhombus	firstname	varchar(255)
blue rhombus	lastname	varchar(255)
hollow rhombus	dob	Date
hollow rhombus	managerid	int(11)
hollow rhombus	notes	Text
blue rhombus	created	timestamp

Diagram 1.5: The constraints and data types of the fields of *person*.

Let's start with data types. Each column can be assigned a **data type** (the third column of the previous table) which denotes the type of value the column will store. The following table summarizes the data types used for the columns of *person*.

DATA TYPE	SIZE SPECIFIED	MEANING
INT	Optional	A positive or negative whole number.
VARCHAR	Yes	Strings of various lengths up to a certain maximum length which must be specified.
CHAR	Yes	Strings of fixed length (no more, no less). The length must be specified.
TEXT	No	Large amounts of text, such as sentences and paragraphs, of no fixed length.
DATE	No	A date value.
TIME	No	A time value.
TIMESTAMP	No	A combined date and time value.

Diagram 1.6: A partial list of the many data types that can be assigned to a table's fields.

The data types listed in the previous tables are not the only ones you can assign to a column of a table in a database. Examples of other data types are *boolean, interval, decimal, real,* and others.

Now, let's look at constraints. These are restrictions imposed on the values of a table's columns.

The first set of constraints is represented by the yellow key icon 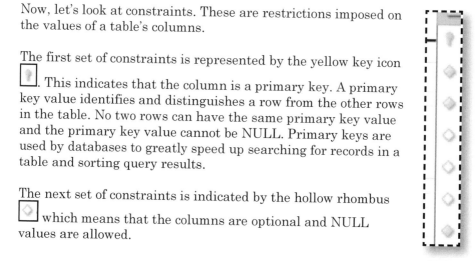. This indicates that the column is a primary key. A primary key value identifies and distinguishes a row from the other rows in the table. No two rows can have the same primary key value and the primary key value cannot be NULL. Primary keys are used by databases to greatly speed up searching for records in a table and sorting query results.

The next set of constraints is indicated by the hollow rhombus which means that the columns are optional and NULL values are allowed.

The third set of constraints is indicated by the blue-shaded rhombus which means that the columns are required fields. Required fields must have a non-NULL value.

QUESTIONS FOR REVIEW

1. What is a data type of a field or column?
   a. The maximum and minimum values of a field or column.
   b. The valid values that a field or column can hold.
   c. The limiting size of a field's data.
   d. The type of value the field or column will store.

2. What do the boxes in an entity-relationship diagram represent?
   a. Attributes.
   b. Relationships.
   c. Columns.
   d. Entities.

3. What is a constraint, as applied to a field of a table?
   a. The non-integer values that a field can store.
   b. The limitations on the size of the values of a field.
   c. The type of data that can be stored in a field.
   d. The restrictions imposed on a field's values.

4. A table can only have one primary key.
   a. True.
   b. False.

LAB ACTIVITY

Consider the ERD you conceptualized in section one. Determine appropriate data types for the fields of those tables.

LAB SOLUTION

borrowers:

idborrowers	INT(11)
namelast	VARCHAR(255)
namefirst	VARCHAR(255)
namemiddle	VARCHAR(255)
datebirth	DATE
dateregister	DATETIME

booksborrowed:

idborrower	INT(11)
idbook	INT(11)
dateborrowed	DATETIME
datedue	DATETIME
datereturned	DATETIME

books:

idbooks	INT(11)
title	VARCHAR(255)
isbn	CHAR(17)

booksauthors

idbooks	INT(11)
idauthors	INT(11)

authors

idauthors	INT(11)
namelast	VARCHAR(255)
namefirst	VARCHAR(255)
namemiddle	VARCHAR(255)

1.4 KEYS, RELATIONSHIPS AND REFERENTIAL INTEGRITY

In this section we discuss the important and intertwined concepts of keys, relationships and referential integrity.

Every table in a database must have a primary key index. The primary key index is a unique identifier for each record in the table and can be comprised of the value of one or more columns in the table. A primary key's value cannot be NULL.

Primary Key

Let's take a look at the following ERD of three tables: *contacttype, person* and *contact*.

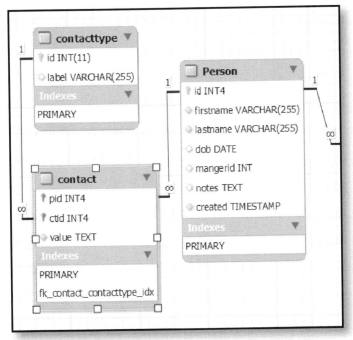

Figure 1-37: ERD for the tables *contacttype, person* and *contact*.

The primary key of each table is indicated by a colored icon of a key. The following diagram provides a summary of the fields that make up the primary key of each table.

Table	Primary Key Fields	Foreign Key Fields
person	id	
contacttype	id	
contact	pid, ctid	pid, ctid

Diagram 1-7: The primary and foreign keys of *person, contacttype* and *contact.*

Note that the primary key of the table *contact* consists of two fields. This is a **compound** or **composite** key. A primary key's value has to be unique. In the case of the table *contact,* neither of the fields *pid* or *ctid* by themselves will guarantee a unique value, but if we combine the two we can guarantee a unique value.

Composite Key

> **NOTE**: Primary keys are almost always of type integer because, with the MySQL AUTO_INCREMENT clause, the DBMS automatically generates a primary key for a row as it is added to the database. Users can opt out of this AUTO_INCREMENT capability and generate their own primary key values, but most choose not to.

Also indicated in the previous list are the foreign keys of *contact.* A foreign key is a table column, or combination of columns, that establishes and enforces a link between two tables. A primary key in the referenced, or parent, table can serve as a foreign key in the referencing, or child, table. For example, the primary keys in the parent tables *person* and *contacttype* are foreign keys in the child table *contact.*

> **NOTE**: A primary key can serve (and very often does, in fact) as a foreign key, but a foreign key cannot serve as a primary key.

The purpose of linking database tables together using foreign keys is to maintain database integrity and to retain logical, real world connections. In our example, each employee is a single individual who will have access to multiple types of contact. Also, each type of contact will be used by multiple employees. Joe Briggs, from *person*, has an email address and a phone number, which are two of the records in *contact*. Email addresses, from *contacttype*, are used by six employees, which are six of the records in *contact*.

Within a record in *contact* is the value of the contact—the specific email address or phone number—a reference to the individual in *person* who uses that contact and a reference to the type of contact in *contacttype* that it is. We know that in reality a "contact" cannot exist without an actual person and a physical medium, so we enforce this idea in our database with the foreign key constraint.

The foreign key constraint says that the value of the foreign key in a table must correspond to a row in the referenced table. It is common to use the primary key of the referenced table as a foreign key, but this is not a requirement. The only requirement is that the referenced field be a unique field in the parent table.

This concept is also known as **referential integrity**. Most DBMSs, including MySQL, provide mechanisms to enforce referential integrity. Referential integrity is what will keep you from creating a record in *contact* for an employee who does not exist, or stop you from deleting an employee from *person* who is assigned to a project in *projectperson*.

Referential Integrity

A table does not require either a primary or foreign key, however, it is good practice to implement a primary key in order to distinguish records. Also, logic will almost always dictate the primary key for a table.

If a table utilizes a primary key it must only have a single primary key, however, that single primary key can be a composite or compound primary key. There is not a specific limit on the potential number of foreign keys that a table can have. As a rule, any attribute which can be represented with only known and valid values is a good candidate for a foreign key.

Let's look at actual examples from our *projmon* database. Take a look at our ERD diagram of the three tables on the previous page. Focus on the line joining the tables *person* and *contact*.

This line represents the relationship between *person* and an entity. The start of the line, at the *person* entity, has the number one just above it while the end, at the *contact* entity, has the infinity symbol (∞) just above it.

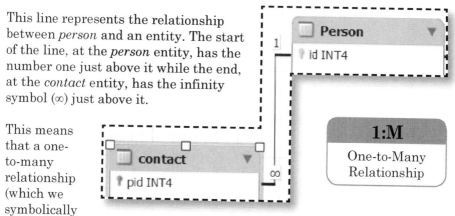

This means that a one-to-many relationship (which we symbolically designate as **1:M**) exists between *person* and *contact*. Stated in practical terms, this type of relationship means that one person can be contacted through their mobile phone, email, postal address, IM account, and so on.

You can also note that ends of both lines are positioned exactly on a field. On the *person* entity, the line is at the field *id* while the other end at *contact* is at the field *pid*. The field *id* is the primary key of the *person* entity while the attribute *pid* is a foreign key of *contact*.

Note that in a one-to-many relationship, the parent table is at the one-side of the relationship while the child table is on the many- side.

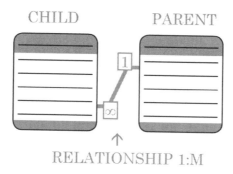

Now, the line between *contacttype* and *contact* is identical to the line between *person* and *contact*. Thus, a one-to-many relationship (which we symbolically designate as **1:N**) also exists between *contacttype* and *contact*, mirroring the real-life situation wherein a type of information (email, IM, address and mobile phone) can have many values. Put another way, the company has many email addresses, mobile phone numbers, and so on for its employees.

> **NOTE:** We designated the one-to-many relationship between *person* and *contact* as 1:M while 1:N is our designation for the one-to-many relationship between *contacttype* and *contact*. There is a reason for this, as you will soon see.

This diagram summarizes the foreign keys of *person* and *contacttype* and lists the primary key field(s) of the table they reference, as well as the type of relationship defined.

Table (parent)	Primary Key	Foreign Key	Relationship
person	id int(4)	pid of contact	1:M
contacttype	id int(11)	ctid of contact	1:N

Diagram 1-8: The foreign keys of *contact* and the primary keys they reference.

Now, what about the table *contact*? This is a table with foreign keys as a composite primary key. This table is called an intermediate table. It doesn't really represent an entity in the same way that the tables *person, contacttype, project,* and *role* represent real-world entities. The table *contact* serves to define a many-to-many relationship (which we can either designate as M:N or N:M) between *contacttype* and *person*. This reflects the situation wherein a person can have several types of contact information, that is, they can be contacted either through email, mobile phone, IM, or home address. It also reflects the fact that many employees can be contacted either through email, mobile phone, IM, or home address.

> **NOTE:** Our present set up of the columns and primary and foreign keys of the tables *contacttype, contact,* and *person* only allows a person one of each type of contact information. What changes would you need to make to the table structures, as well as to the primary and foreign key fields, in order to handle the situation where a person has several email addresses, uses two mobile phones, or lives at one address during the week and another address during the weekend?

In general, there are three types of relationships in a relational database.

First is the one-to-one relationship, which occurs when one *entity* is related to only one other *entity*. This type of relationship, abbreviated as 1:1, occurs infrequently. In our *projmon* database, we do not have any one-to-one relationship between tables.

> ONE-TO-ONE RELATIONSHIP: **1:1**

The second and most common type of relationship is a one-to-many relationship, which occurs when one entity is related to two or more entities. This relationship is abbreviated as 1:M, M:1, 1:N, N:1, 1:X, X:1 or other similar types of abbreviations. Our *projmon* database has five occurrences of this type of relationship.

> ONE-TO-MANY RELATIONSHIP:
> **1:M | M:1 | 1:N | N:1 | 1: X | X:1**

The third type of relationship, also very common, is a many-to-many relationship which occurs when many entities are related to many other entities. This relationship is commonly abbreviated as M:N, X:Y, X:Z and other similar abbreviations. In our *projmon* database, we have two occurrences of many-to-many relationships.

> MANY-TO-MANY RELATIONSHIP:
> **M:N | X:Y | X:Z**

QUESTIONS FOR REVIEW

1. Which of the following are constraints used in database design?
   a. Primary Key Constraint.
   b. Unique Key Constraint.
   c. Composite Key Constraint.
   d. Unlimited Value Constraint.

2. What concept or rule states that a foreign key's value must correspond to an existing value of a unique row in the referenced table?
   a. Referential integrity.
   b. Personal Integrity.
   c. Non-null constraint.
   d. Duplicates not allowed.

3. What relationship occurs when one entity is related to two or more entities?
   a. many-to-one.
   b. one-to-many.
   c. one-to-one.
   d. many-to-many.

4. What uniquely identifies a row in a table and distinguishes it from the other rows?
   a. Composite key.
   b. Primary key.
   c. Foreign key.
   d. Compound key.

In our *projmon* database, consider the four tables: *person, projectperson, project,* and *role*. The following is the portion of our ERD for those four tables:

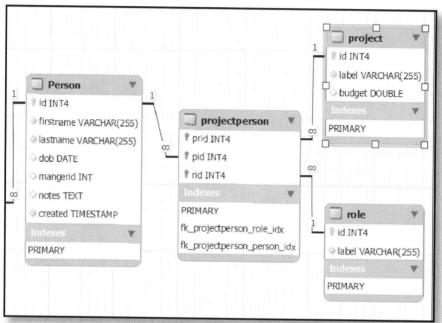

ERD for the tables *person, projectperson, project* and *role*.

Based on this ERD, complete the following two diagrams.

Table	Primary Key Fields	Foreign Key Fields
person		
project		
role		
projectperson		

Fill in the primary and foreign keys of *person, project, role* and *projectperson*.

Table	Referenced Field	Foreign Key (field of child table)	Relationship
person			
project			
role			

Fill in the foreign keys of *person, project* and *role* and the respective fields of the primary key they reference.

CHAPTER 1 LAB SOLUTION

Table	Primary Key Fields	Foreign Key Fields
person	id	
project	id	
role	id	
projectperson	prid, pid, rid	prid, pid, rid

The primary and foreign keys of *person, project, role* and *projectperson*.

Table (parent)	Referenced Field	Foreign Key (field of child table)	Relationship
person	id	prid of project person	1:K
project	id	ctid of contact	1:M
role	id	rid of role	1:N

The foreign keys of *person, project* and *role* and the respective fields of the primary key they reference.

CHAPTER SUMMARY

In this chapter, we discussed the fundamental structural elements of a database: tables, fields, data types, constraints, indexes, primary and foreign keys, relationships, and others. We learned how to read and interpret an entity-relationship diagram which represents the database schema.

More importantly, we gained actual experience with the MySQL language syntax as we created our sample Project Monitoring Database, *projmon,* using MySQL Workbench.

In the next chapter, we will learn the history of the SQL standard and look into some of the SQL platform variations that are available. We will also understand the syntactic structure of SQL statements.

CHAPTER 2

SQL STATEMENTS: COMPONENTS, STRUCTURE, AND ELEMENTS

CHAPTER OBJECTIVES:

- You will be introduced to the top five dialects of SQL as well as the ANSI SQL Standard.
- You will survey the components of SQL: DDL, DML, DQL, DCL, and others.
- You will learn the structure of a SQL statement.
- You will review the elements that comprise a SQL statement.

2.1 A BRIEF HISTORY OF SQL

SQL is a programming language designed for Relational Database Management Systems (RDBMSs or just DBMSs). It is not a general-purpose programming language to be used to create stand-alone programs or web applications. It cannot be used outside of the DBMS world.

SQL

Structured
Query
Language

The origins of SQL are intertwined with the history of the origins and development of relational databases. It all started with an IBM researcher, Edgar Frank "Ted" Codd, who in June of 1970, published an article entitled "A Relational Model of Data for Large Shared Data Banks" in the journal *Communications of the Association for Computing Machinery*. In this paper, Codd outlined a mathematical theory of how data could be stored and manipulated using a tabular structure. This article established the foundational theories for relational databases and SQL.

Codd's article ignited several research and development efforts and this eventually led to commercial ventures.

The company Relational Software, Inc. was formed in 1977 by a group of engineers in Menlo Park, California and in 1979 they shipped the first commercially available DBMS product, named Oracle. The company Relational would eventually be renamed Oracle.

In 1980, several Berkeley University professors resigned and founded Relational Technology, Inc. and in 1981, they released their DBMS product named Ingres.

In 1982, IBM finally started shipping its DBMS product, named SQL/ Data System or SQL/DS. In 1983, IBM released Database 2 or DB2 for its mainframe systems.

By 1985, Oracle proclaimed that they had over 1,000 Oracle installations. Ingres had a comparable number of sites and IBM's DB2 and SQL/DS products were approaching 1,000.

As these vendors were developing their DBMS products, they were also working on their products' query language – SQL.

IBM developed SQL at its San Jose Research Laboratory in the early 1970s and formally presented it in 1974 at a conference of the Association of Computing Machinery, ACM. The language was originally named "SEQUEL" for Structured English Query Language but it was later shortened to just SQL.

It was Oracle Corporation, however (then known as Relational Software Inc.), who came out with the first implementation of SQL for its Oracle DBMS. IBM came out with its own version in 1981 for its SQL/DS DBMS.

Because of the increasing popularity and proliferation of DBMSs and consequently, SQL, the American National Standards Institute, ANSI, began working on a SQL standard in 1982. This standard, released in 1986 as X3.135, was largely based on IBM's DB2 SQL. In 1987, the International Standards Organization, ISO, adopted the ANSI standard also as an ISO standard.

Since 1986, ANSI has continued to work on the SQL standard and released major updates in 1989, 1992, and 1999.

The 1999 standard added extensions to SQL to allow the creation of functions either in SQL itself or in another programming language. Since its official appearance, the 1999 standard has been updated three times: in 2003, in 2006, and in 2008. This last update is known as SQL:2008. There have been no updates since then.

Current vendors exert admirable efforts to conform to the standard, but they still continue to extend their versions of the SQL language with additional features.

The largest vendor, with a market share of 48% as of 2011, is Oracle Corporation. Its flagship DBMS, Oracle 11g, has dominated the UNIX market since the birth of the DBMS market. Oracle 11g is a secure, robust, scalable, high-performance database. However, Oracle 11g holds only second place in the transaction processing benchmark.

Next, IBM's DB2, holds the record in transaction speed. DB2's current version is 9.7 LUW (Linux, UNIX and Windows). IBM holds 25% of the DBMS market.

Third is Microsoft with an 18% share. Their product is SQL Server and the latest version is 2008 Release 2. Microsoft also has Microsoft Office Access, which is touted as a desktop relational database. Unlike the other DBMSs mentioned in this book, Access is a file-based database and as such has inherent limitations in performance and scalability. It also only supports a subset of the SQL Standard.

The remaining 12% market share is staked out by Teradata, Sybase and other vendors including open source databases, one of which is MySQL.

MySQL was initially developed as a lightweight, fast database in 1994. The developers, Michael Widenius and David Axmark, intended MySQL to be the backend of data-driven websites. It was fast, had many features, and it was free. This explains its rise in popularity. In 2008, MySQL was acquired by Sun Microsystems, and Sun Microsystems was later purchased by Oracle. Oracle then offered a commercial version of MySQL in addition to the free version. The free version was named "community edition."

In programming, a relatively small addition or extension to a language that does not change the intrinsic nature of that language is called a **dialect**. There are five dominant SQL dialects: 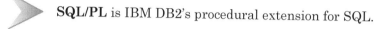 **dialect**

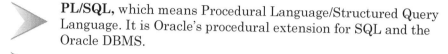 **PL/SQL,** which means Procedural Language/Structured Query Language. It is Oracle's procedural extension for SQL and the Oracle DBMS.

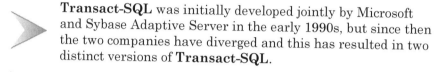 **SQL/PL** is IBM DB2's procedural extension for SQL.

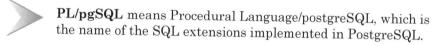 **Transact-SQL** was initially developed jointly by Microsoft and Sybase Adaptive Server in the early 1990s, but since then the two companies have diverged and this has resulted in two distinct versions of **Transact-SQL**.

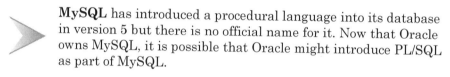 **PL/pgSQL** means Procedural Language/postgreSQL, which is the name of the SQL extensions implemented in PostgreSQL.

MySQL has introduced a procedural language into its database in version 5 but there is no official name for it. Now that Oracle owns MySQL, it is possible that Oracle might introduce PL/SQL as part of MySQL.

The above SQL dialects implement the ANSI/ISO standard. Programmers should have few problems migrating from one dialect to another.

It is also interesting to note the computer technology landscape during the period that relational databases and SQL began to emerge—the late 1970s to early 1980s. During that period, IBM dominated the computer industry with its mainframe computers, but was facing strong competition from minicomputer vendors Digital Equipment, Data General, and Hewlett-Packard, among others. Cobol, C, and Pascal were the predominant languages. Java was non-existent, and object-oriented programming had just emerged. Almost all software was proprietary with license fees in the tens or hundreds of thousands. The internet was just a couple of laboratories interconnected to share research papers. The World Wide Web was just a fantasy.

Today, most of the dominant software and hardware of that era have gone the way of the dinosaur and much more powerful and innovative technologies have replaced them.

The only exception to this is the DBMS and its Structured Query Language, SQL, which continues to grow and dominate the computer world with no sign of becoming overshadowed or obsolete.

QUESTIONS FOR REVIEW

1. Who was the DBMS vendor that came out with the first commercial DBMS?
   a. IBM.
   b. Relational Technology, Inc.
   c. Relational Software, Inc.
   d. None of the above.

2. Why do DBMS vendors persist in adding features to their implementations of SQL that do not comply with the ANSI/ISO standard?
   a. To maintain a distinct identity separate from IBM's DB2.
   b. To preserve the profit margins of their products.
   c. To protest the implementation of ANSI standards.
   d. To fully exploit the unique features of their DBMS.

3. What DBMS product claimed to be a relational database system for desktops?
   a. IBM's DB2.
   b. Oracle.
   c. Ingress.
   d. Microsoft Access.

4. What event sparked the birth of the DBMS market?
   a. Codd's publication of his article "A Relational Data Model..."
   b. The founding of Relational Software by ex-Berkeley professors.
   c. IBM's presentation at the ACM of its version of SQL.
   d. Relational Technology's acquisition by Oracle Corporation.

2.2 DML, DDL, DQL, DCL: Components of SQL

SQL's statements can be conceptually grouped into what we call components. One purpose of this grouping is security. Most users of a database are granted privileges to use only certain components, such as querying, but are denied the components that define or manipulate the data in the database.

SQL consists of the following components. They are:

1. **DML** or **Data Manipulation Language**
2. **DDL** or **Data Definition Language**
3. **DQL** or **Data Query Language**
4. **DCL** or **Data Control Language**
5. **Transaction Control**
6. **Programmatic SQL**.

We will be covering the data manipulation, data definition and data query groups in depth in this book, and we will touch on transaction control and programmatic SQL.

Some bundle DQL as part of DML, arguing that DQL also manipulates data and that DQL consists of only one statement, SELECT, so it should not have a separate category. For the purposes of this book, however, we will keep DQL as a separate component.

DATA MANIPULATION LANGUAGE

This DML component involves inserting data into database tables, deleting data from existing tables, and modifying existing data. These tasks are reflected in the three major commands that form the core of any DML language. They are:

> **DML**
>
> Data Manipulation Language

> INSERT: This command adds one or more records to a database table. Its syntax is INSERT INTO *tablename* [column(s)] VALUES [value(s)].

> DELETE: This command removes one or more records from a table according to specified conditions. Its syntax is DELETE FROM *tablename* where [condition].

➤ UPDATE: This command modifies data of one or more records. Its syntax is UPDATE *tablename* SET *columnname* = value where [condition].

> **NOTE:** SQL is a set-based language. Set-based programming languages are based on the mathematical theory of a set, which is simply a collection of objects. In set-based programming you can modify a member of the set; in SQL that would be a record in a table, but you cannot change how that member is defined. In practical terms, you can modify the value of a field in a record, but you cannot delete a field from a record.

DATA DEFINITION LANGUAGE

> **DDL**
>
> Data Definition Language

This DDL component creates and modifies database schema.

> **NOTE**: The SQL standard specifically avoids using the term *database* because of its many meanings derived from its frequent use. The SQL standard instead uses the term *catalog* to describe a named collection of tables.

There are many DDL commands, but the most frequently used are:

➤ CREATE: This command can be used to build a new schema object.

In chapter 1, we encountered the detailed syntax of the CREATE TABLE command which we used six times to create six different tables. We will go into DDL in more depth later in the book.

➤ ALTER: This command modifies an existing schema object.

➤ DROP: This command is used to delete schema objects.

DATA QUERY LANGUAGE

> **DQL**
>
> Data Query Language

This DQL component contains only one statement: SELECT. But it is the statement that you will be using most of the time.

DATA CONTROL LANGUAGE

This DCL component is used to assign and revoke database rights and permissions. Its main statements are GRANT and REVOKE.

➤ GRANT: This command gives a privilege to a user.

➤ REVOKE: This command takes back privileges granted to a user.

In your time as a database application developer, you will likely most often be working with about thirty SQL statements.

The following table lists those thirty statements grouped by their component classification.

MAJOR SQL STATEMENTS DIAGRAM

Statement	Description
Data Manipulation	
INSERT	Adds new rows of data to a table.
UPDATE	Modifies existing data of a table.
MERGE	Conditionally inserts/updates/deletes new and existing rows.
DELETE	Removes rows of data from a table.
Data Definition	
CREATE TABLE	Adds a new table to a database.
DROP TABLE	Removes a table from a database.
ALTER TABLE	Modifies the structure of a table.
CREATE VIEW	Adds a new view to a database.
DROP VIEW	Removes a view from a database.
CREATE INDEX	Builds an index for a column.
DROP INDEX	Removes the index for a column.
CREATE SCHEMA	Adds a new schema to a database.
DROP SCHEMA	Removes a schema from a database.

CREATE DOMAIN	Adds a new data value domain.
ALTER DOMAIN	Changes a domain definition.
DROP DOMAIN	Removes a domain from the database.
Data Query	
SELECT	Retrieves data from the database.
Access Control	
GRANT	Grants user access privileges.
REVOKE	Removes user access privileges.
CREATE ROLE	Adds a new role to the database.
GRANT ROLE	Grants role containing user access privileges.
DROP ROLE	Removes a role from the database.
Transaction Control	
COMMIT	Ends the current transaction.
ROLLBACK	Aborts the current transaction.
SET TRANSACTION	Defines data access characteristics of the current transaction.
START TRANSACTION	Explicitly starts a new transaction.
SAVEPOINT	Establishes a recovery point for a transaction.
Programmatic SQL	
DECLARE	Defines a cursor for a query.
EXPLAIN	Describes the data access plan for a query.
OPEN	Opens a cursor to retrieve query results.
FETCH	Retrieves a row of query results.
CLOSE	Closes a cursor.
PREPARE	Prepares a SQL statement for dynamic execution.
EXECUTE	Executes a SQL statement dynamically.
DESCRIBE	Describes a prepared query.

Diagram 2.1: Major SQL Statements

1. The three statements MERGE, UPDATE, and DELETE belong to what SQL component?
   a. Manipulation.
   b. Definition.
   c. Control.
   d. Programmatic.

2. What is one purpose of grouping SQL statements into components?
   a. Pedagogical.
   b. Classification.
   c. Access control.
   d. Future expansion.

3. The SELECT statement is sometimes bundled with the data manipulation language.
   a. True.
   b. False.

4. What would you use to create and modify database schema?
   a. DDL.
   b. DML.
   c. DQL.
   d. Run DMC.

2.3 SQL STATEMENTS – STRUCTURE AND ELEMENTS

In this section, we will discuss the structure of a SQL statement and the elements that comprise it.

The discussion here will cover the ANSI standard, but keep in mind that vendors often implement these standards along with substantial additions.

SQL STATEMENT STRUCTURE

1. Every SQL statement begins with a **verb**, a keyword or reserved word that unambiguously declares what the statement does. For example, CREATE, INSERT, DELETE, and others.
2. The statement continues with one or more **clauses**.
3. A clause may identify data or a database object to be operated on by the statement or it may provide more details about what the statement is going to do.
4. The clause also begins with a **keyword**, such as WHERE, FROM, INTO, and HAVING.
5. Some clauses are mandatory. Others are optional.
6. The format and content of clauses vary from one clause to another.

verb

clause

keyword

The following screenshot identifies all the elements of a DELETE statement (with two clauses), which removes a specific record from a table.

DELETE

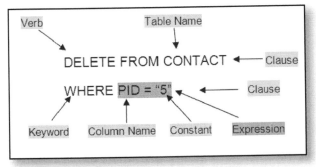

Figure 2-1: The structure and elements of a SQL statement.

NAMES

Names identify the schema objects that a SQL statement will manipulate or use. In our previous screenshot of a DELETE statement, there is the name of a table, *contact,* and the name of a column or field, *pid.*

The ANSI standard specifies that names can contain up to 127 characters, must begin with a letter, and must not contain any spaces or special characters.

In the case of column names, as in our *projmon* database example, you may have noticed that the field *id* is present in four tables: *contacttype, person, role,* and *project.* To distinguish which *id* field we are referring to, we place the table name, followed by a period (.) before the field name.

For example, *person.id* refers to the *id* field of the table *person* and *role.id* refers to the *id* field of the table *role.*

DATA TYPES

The following table lists some of the data types specified in the ANSI standard. MySQL has additional data types that we will discuss as we utilize them later in the book.

ANSI SQL DATA TYPES DIAGRAM

Data Type	Abbreviation	Description
CHARACTER(len)	CHAR	Fixed-length character strings.
CHARACTER VARYING(len)	CHAR VARYING, VARCHAR	Variable-length character strings.
CHARACTER LARGE OBJECT(len)	CLOB	Large fixed-length character strings.
NATIONAL CHARACTER(len)	NATIONAL CHAR, NCHAR	Fixed-length national character string.
NATIONAL CHARACTER VARYING(len)	NATIONAL CHAR VARYING, NCHAR	variable-length national character strings.

NATIONAL CHARACTER LARGE OBJECT(len)	NCLOB	Large variable-length national character strings.
BIT(len)		Fixed-length bit strings.
BIT VARYING(len)		Fixed-length bit strings.
INTEGER	INT	Integers.
SMALLINT		Small integers.
NUMERIC(precision, scale)		Decimal numbers.
DECIMAL(precision, scale)	DEC	Decimal numbers.
FLOAT(precision)		Floating-point numbers.
REAL		Low-precision floating point numbers.
DOUBLE PRECISION		High-precision floating point numbers.
DATE		Calendar dates.
TIME(precision)		Clock times.
TIME WITH TIME ZONE(precision)		Clock times with time zone.
TIMESTAMP(precision)		Dates and times.
TIMESTAMP WITH TIME ZONE(precision)		Dates and times with time zones.
INTERVAL		Time intervals.
XML(type modifier [secondary type modifier])		Character data formatted as Extensible Markup Language (XML).

Diagram 2.2: ANSI SQL Data Types

CONSTANTS

We can classify constants into three groups: **numeric**, **string**, and **date and time**.

Numeric constants, sometimes called exact numeric literals, consist of integer and decimal constants. Decimal constants are written as ordinary decimal numbers in SQL statements, with an optional leading plus or minus sign. Here are some examples.

```
 34    -456    3001.00    +936.29
```
Numeric Constant

There should be no comma between the digits of a numeric constant. MySQL allows a leading plus sign, but some other dialects do not.

String constants have to be enclosed in single quotes (ASCII decimal code 39, or hexadecimal code 0027), as in these examples.

```
'Kirk, John'

'Mexico'

'I can''t'
```
String Constant

Note the third and final example that shows that if a single quote is to be part of the string constant, it is written as two consecutive single quote characters.

Date and Time constants are treated as strings with a specified format. DBMS vendors implement these formats differently and complicate the situation by adding further date and time options. Also, DBMS systems, including MySQL, implement a DateTime constant which consists of a combined date and time value.

Date & Time Constant

The following table summarizes the more common date and time formats, including the ANSI standard.

COMMON DATE AND TIME FORMATS DIAGRAM

Format Name	Date Format	Time Format
ANSI	yyyy-mm-dd	hh.mm.ss
American	mm/dd/yy	hh:mm am/pm
European	dd.mm.yy	hh.mm.ss
MySQL	yyyy-mm-dd	hh:mm:ss

Diagram 2.3: Date and Time Formats

EXPRESSIONS

In SQL, an expression is any combination of field names, operators, constants, values, and functions that return a value when evaluated.

For example, using the *project* table of our *projmon* database to calculate what the budget of a project would be if we increase it by 10%, we would use the expression:

```
project.budget * 1.10
```

Another example is the expression you would use to calculate the approximate age of an employee:

```
year(now()) - year(dob)
```

In a database, expressions are used primarily to calculate values retrieved from a database and calculate values used when searching a database.

BUILT-IN FUNCTIONS

The ANSI standard specifies a number of quite useful built-in functions and each vendor adds some of their own. In an expression, a SQL function can replace a constant of the same data type. Recall that a function must return a value of a specific data type.

The following table lists the more commonly used functions of the ANSI SQL specification.

Common ANSI SQL Functions Diagram

Function	Returns
BIT_LENGTH(string)	The number of bits in a bit string.
CAST(value AS data_type)	The value, converted to the specified data type (for example, a date converted to a character string).
CHAR_LENGTH(string)	The length of a character string.
CONVERT(string USING conv)	A string converted as specified by a named conversion function.
CURRENT_DATE	The current date.
CURRENT_TIME(precision)	The current time, with the specified precision.
CURRENT_ TIMESTAMP(precision)	The current date and time, with the specified precision.
EXTRACT(part FROM source)	The specified part (DAY, HOUR, etc.) from a DATETIME value.
LOWER(string)	A string converted to all lowercase letters.
OCTET_LENGTH(string)	The number of 8-bit bytes in a character string.
POSITION(target IN source)	The position where the target string appears within the source string
SUBSTRING(source FROM n FOR len)	A portion of the source string, beginning at the nth character, for a length of len.

TRANSLATE(string USING trans)	A string translated as specified by a named translation function.
TRIM(BOTH *char* FROM *string*)	A string with both leading and trailing occurrences of *char* trimmed off.
TRIM(LEADING *char* FROM *string*)	A string with any leading occurrences of *char* trimmed off.
TRIM(TRAILING *char* FROM *string*)	A string with any trailing occurrences of *char* trimmed off.
UPPER(string)	A string converted to all uppercase letters.

Diagram 2.4: Commonly used ANSI SQL functions

NULL VALUES

Filling out paperwork is an unfortunate but common part of life. When doing so, it's not uncommon to come across a field that you cannot complete because it is not relevant to you, for example, if you live in a house and an address form asks for an apartment number. The apartment number field needs to exist, but the form's creators understand that it will not be applicable to everyone.

The same situation occurs for certain fields in tables of databases. In our sample *projmon* database, a person may be assigned to a project without immediately being assigned a role, so no data is entered into the *rid* field of table *projectperson*. Another example would be a new project for which the budget has not yet been determined. We could enter a zero in the *budget* field of table *project* but we might want **NULL** to reserve this value for pro-bono projects.

It is in these types of situations that the SQL data type NULL value is used. The NULL value is an indicator that data is missing, unknown, or inapplicable. The NULL value is not a true data type like a numeric or string data type.

1. What type of SQL constants must be enclosed in single quotes?
   a. Strings.
   b. Dates.
   c. Numeric.
   d. Datetime.

2. Which of the following is an invalid numeric constant?
   a. -4507
   b. 34
   c. +930
   d. 4,556.70

3. What format does MySQL use for its date data type?
   a. yyyy-mm-dd
   b. yyyy:mm:dd
   c. dd.mm.yy
   d. mm/dd/yy

4. The NULL value is equivalent to zero.
   a. True.
   b. False.

CHAPTER 2 LAB EXERCISE

This activity will give you a little more experience in using MySQL Workbench to become familiar with the data types of the fields of the tables in *projmon*.

The following diagram lists fields taken randomly from each of the six tables of *projmon*. Using Workbench, examine the structures of the tables of *projmon* and provide the correct values for the third column.

Table	Field (Column)	Data Type
project	label	
projectperson	pid	
contact	value	
person	dob	
project	budget	
person	created	
contacttype	id	
person	managerid	

CHAPTER 2 LAB SOLUTION

Table	Field (Column)	Data Type
project	label	varchar(255)
projectperson	pid	int(11)
contact	value	text
person	dob	date
project	budget	double
person	created	timestamp
contacttype	id	int(11)
person	managerid	int

CHAPTER SUMMARY

In this chapter, you learned a little bit about the origins and development of DBMSs and its programming language SQL. This brief history should give you some assurance that investing time and effort in learning and mastering SQL will not be wasted, as SQL's more than 30-year history proves that it is a technology that is here to stay.

You then surveyed the grouping of SQL statements into its components: DDL, DML, DQL, and so on.

You also explored how SQL statements are structured and what elements (names, data types, constants, functions, expressions, null value) go into the making an SQL statement.

In the next chapter, we will start our study of the most powerful, complex, and popular of the SQL statements, the SELECT statement.

CHAPTER 3

THE SELECT STATEMENT
Select, From, and *Order By* clauses

CHAPTER OBJECTIVES

- You will learn the syntax definition of the select statement.
- You will work on examples of the SELECT statement using the SELECT, FROM, and ORDER BY clauses.
- You will understand how to format output using SQL functions.
- You will use column aliases to modify the appearance of the column headings of your query results.

3.1 THE SELECT STATEMENT

The SELECT statement is the heart of SQL. The SELECT statement is the most powerful and complex of the SQL statements and it is the statement that is used most frequently—about 90 percent of the time. The SELECT statement is the one and only statement of the DQL component of SQL.

The SELECT statement retrieves data from a database and returns it in a **query result** or a **resultset** (a term used by some vendors) which is in the form of a virtual table – a table that exists only in memory. This virtual table has all the characteristics of tables that exist permanently in a database.

> **Query Result**
> **Resultset**

This is the syntax of the SELECT statement.

SELECT { all, distinct } { select-item }
   FROM table-specification
   WHERE search-condition
   GROUP BY grouping-column
   HAVING search condition
   ORDER BY sort-specification.

There are six clauses. They all begin with a keyword, shown above in bold and italics. The first two clauses, SELECT and FROM, are required. The rest are optional.

In this chapter, we will explain and illustrate the SELECT, FROM, and ORDER BY clauses. GROUP BY and HAVING will be covered later.

The SELECT clause begins every SELECT statement. It specifies the fields to be retrieved and displayed, the constants to be displayed, and the expressions to be evaluated and displayed. The order that fields, constants, and expressions are listed in the SELECT statement is the order that they will appear in the query result.

SELECT

In a syntax definition, curly brackets denote optional items. Therefore, the previous syntax definition, "{all, distinct}" means that you use either "all" or "distinct" or neither.

Next, "{select-item}" is a comma-separated list of column names, constants, or SQL expressions, which is to be displayed by the SELECT statement.

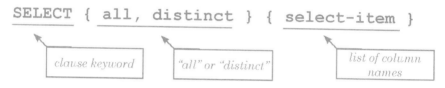

The FROM clause lists the tables which will provide the columns in the SELECT clause.

The ORDER BY clause specifies the order in which the data in the query result will appear.

FROM

ORDER BY

In the following code listing, we have summarized all the SQL SELECT statements that we will cover in this chapter. The keywords are all uppercase to help you identify the SELECT, FROM, and ORDER BY clauses.

These SELECT statements are good examples of the statement's syntax and provide many examples of "{select-item}."

When you type the code examples into your query window they do not need to be all uppercase.

```
SELECT * FROM person;
SELECT * FROM contact;

SELECT firstname, lastname, dob FROM person;
SELECT managerid FROM person;
SELECT distinct managerid FROM person;
SELECT distinct managerid, lastname, firstname FROM
person;

SELECT left(firstname,1), lastname FROM person;
SELECT substr(firstname,1,1), lastname FROM person;

SELECT concat(firstname, ' ', lastname) FROM person;
SELECT concat_ws(' ', firstname, lastname) FROM
person;

SELECT firstname, lastname, year(dob) FROM person;
SELECT firstname, lastname, year(dob), month(dob) FROM
person;
SELECT firstname, lastname, now()-dob FROM person;
SELECT firstname, lastname, year(now()-dob) FROM
person;
SELECT firstname, lastname, year(now()) - year(dob)
FROM person;

SELECT firstname, lastname, datediff(now(), dob) FROM
person;

SELECT firstname, lastname, datediff(now(), dob)/365
FROM person;

SELECT firstname, lastname, round(datediff(now(),
dob)/365) FROM person;

SELECT firstname, lastname, dob FROM person ORDER BY
lastname asc;
SELECT firstname, lastname, dob FROM person ORDER BY
dob desc;

SELECT firstname, lastname, dob FROM person ORDER BY
firstname asc, dob desc;
SELECT firstname, lastname, dob FROM person ORDER BY
managerid asc, dob desc;

SELECT left(firstname, 1) initial, lastname, dob FROM
person;
```

Now, let's start with the simplest form of the SELECT statement.

```
SELECT * FROM table_name;
```

This simplest form of the SELECT statement displays all the columns of all the rows in a table called *table_name*. The asterisk (*) character is considered a wildcard character and here it is interpreted as all fields. Bring up MySQL Workbench and click on *My1stConn* (the connection you created in chapter one) as shown in figure 3-1.

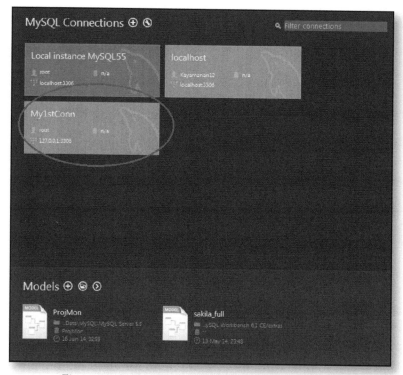

Figure 3-1: Connect to *My1stConn* in MySQL Workbench.

Clicking on *My1stConn* will bring up the Query window as shown in the next screenshot. Make sure that *projmon* is the default database by right clicking on it and selecting "Set As Default."

Type the following code into the query window and then click on the Execute icon.

```
SELECT * FROM projmon.person;
```

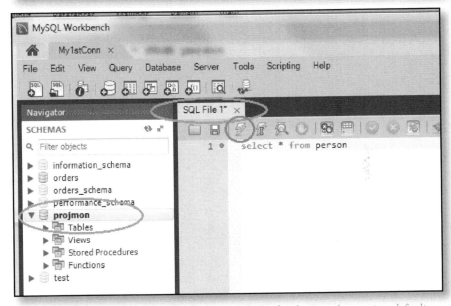

Figure 3-2: The Query window of Workbench with the database *projmon* set as default.

Clicking on the execute icon will bring up the result grid which is shown in the next screenshot. As you can see, all fields of all six records of the table *person* are displayed.

Figure 3-3: The result grid for the query "select * from person;".

Now, if the table *person* had forty fields and a thousand records, all of that would be displayed, but no screen currently exists that can display forty fields and a thousand records in a clear and readable manner. This would also put a considerable strain on network and computer resources.

To practice SELECT more, display the contents of *contact by* typing the following SQL statement in Workbench's query window.

```
SELECT * FROM projmon.contact;
```

Your result grid should look like this:

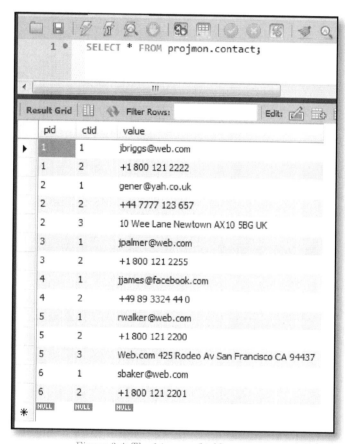

Figure 3-4: The 14 rows of table *contact*.

Now that you have seen how to unconditionally retrieve all fields of all records of a table, in the second section of this chapter, you will see how to restrict the fields to be retrieved. In the third section, you will see how to limit the rows to be retrieved.

QUESTIONS FOR REVIEW

1. What clause in the SELECT statement lists the tables that will be the source of the query's data?
   a. ORDER BY
   b. FROM
   c. GROUP BY
   d. DISTINCT

2. What two terms are used to refer to the data generated by a query?
   a. recordset, dataset.
   b. resultset, query result.
   c. query output, resultgrid.
   d. resultset, recordset.

3. What two clauses in the SELECT statement are required?
   a. HAVING, ORDER BY.
   b. FROM, SELECT.
   c. GROUP BY, HAVING.
   d. SELECT, WHERE.

4. What special character in the SELECT statement means "ALL"?
   a. &
   b. +
   c. #
   d. *

LAB ACTIVITY

In this section, we retrieved and displayed all fields of all records of the tables *person* and *contact* - two tables in our sample database *projmon*. Now, do the same for the other four tables of *projmon*, namely, *contacttype*, *project*, *role* and *personproject*.

The following four screenshots show the result grid of MySQL Workbench for the four tables, *contacttype, project, role,* and *personproject.*

The four rows of table *contacttype:*

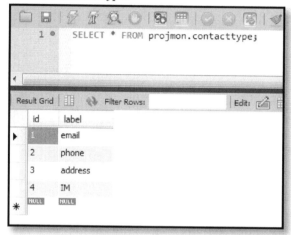

The three rows of table *project:*

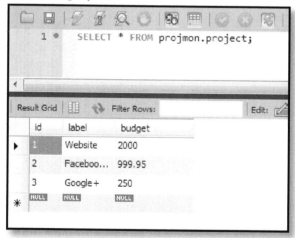

The four rows of table *role:*

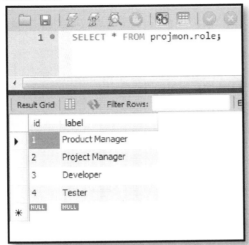

The nine rows of table *projectperson:*

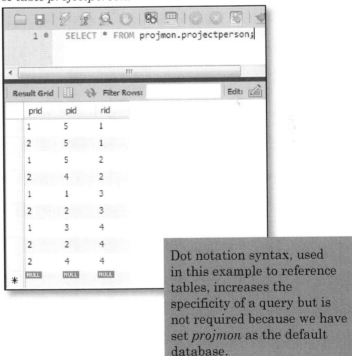

Dot notation syntax, used in this example to reference tables, increases the specificity of a query but is not required because we have set *projmon* as the default database.

3.2 THE SELECT CLAUSE

In our first use of the SELECT statement, we unconditionally displayed all fields of all records. Now, we will use clauses in the SELECT statement to display only specific fields in the order we choose.

In your MySQL Workbench query window, type the following query:

```
SELECT firstname, lastname, dob FROM person;
```

Your result should look something like figure 3-5.

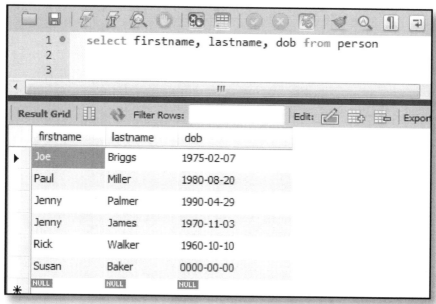

Figure 3-5: Displaying only the columns *firstname*, *lastname* and *dob* from the table *person*.

Now, execute the following query in Workbench:

```
SELECT dob, firstname, lastname, dob FROM
person;
```

Figure 3-6 shows what you should get in your result grid.

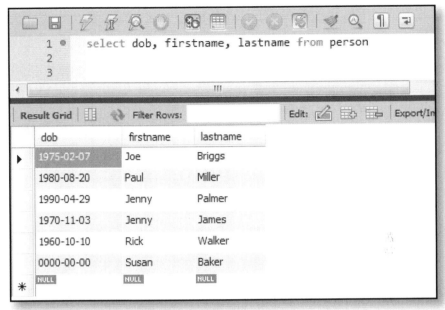

Figure 3-6: Displaying only the columns *dob, firstname,* and *lastname* from the table *person.*

You might have realized that the order you list the columns or fields in your query in is the same order in which they appear in your query result. Pretty simple!

Now, type and execute the following in the Query Panel.

```
SELECT FROM person;
```

Nothing will appear in your result grid, but you should see the following in your output panel:

Figure 3-7: The output panel indicates any error in the SQL statement that causes it to fail to execute.

It's an error message! The SELECT statement you typed has a syntax error because the select clause is incomplete. The purpose of this exercise is to emphasize that after you execute a query, even if the output on the result grid is what you expected, you should always look at your output panel to check for any errors or warnings.

Now, before we go on with our examples, we have to make a correction to the *managerid* field of the table *person*. Input the following SQL script into the Query Panel:

```
UPDATE person SET managerid="5" WHERE
id="1";
UPDATE person SET managerid="4" WHERE
id="2";
UPDATE person SET managerid="5" WHERE
id="3";
UPDATE person SET managerid="5" WHERE
id="4";
UPDATE person SET managerid="5" WHERE
id="6";
```

Make sure that *projmon* is the default database, then execute the script. Check your output panel to make sure you see all white checkmarks on a green circular background, as shown in figure 3-8.

		Time	Action
✓	12	15:01:16	UPDATE person SET managerid="5" WHERE id="1"
✓	13	15:01:16	UPDATE person SET managerid="5" WHERE id="2"
✓	14	15:01:16	UPDATE person SET managerid="5" WHERE id="3"
✓	15	15:01:17	UPDATE person SET managerid="5" WHERE id="4"
✓	16	15:01:17	UPDATE person SET managerid="5" WHERE id="6"

Figure 3-8: All white checkmarks on a green circular background means that the SQL statements executed flawlessly.

This script modifies the values of the field *managerid* with the use of the UPDATE statement (which we will study in a later chapter).
Now, back to our examples. We want to see only the values of the field *managerid*. We type the following SELECT statement in the Query Panel and execute it.

```
SELECT managerid FROM person;
```

This should be the output in our result grid.

Figure 3-9: Displaying only the field *managerid* of all rows of the table *person*.

As you can see here, only the *managerid* field is displayed. However, look at the output—there are a lot of duplicates. To eliminate these duplicates, use the **DISTINCT** keyword. Type the following SQL statement in the Query Panel and execute it:

```
SELECT DISTINCT managerid
FROM person;
```

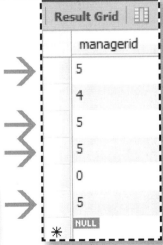

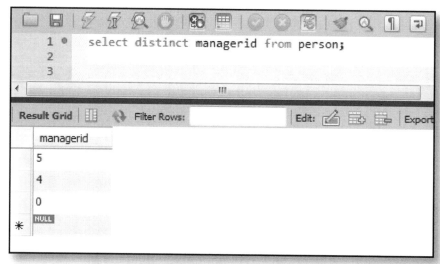

Figure 3-10: Removing duplicate occurrences with the DISTINCT keyword.

As you can see, the duplicate values have been eliminated. Remember that the DISTINCT keyword only applies to records and not to fields.

DISTINCT

Now, what if we add *firstname* to the name list of the previous code as in the following SELECT statement?

```
SELECT DISTINCT managerid, firstname FROM
person;
```

The following figure shows the output of the code:

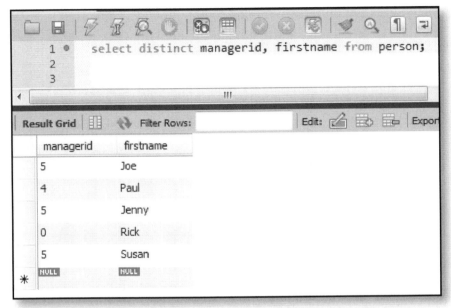

Figure 3-11: Applying the DISTINCT keyword to two fields.

As we analyze the output, note that:

1. Duplicate values have appeared in the *managerid* column.
2. Only five out of a total of six records have appeared.

To understand this output, let's remove the DISTINCT keyword from the query and execute the following SQL statement.

```
SELECT managerid, firstname FROM person
```

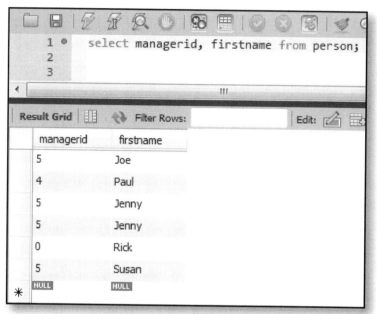

Figure 3-12: Since the DISTINCT keyword was removed from the SQL statement, duplicates in rows 3 and 4 appeared.

In figure 3-12, we can see that the third and fourth rows are identical. This is the duplicate that the DISTINCT keyword removed. Note that DISTINCT will consider and operate on all the fields listed after it—not just on the first field.

QUESTIONS FOR REVIEW

1. How many column names can be listed in the SELECT clause of a query statement?
    a. 1.
    b. 2.
    c. 3.
    d. None of the above.

2. Which of the following will display *dob*, *firstname*, and *lastname*, in that order?
    a. SELECT firstname, lastname, dob FROM person
    b. SELECT firstname, dob, lastname FROM person
    c. SELECT * FROM person
    d. SELECT dob, firstname, lastname FROM person

3. Which of the following will give compilation errors?
    a. SELECT id FROM person
    b. SELECT id, firstname, lastname, dob, managerid, notes, creation, projected FROM person
    c. SELECT person
    d. SELECT id, firstname FROM person

4. Refer to figure 3-11 and 3-12. What are the differences between these two outputs? (Choose all that apply.)
    a. There are five outputs in 3-11 and six in 3-12.
    b. The name Jenny is repeated twice in 3-12.
    c. The query used to produce the output in 3-11 used the DISTINCT keyword.
    d. 3-12 had records where first names were distinct.

LAB ACTIVITY

Use the DISTINCT keyword in a SELECT statement on the *managerid* field in table *person* and then on the *pid* field in table *projectperson*. Display the output of these two queries in the results grid.

LAB SOLUTION

```
SELECT DISTINCT managerid FROM Person

SELECT DISTINCT pid FROM projectperson;
```

3.3 FORMATTING AND SORTING OUTPUT

In the previous section, we learned how to limit the number of fields retrieved by a query. Now, we introduce you to some simple techniques for formatting the output of a query. These techniques use a few of MySQL's built-in functions.

Recall that functions are self-contained compilations of program statements that perform a specific task. A function optionally accepts one or more arguments that modify its tasks, and a function returns a value, either as a result of carrying out its tasks or as an indicator of its behavior.

In this section, we discuss specific MySQL functions that may not adhere to the ANSI standard.

The following table alphabetically lists the functions that we will be using in this section. The function's defined parameters are also listed.

MySQL Built-In Functions Diagram

Name	Description
concat(str1, str2, ..., strN)	Returns concatenated string consisting of str1, str2, ..., and strN.
concat_ws(separator, str1, str2, ..., strN)	Concatenate with separator. The separator is added between the strings to be concatenated.
datediff(date1, date2)	Calculates the expression date1–date2 as the number of days between the two dates. *Date1* and *date2* are date or datetime expressions.
left(str, len)	Returns the leftmost *len* characters from the string *str*.
month(date)	Returns the month for *date,* in the range 1 to 12 for January to December or 0 for dates that have a zero month part.
now()	Returns the current date.
round(x, d)	Rounds the argument x to d decimal places.

substr(str, pos, len)	Returns a string of length *len* consisting of a portion of *str* beginning from position *pos*).
year(date)	Returns the year for *date* in the range 1000 to 9999.

Diagram 3-1: A summary of the SQL functions used in this chapter.

Look over those functions briefly. Pay particular attention to the order in which the parameters are listed.

TIP: To get a complete list and comprehensive description of MySQL functions, you can go to http://dev.mysql.com/doc/refman/5.0/en/functions.html. You can also refer to Chapter 12 of the MySQL 5.6 Reference Manual. As of July 2014, version 5.6 is the latest release.

For our first example, start with the **left()** function. Type the following SQL statement in Workbench's Query Panel:

left()

```
SELECT LEFT(firstname, 1), lastname FROM
person;
```

Figure 3-13 shows what should appear in the result grid.

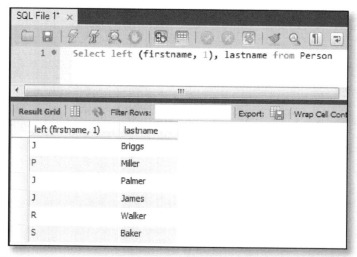

Figure 3-13: Using the **left()** function to get the first character of *firstname*.

From this screenshot, we can see that the function "LEFT(firstname, 1)" extracted the leftmost character of the field *firstname*. The function's second argument, "1," instructed it to extract only one character.

> **NOTE**: Many of these functions are not standardized and may vary across different dialects of SQL. If you move to a different DBMS, make sure that you read its documentation.

You can obtain exactly the same result by using **substr()**, as shown in the following SELECT statement:

substr()

```
SELECT SUBSTR(firstname, 1, 1), lastname
FROM person;
```

This should be the output of your result grid from using the **substr()** function:

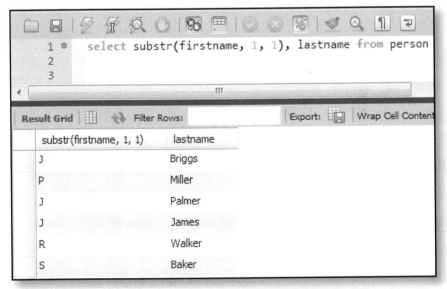

Figure 3-14: Using the **substr()** function to get the first character of *firstname*.

In the **substr()** function, the second argument indicates the starting position in the string from which to begin extracting characters.

The third argument specifies the number of characters to extract, beginning from the starting position.

Next, we come to the **concatenation** function, **concat()**. To concatenate means to join together and so **concat()** is used to join any number of strings into one string. In our SELECT statement example, we will be joining the *lastname* and *firstname* with a space between them.

concat()

This is the select statement to type in Workbench's Query panel.

```
SELECT CONCAT(firstname, ' ', lastname) FROM
person
```

This is what your result grid should look like:

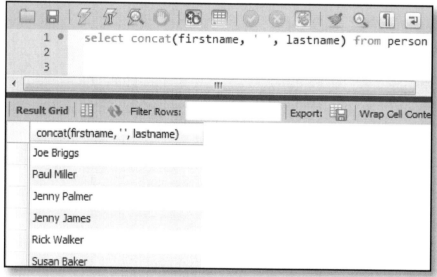

Figure 3-15: Concatenating two fields into one result column by using **concat()**.

It's important to note that **concat()** takes any number of strings as arguments, so in our example it joined together the field *firstname*, then a space, and then the field *lastname*.

We can concatenate any number of strings or expressions that evaluate to strings. We could very well use **concat()** in the following manner to join four strings with spaces between them.

```
CONCAT(string1, ' ', string2, ' ', string3,
' ', string4)
```

But in the case of the previous example, it would be easier to use the **concat_ws()** function. The "ws" means "with separator."

concat_ws()

Please type the following in Workbench's query panel:

```
SELECT CONCAT_WS(' ',firstname, lastname)
FROM person;
```

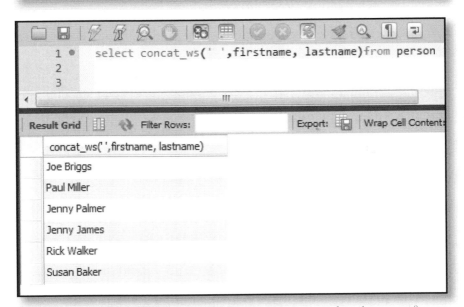

Figure 3-16: The **concat_ws()** function is more convenient to use than the **concat()** function if you have many strings or expressions to concatenate.

In this case using either **concat()** or **concat_ws()** yields the same results, however **concat_ws()** is very useful when you have a large number of strings to be concatenated.

Now, we tackle some date functions. Recall the output of the SELECT statement shown in figure 3-17:

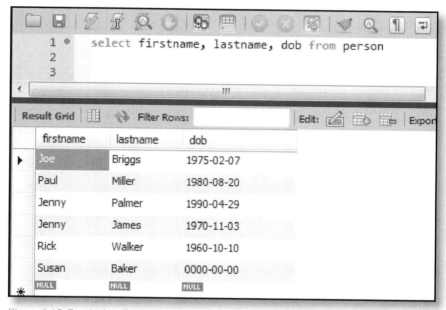

Figure 3-17: Retrieving *firstname*, *lastname*, and *dob* from *person*.

As you can see from the previous screenshot, *dob* is displayed in the format "yyyy.mm.dd." Note also the last record, which holds the data of "Susan Baker," was instructed to hold the value 0 but instead displays "0000-00-00". This *dob* field should be set to NULL but it has been purposely left at zero to indicate the problems that arise by setting this field to zero instead of NULL. This also shows that NULL is useful and practical.

Type the following SELECT statement in the query panel:

```
SELECT firstname, lastname, YEAR(dob) FROM
person;
```

The next screenshot shows the output we should get.

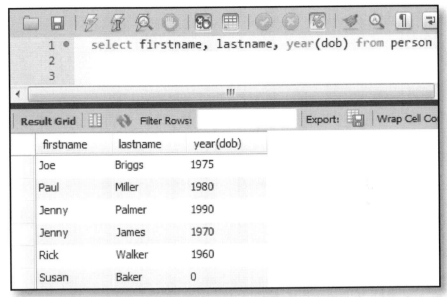

Figure 3-18: Using the **year()** function to display the birth year from *dob*.

The **year()** function extracts the year from a field with a date data type. Again, note how the *dob* of Susan Baker's record shows the value zero, the value calculated by the SQL function **year()**.

year()

Now, let's use the **month()** function. Execute the following SQL statement:

month()

```
SELECT firstname, lastname, YEAR(dob),
MONTH(dob) FROM person;
```

This should be the output in your result grid:

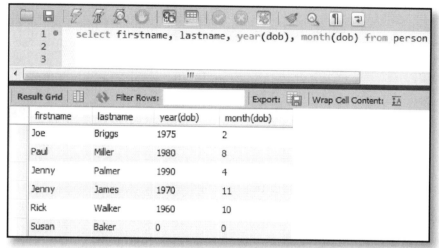

Figure 3-19: Using the **year()** and **month()** function to display the birth month and birth year.

Like **year()**, **month()** outputs only the month from a field with a date data type. Note that it is the numerical month value, not the month's name.

Now, let's use SQL to calculate the age of the person. For this we need to use the **now()** function. This is the query to execute:

now()

```
SELECT firstname, lastname, dob-NOW() FROM
person;
```

The output of the previous code is shown in figure 3-20:

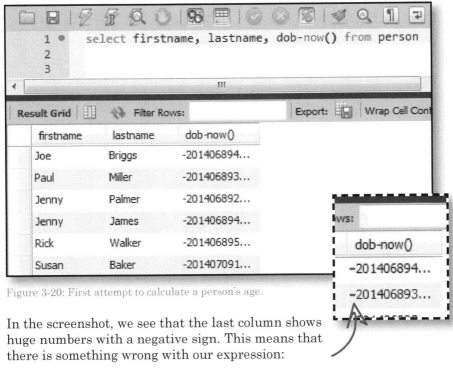

Figure 3-20: First attempt to calculate a person's age.

In the screenshot, we see that the last column shows huge numbers with a negative sign. This means that there is something wrong with our expression:

```
dob - NOW()
```

Looking at what we have entered, we can deduce that we are subtracting the value of **now()** {which will be a date data type representing the date and time when the function is executed) from the value of each record's *dob*. Let's try reversing the order.

```
SELECT firstname, lastname, NOW()-dob FROM
person;
```

If we execute this SQL statement, the following screenshot shows what our output should be.

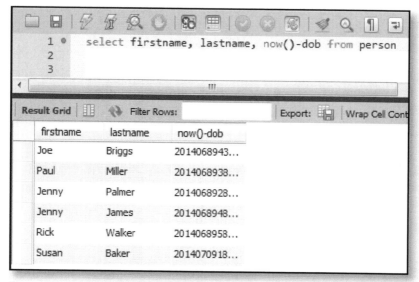

Figure 3-21: Second attempt to calculate a person's age.

As the screenshot shows, the negative signs are gone but the large numbers are still meaningless. Those numbers can't be the correct dates of birth. Let's try this SELECT statement.

```
SELECT firstname, lastname, YEAR(NOW()-dob)
FROM person;
```

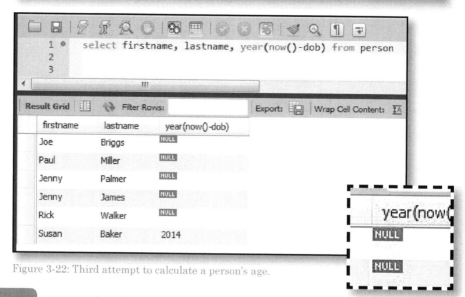

Figure 3-22: Third attempt to calculate a person's age.

This output, showing NULL values, is still incorrect.

Let's try this SELECT statement. This should get it right.

```
SELECT firstname, lastname, YEAR(NOW())-
YEAR(dob) FROM person;
```

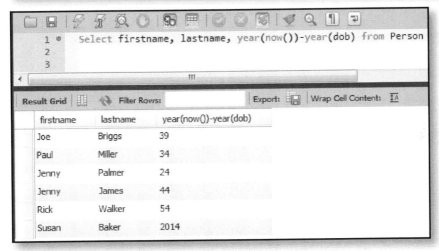

Figure 3-23: Finally, we got it right.

The output looks correct for everyone except Susan Baker. She can't be 2014 years old.

This odd result is due to the fact that her *dob* has been set to '0000-00-00' when it should have been set to NULL, an oversight we purposely left uncorrected to help understand the proper use of NULL. We'll go into more detail about NULL later.

This is not exactly the ideal way to get correct results in SQL. A careful reading and understanding of the **year()** and **now()** functions and an understanding of how the date data type is internally stored should have led us to the correct expression without a lot of failed attempts.

Many people find it difficult to understand a function or a concept just by reading about it, so they like to immediately try it out.

There's nothing wrong with that, but before you start banging out SQL statements, try to make a serious effort to read the documentation. Then you can try some commands to refine whatever you absorbed from your reading. It's a continuous cycle between reading, understanding, and executing the code to see the results.

Now, in the last example, we got it right with the somewhat awkward and complex expression:

```
YEAR(NOW())-YEAR(dob)
```

To make life simpler for SQL programmers, **datediff()** was created. Execute the following SQL statement:

datediff()

```
SELECT firstname, lastname,
DATEDIFF(NOW(),dob) FROM person;
```

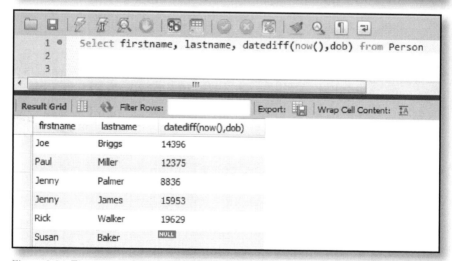

Figure 3-24: First attempt to use **datediff()** to calculate a person's age.

The output still doesn't make sense, but it is correct. **datediff()** calculates the number of days between two dates, so what we have here are ages in days! We just have to convert the days to years. This is the SQL statement to execute that:

```
SELECT firstname, lastname,
DATEDIFF(NOW(),dob)/365 FROM person
```

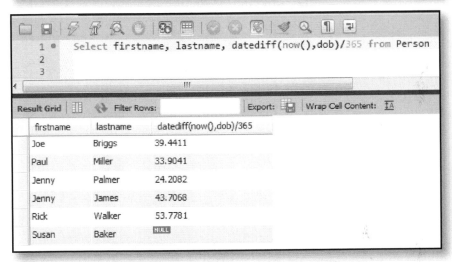

Figure 3-25: Second attempt to use **datediff()** to calculate a person's age.

Now, the ages are being shown not only in years, but also in decimal format. Since you don't typically tell people that you are 38.7370 years of age, we will use **round()** to correct this amusing situation. This is our final SQL statement to calculate ages.

round()

```
SELECT firstname, lastname,
ROUND(DATEDIFF(NOW(),dob)/365) FROM person;
```

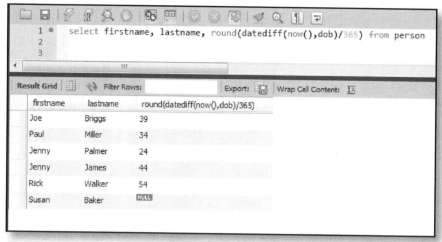

Figure 3-26: Got it right on the third try.

That ends our introductory coverage of SQL functions.

Now, we will tackle the ORDER BY clause which specifies the order in which the data in the query result will appear. Let's execute the following SQL statement:

```
SELECT lastname, firstname, dob FROM person
ORDER BY lastname ASC;
```

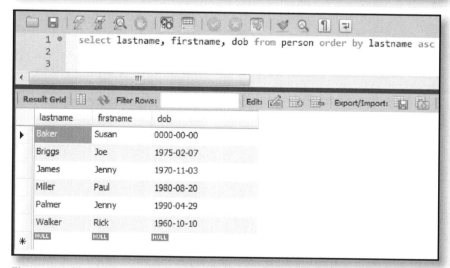

Figure 3-27: Sorting the query results by *lastname*.

As we can see from figure 3-27, the rows are arranged alphabetically by *lastname*. "ASC" means ascending.

Here is another SQL statement to execute.

```
SELECT firstname, lastname, dob FROM person
ORDER BY dob DESC;
```

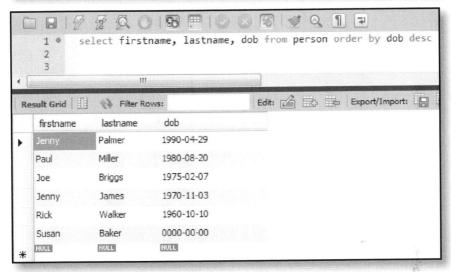

Figure 3-28: Sorting the query results by *dob*.

This time, the rows are arranged by descending date of birth. The youngest person is the first row and the oldest person is the last row. "DESC" means descending.

In the last two examples, we have sorted one field only, but we can sort two fields as this SQL statement shows. Execute this query:

```
SELECT firstname, lastname, dob FROM person
ORDER BY firstname ASC, dob DESC;
```

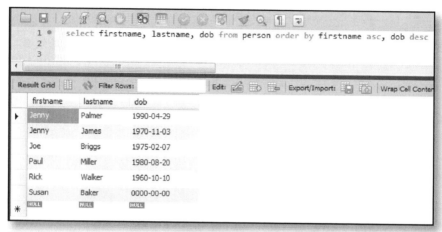

Figure 3-29: Sorting on two fields.

The results will first be sorted by *firstname* in ascending order and then they will be sorted again by *dob* in descending order. You can see this in the first two rows which have identical *firstname* values. Now look at the *dob* field of the first two rows.

It is also possible to sort the rows of a table by a field which will not be shown in the *query result*. First, let's execute the following SQL statement which shows the sort fields *managerid* and *dob* in the *query result*.

```
SELECT firstname, lastname, dob, managerid
FROM person ORDER BY managerid ASC, dob
DESC;
```

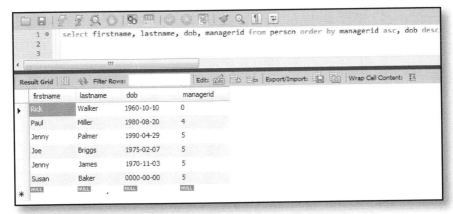

Figure 3-30: Sorting on two fields *managerid* and *dob*.

Now, let's execute the following SQL statement which eliminates the field *managerid* from the *query result*.

```
SELECT firstname, lastname, dob FROM person
ORDER BY managerid ASC, dob DESC;
```

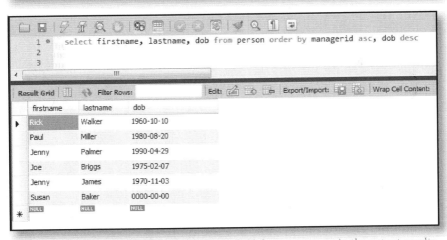

Figure 3-31: We can sort on a field even if that field does not appear in the output results.

As you can see in figure 3-31, except for the missing *managerid* column, we get exactly the same result as in figure 3-30.

1. What function allows you to access portions of a string?
   a. concat()
   b. substr()
   c. datediff()
   d. append()

2. Which of the following is not a SQL date function?
   a. month()
   b. datediff()
   c. now()
   d. round()

3. Which query cannot be executed because of a syntax error?
   a. SELECT * FROM person ORDER BY firstname DESC;
   b. SELECT * FROM person ORDER BY managerid ASC, dob DESC;
   c. SELECT firstname FROM person ORDER BY managerid ASC firstname DESC;
   d. SELECT firstname, lastname, dob FROM person;

4. Which of the following is not a function for text operations?
   a. left()
   b. right()
   c. concat()
   d. round()

LAB ACTIVITY

Write the output of the following functions:

1. Left ('John', 2)

_____

2. Datediff ('2013-10-24', '1986-07-14')

_____

3. Concat ('John', ' n', 'Doe')

_____

4. Substr ('John', 1, 3)

_____

5. Round (38.14567)

_____

LAB SOLUTION

1) Jo

2) 9922

3) JohnnDoe

4) Joh

5) 38

3.4 COLUMN ALIASES

In the last two sections, as we executed SQL SELECT statements, our focus was on the rows outputted in the query results. Now, let's focus on the column headings that identify the contents of each column.

If you review all the queries we executed, you will notice that if our query included an expression as one of its output, that expression would be used as a column heading. For example, we used the following expression to calculate a person's age:

```
DATEDIFF(NOW(),dob)/365
```

Take a look at figure 3-32:

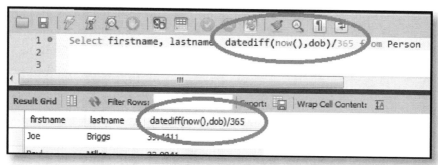

Figure 3-32: The expression in the SELECT statement becomes a column heading in the query result.

You can see where the expression in the query became a column heading in the query result. This is not exactly a user-friendly heading.

Execute the following query in Workbench:

```
SELECT firstname AS fn_name, lastname, dob
FROM person;
```

As you can see in figure 3-33, instead of *firstname* as a column heading, we changed it to "fn_name" with the **AS** keyword.

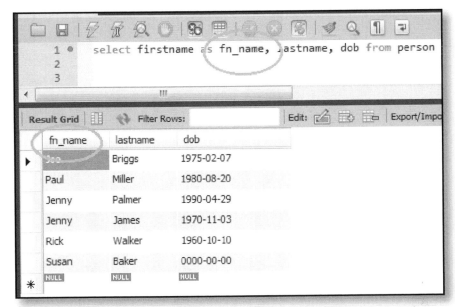

Figure 3-33: Using the AS keyword to change a column heading.

Now, execute the following query:

```
SELECT firstname AS fn_name, lastname 'Last
Name', dob FROM person;
```

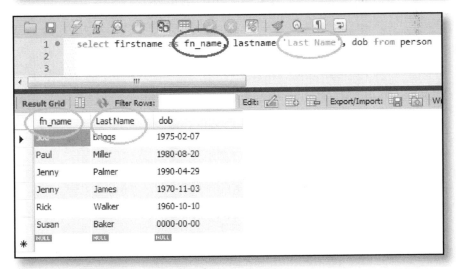

Figure 3-34: The AS keyword is optional.

As you can see in figure 3-34, we changed two column headings but we never used the AS keyword. That's because it is optional.

Now, execute this SELECT statement:

```
SELECT firstname AS fn_name, lastname 'Last
Name', dob Birthday FROM person;
```

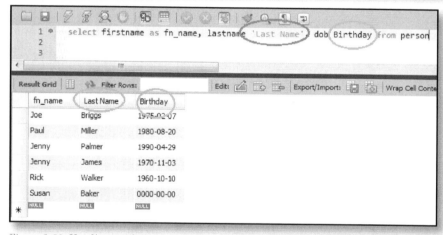

Figure 3-39: Headings with spaces should be enclosed in single quotes.

In this query, we changed three column headings but the important point to remember is in the second heading "Last Name" which we had to enclose in single quotes because of the space between the two words.

Now, execute this query:

```
SELECT LEFT(firstname, 1) initial, lastname,
dob FROM person;
```

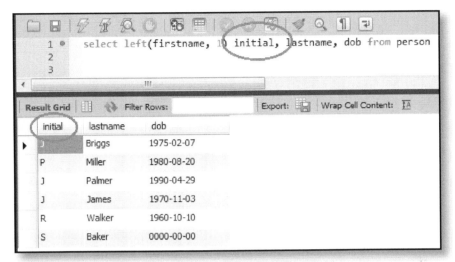

Figure 3-40: The heading of the first column is changed to "initial."

There's nothing unusual here. The heading of the first column has been changed to 'initial'. Now, execute this query:

```
SELECT LEFT(firstname, 1)initial, lastname,
dob FROM person ORDER BY initial ASC;
```

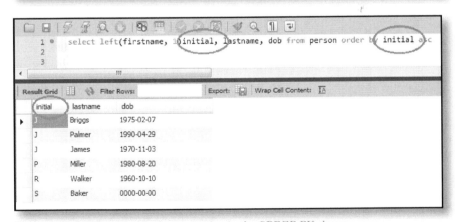

Figure 3-41: An alias used in the expression in the ORDER BY clause.

Notice that the expression we used in the ORDER BY clause is the alias we used, 'initial', to replace the default heading of the first column.

1. Which of the following queries will result in a compilation error?
    a. SELECT firstname AS FirstName FROM person;
    b. SELECT lastname LastName FROM person;
    c. SELECT lastname last name FROM person;
    d. SELECT dob birthday FROM person;

2. What is the maximum number of columns that can be used in an ORDER BY clause?
    a. 1.
    b. 2.
    c. 3.
    d. None of the above.

3. An alias must only be one word.
    a. True.
    b. False.

4. The AS keyword is optional.
    a. True.
    b. False

LAB ACTIVITY

The following screenshot is the result of executing this SELECT statement:

```
SELECT RIGHT(firstname,1), lastname FROM
person;
```

Now, revise the SELECT statement according to the following requirements:

1. Give "RIGHT(firstname,1)" the alias "Last Letter"
2. Give "lastname" the alias "ln"
3. Implement the aliases from steps one and two of the exercise, and then sort the query results according to *lastname* in ascending order.

1.
```
SELECT RIGHT(firstname, 1)'Last Letter,
lastname FROM person;
```

2.
```
SELECT RIGHT(firstname, 1), lastname ln
FROM person;
```

3.
```
SELECT right(firstname, 1) 'Last Letter',
lastname ln FROM person ORDER BY initial
ASC;
```

CHAPTER 3 LAB EXERCISE

1. Write a query returning all the records in the *project* table.
2. Write a query returning the name and budget of each *project*.
3. Sort the query results in number two by ascending budget amount.
4. Improve the budget column of the query in number four by rounding to two digits.
5. Name the rounded budget column of the query in number five "Budget".
6. Write a query returning a list of project names.
7. Modify the query in number six to limit the returned project names to five characters.
8. In the query in number seven, rename the project name column to "prcode".

CHAPTER 3 LAB SOLUTION

1.
```
SELECT * FROM project;
```

2.
```
SELECT label, budget FROM project;
```

3.
```
SELECT label, budget FROM project ORDER
BY budget ASC;
```

4.
```
SELECT label, ROUND(budget, 2) FROM
project ORDER BY budget ASC;
```

5.
```
SELECT label, ROUND(budget, 2) budget
FROM project ORDER BY budget ASC;
```

6.
```
SELECT label FROM project;
```

7.
```
SELECT LEFT(label, 5) FROM project;
```

8.
```
SELECT LEFT(label, 5) prcode FROM project;
```

Chapter Summary

In this chapter, we began our study of the SELECT statement – the most complex and frequently used of all the SQL statements. We know that when we execute a SELECT statement, we are executing a query. The data retrieved by a query is stored in a query result or resultset, which is a virtual table identical in structure to a permanent database table.

We looked into numerous examples of the SELECT, FROM, and ORDER BY clauses of the SELECT statement.

We saw how to use the DISTINCT keyword, which eliminates duplicates.

We used several SQL functions such as **concat()**, **concat_ws()**, **datediff()**, **left()**, **month()**, **now()**, **round()**, and **substr()** to format the output of our fields.

We learned how to use the ORDER BY clause to control the order in which the output rows are presented in the query result or resultset.

Finally, we studied how to use column aliases to modify the column headings of query results to make them more understandable.

We will continue our study of the other clauses of the SELECT statement in the next chapters.

CHAPTER 4
THE SELECT STATEMENT – PART II

CHAPTER OBJECTIVES

- You will learn how to build conditional expressions for the predicate of the WHERE clause.
- You will learn about comparison operators, logical operators, test operators, the negation operator, and wildcard characters.
- You will learn when to effectively use the NULL value.
- You will learn how to test for the NULL value in conditional expressions.

4.1 THE WHERE CLAUSE

In the previous chapter, we began studying the most powerful and complicated of the SQL statements, SELECT, and we concentrated on that statement's SELECT, FROM, and ORDER BY clauses. Let's review the syntax of the SELECT statement:

SELECT { all, distinct } { select-item }
   FROM table-specification
   WHERE predicate (or search-condition)
   GROUP BY grouping-column
   HAVING search condition
   ORDER BY sort-specification.

We saw that the SELECT statement in its simplest form,

```
SELECT * FROM person;
```

displayed all fields of all rows—a very unwieldy query result. But we learned how to limit the retrieved fields by specifying the exact names of the fields to be included.

In this chapter, we are going to limit the rows to be retrieved by using the WHERE clause.

WHERE predicate (or search-condition)

This clause requires a **predicate** or **search-condition**, which is just a conditional expression that evaluates to one of the Boolean values, TRUE or FALSE. If the data in a row fulfills the search-condition, the expression evaluates to TRUE and that row is included in the query result or resultset.

> **WHERE**

> **Predicate**
>
> **Search-Condition**

We can create two types of predicates or search-conditions.

1. Simple predicates, which use one of the comparison or relationship operators.
2. Complex predicates, which use comparison operators as well as logical operators.

In creating predicates, we need several types of operators, namely:

1. comparison or relationship operators
2. logical operators
3. test operators

First, we will summarize the comparison operators in the following diagram where "LS" means "(the) Left Side" and "RS" means "(the) Right Side."

COMPARISON OPERATORS DIAGRAM

Operator	Example	Result
= (equal)	LS = RS	TRUE if the expression stored on the LS is equal to the expression on the RS; FALSE otherwise.
!	!(cond)	Negates a Boolean condition. TRUE becomes FALSE and FALSE becomes TRUE. It is most often used to negate equality as in !=.
!= or <> (not equal to)	LS != RS or LS <> RS	TRUE if the expression stored on the LS does not equal the expression stored on the RS; FALSE otherwise.
> (greater than)	LS > RS	Tests if the expression on the left side of the operator is greater than the expression on the right side of the operator.

< (less than)	LS < RS	Tests if the expression on the left side of the operator is less than the expression on the right side of the operator.
>= (greater than or equal to)	LS >= RS	Tests if the expression on the left side of the operator is greater than or equal to the expression on the right side of the operator.
<= (less than or equal to)	LS <= RS	Tests if the expression on the left side of the operator is less than or equal to the expression on the right side of the operator.

Diagram 4-1: The comparison or relationship operators.

We use these comparison operators to create simple predicates. The following summary lists the simple predicates used in the SELECT statement examples in this chapter.

```
SELECT * FROM Person WHERE id = 3;
SELECT firstname, lastname, dob FROM person
WHERE id = 3;

SELECT * FROM person WHERE id <> 2;
SELECT * FROM person WHERE id != 2;
SELECT * FROM person WHERE id >= 2;
SELECT * FROM person WHERE id <= 2;

SELECT * FROM person WHERE lastname =
'Briggs';
SELECT * FROM person WHERE lastname >
'Briggs';
SELECT * FROM person WHERE lastname >=
'Briggs';

SELECT * FROM person WHERE lastname >= 'M';

SELECT * FROM person WHERE dob = '1980-08-
20';
```

Now, using the rules of logic, we can use the logical operators to combine simple predicates to form more complex predicates.

This is a summary of the logical operators AND and OR where "exp1" and "exp2" are simple predicates.

LOGICAL OPERATORS DIAGRAM

Operator	Example	Result
AND	exp1 AND exp2	TRUE only if both exp1 and exp2 evaluate to TRUE; FALSE otherwise.
OR	exp1 OR exp2	TRUE if either exp1 and exp2 evaluate to TRUE or both exp1 and exp2 are TRUE; FALSE only if both exp1 and exp2 are FALSE.

Diagram 4-2: The logical operators.

The following summary shows the SELECT statements in this chapter that use complex predicates.

```
SELECT firstname, lastname, dob FROM person
WHERE managerid=5 AND firstname = 'Jenny'

SELECT * FROM person WHERE managerid=5 AND
firstname = 'Jenny'

SELECT * FROM person WHERE dob > '1970-12-
31' AND managerid=5
SELECT * FROM person WHERE dob > '1970-12-
31' OR managerid=5


SELECT * FROM person WHERE dob > '1970-12-
31' AND managerid=5 AND id > 1

SELECT * FROM person WHERE dob > '1970-12-
31' AND managerid=5 OR id > 2
```

```
SELECT * FROM person WHERE (dob > '1970-12-
31' AND managerid=5) OR id > 2

SELECT * FROM person WHERE dob > '1970-12-
31' AND (managerid=5 OR id > 2)
```

In addition to the comparison and logical operators, SQL provides the following test operators which can be used to form simple predicates. The logical operators AND and OR can also be used to combine the predicates formed with these test operators into more complex ones.

TEST OPERATORS DIAGRAM

Operator	Name	Description
not	Not (Negation) Operator	Negates a Boolean condition. TRUE becomes FALSE and FALSE becomes TRUE.
between (not between)	Range Test	Checks whether a data value lies between two specified values.
like (not like)	Pattern Matching Test	Checks to see whether the data value in a column matches a specified *pattern* that contains the wildcard characters % (percent) and _ (underscore).
is null (is not null)	Null Value Test	Checks to see whether the data value is null.
in (not in)	Set Membership Test	Tests whether a data value matches one of a list of target values.

Diagram 4-3: The test operators.

The following diagram summarizes the wildcard characters used by the like operator.

WILDCARD DIAGRAM

Wildcard	Name	Result
%	Percent	Matches any sequence of zero or more characters.
_	Underscore	Matches any single character.

Diagram 4-4: Wildcard characters.

Here is a summary of the SELECT statements in this chapter that use the test operators and wildcard characters in the predicates.

```
SELECT * FROM person WHERE id BETWEEN 2 AND
5

SELECT * FROM person WHERE lastname IN
('Palmer','James')

SELECT * FROM person WHERE notes LIKE
'%CEO%'
SELECT * FROM person WHERE notes LIKE
'rick%'
SELECT * FROM person WHERE lastname LIKE
'_a%'

SELECT * FROM person WHERE notes = NULL
SELECT * FROM person WHERE managerid IS
NULL
SELECT * FROM person WHERE managerid IS NOT
NULL
```

In the next section, we will study the simple and complex predicates used in the WHERE clause.

QUESTIONS FOR REVIEW

1. In the WHERE clause of the SELECT statement, what should the keyword WHERE be followed by?
   a. A logical operator.
   b. An unlimited number of tests.
   c. A predicate.
   d. A subject.

2. What operator uses the wildcard characters % and _?
   a. BETWEEN.
   b. comparison.
   c. logical.
   d. LIKE.

3. The logical operators AND and OR can be used to connect a maximum of four conditional expressions.
   a. True.
   b. False.

4. Which is a valid comparison operator?
   a. !<=
   b. !<>
   c. !>=
   d. !=

4.2 SIMPLE PREDICATES AND THE COMPARISON OPERATORS

Let's start with simple predicates.

If you have forgotten, first you have to start WampServer, then start MySQL Workbench and connect to our database.

Once you're up and running, display all the fields of all the records in the table *person*.

```
SELECT * FROM person;
```

The following screenshot shows the SELECT statement in the query panel and the query result in the result grid.

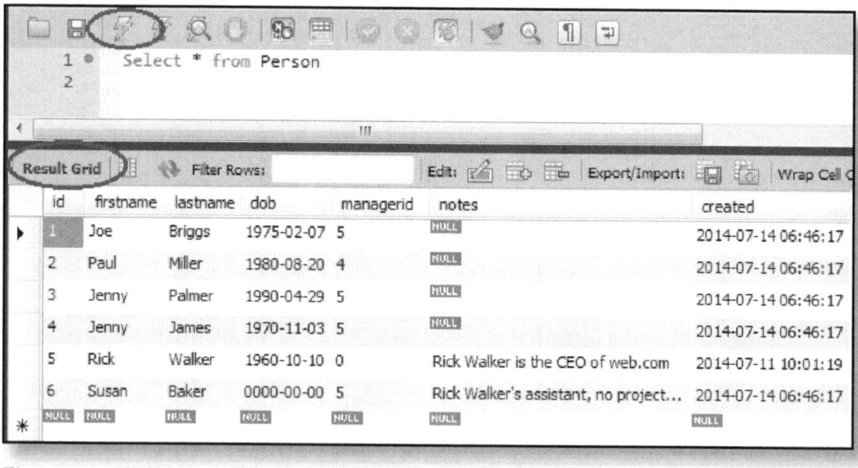

Figure 4-1: All fields of all records of *person*.

We will use this query result, showing all fields of all records of the table *person,* as a basis for comparing the results we get when we use the WHERE clause.

Now, the next screenshot (figure 4-2) shows a SELECT statement with a WHERE clause in the query panel.

```
SELECT * FROM person WHERE id=3;
```

Type that same SELECT statement in the query panel of your
Workbench and execute it by clicking on the "Execute SQL Script"
icon. Your Result Grid should show the same result as that shown
in figure 4-2:

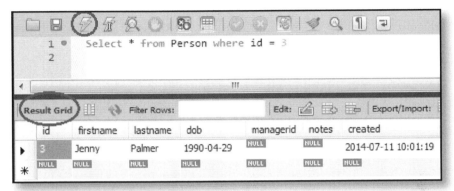

Figure 4-2: Searching on the primary key *id*.

You should always check your output panel for the white checkmark on
a green circular background, which indicates that the query executed
correctly. Figure 4-3 shows the Output Panel for the execution of the
SELECT statement of the previous screen.

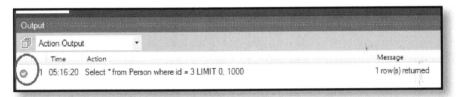

Figure 4-3: The output screen for "SELECT * FROM person WHERE id=3;"

Now, our SELECT statement retrieved the record whose *id* holds the
numeric value 3. Since *id* is the primary key of *person*, its value is unique
and we will get only one record in our query result.

Since we used the wildcard character (*), all the fields of the record are
displayed. But just like in the previous chapter, we can select the fields
we want displayed. The field used in the predicate of our WHERE clause
need not be in the fields we chose to retrieve.

```
SELECT firstname, lastname, dob FROM person
WHERE id=3;
```

In figure 4-4, execute the SELECT statement you see in the query window.

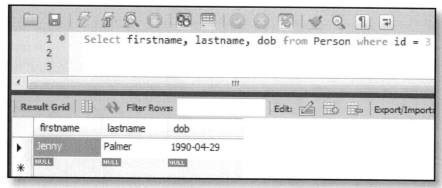

Figure 4-4: Displaying only three fields of a record.

We expect to still get only one record and we display only three fields of that record.

Take a look at our next SELECT statement in figure 4-5.

```
SELECT firstname, lastname, dob FROM person
WHERE managerid=5;
```

Execute this statement in your Workbench and match your results with the query results shown in the Result Grid.

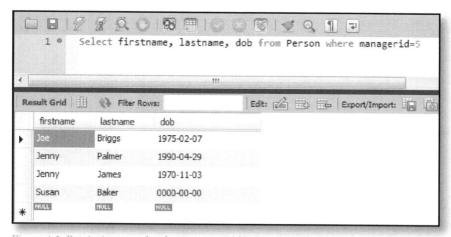

Figure 4-5: Retrieving records whose *managerid* holds the value 5.

Now, after using the equal comparison operator (=), let's try the not equal to operator (!= or <>).

```
SELECT * FROM person WHERE id<>2;
```

or

```
SELECT * FROM person WHERE id!=2;
```

Here is the SELECT statement to execute and your expected output in the result grid.

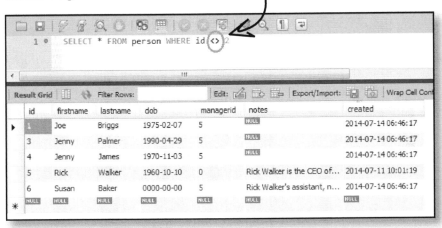

Figure 4-6: The not equal to comparison operator (<>). Using (!=) would produce identical results.

As expected, all the records of the *person* were retrieved except for the one record whose *id* is 2.

Figure 4-7 shows the same result, but this time we used the != operator.

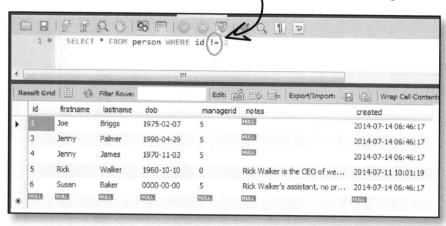

Figure 4-7: The not equal to comparison operator (!=).

So far, we have been using numeric values in our predicates. Now, let's use string values.

```
SELECT firstname, lastname, dob, managerid
FROM person WHERE lastname='Briggs';
```

Figure 4-8 shows the SELECT statement to execute and the results to expect in your Result Grid.

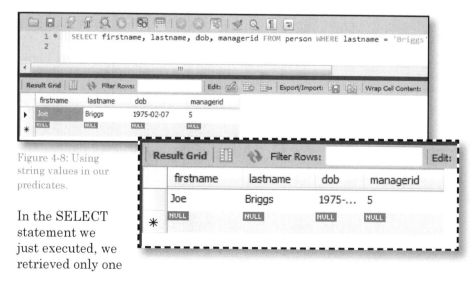

Figure 4-8: Using string values in our predicates.

In the SELECT statement we just executed, we retrieved only one record, meaning that we have only one person whose last name is Briggs. Now, let's modify our predicate and then execute this next SELECT statement:

```
SELECT firstname, lastname, dob, managerid
FROM person WHERE firstname='Jenny';
```

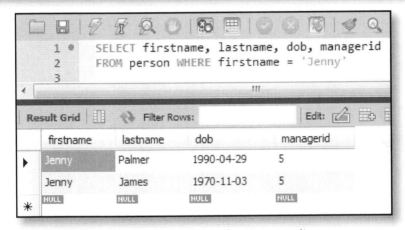

Figure 4-9: Still using string values in our predicates.

Our result grid shows two records, meaning there are two persons both with first name Jenny.

Let's use a date value in our predicate.

```
SELECT * FROM person WHERE dob='1980-08-
20';
```

Figure 4-10: Retrieving a specific date value.

In the previous SELECT statement, we searched for a person whose birth date is a specific value and we obtained one record.

Now, in the next screenshot, we have changed our comparison operator from equals (=) to greater than (>).

```
SELECT * FROM person WHERE dob>'1980-08-
20);
```

Figure 4-11: Using the comparison operator greater than (>) on a date value.

We find one person ten years younger than Paul Miller.

Now, in our final screenshot (figure 4-12) for this section, we have changed our comparison operator from greater than (>) to less than (<).

```
SELECT * FROM person WHERE dob<'1990-08-
20';
```

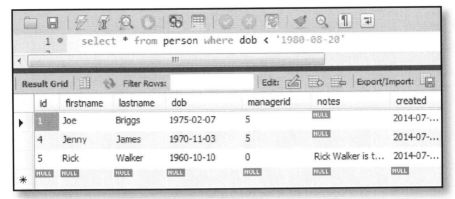

Figure 4-12: Using the comparison operator less than (<) on a date value.

This time, we found three people older than Paul Miller.

Note that in our use of the =, > and < operators against the date value '1980-08-20' we did not retrieve the record of Susan Baker. This is because her *dob* is set to the NULL value.

Carfully study the three conditional expressions we used, namely:

```
dob = '1980-08-20'
dob > '1980-08-20'
dob < '1980-08-20'
```

Observe that in neither of the previous conditional expressions was the null value in Susan Baker's *dob* field retrieved.

This leads to an important conclusion. In conditional expressions where a field is compared against a NULL value, the conditional expression evaluates to neither TRUE nor FALSE.

We will discuss this peculiarity of the null value later on in this chapter.

QUESTIONS FOR REVIEW

1. What is the function of the predicate in the WHERE clause?
    a. It sets the maximum number of records that can be retrieved.
    b. It establishes the sorting order of the primary key fields.
    c. It determines the order of the rows to be retrieved.
    d. It provides the search condition, which determines what records to retrieve.

2. What will "SELECT * FROM sometable" return?
    a. An error.
    b. All of the records from *sometable* but only the first field.
    c. All of the fields and records from *sometable*.
    d. All of the records from *sometable* that contain the character "*".

3. What is the window or panel in MySQL Workbench called that displays status or error messages for every SQL statement that is executed?
    a. Output panel.
    b. Result grid.
    c. Query panel.
    d. Message window.

4. A conditional expression compared against a NULL value returns FALSE.
    a. True.
    b. False.

LAB ACTIVITY

Write three queries that return data from *contact*. Have the first query return only phone numbers, have the second query return only email addresses, and have the third query return phone numbers and street addresses.

LAB SOLUTION

Use the value of *ctid* to determine the type of contact you're displaying.
Email addresses are 1, phone numbers are 2, and street addresses are 3.
Your queries should look like the following:

```
SELECT * FROM contact WHERE ctid=2;

SELECT * FROM contact WHERE ctid=1;

SELECT * FROM contact WHERE ctid>=2;
```

4.3 COMPLEX PREDICATES AND THE LOGICAL OPERATORS

We are now ready to use the logical operators AND and OR to form complex predicates.

The AND operator requires and evaluates two conditional expressions and returns either the Boolean value TRUE or FALSE based on the following truth table.

AND

Cond1	Cond2	Cond1 AND Cond2 Returns
TRUE	TRUE	TRUE
TRUE	FALSE	FALSE
FALSE	TRUE	FALSE
FALSE	FALSE	FALSE

Diagram 4-5: AND truth table for two conditional expressions.

> **Tip:** The only time the AND operator returns TRUE is when the two conditional expressions it operates on are both TRUE.

The OR operator also requires and evaluates two conditional expressions and returns either TRUE or FALSE based on the following truth table.

OR

Cond1	Cond2	Cond1 OR Cond2 Returns
TRUE	TRUE	TRUE
TRUE	FALSE	TRUE
FALSE	TRUE	TRUE
FALSE	FALSE	FALSE

Diagram 4-6: OR truth table for two conditional expressions.

> **TIP:** The only time the OR operator returns FALSE is when the two conditional expressions it operates on are both FALSE.

Figure 4-13 shows a SELECT statement using the AND operator and the expected output in the Result Grid.

```
SELECT firstname, lastname, dob, managerid
FROM person WHERE managerid=5 AND
firstname='Jenny';
```

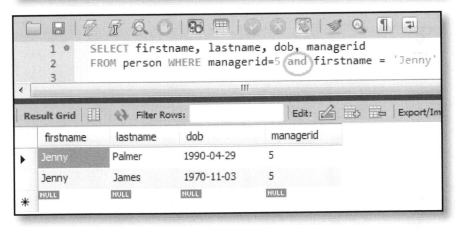

Figure 4-13: The AND logical operator.

Let's study the two conditional expressions in the WHERE clause.

```
managerid = 5
firstname = 'Jenny'
```

To verify the previous results, first we reproduce a screenshot of all the records of *person*. The two rows that were retrieved by our query are indicated by the two arrows.

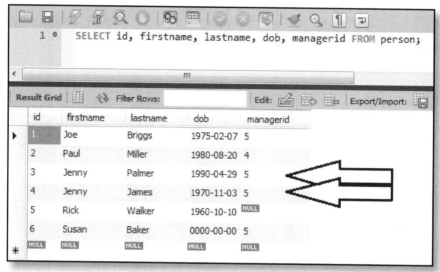

Figure 4-14: All the records of *person*.

Then, we create a truth table for the conditions in the predicate of the WHERE clause.

id	managerid=5	firstname='Jenny'	managerid=5 AND firstname='Jenny'
1	TRUE	FALSE	FALSE
2	FALSE	FALSE	FALSE
3	TRUE	TRUE	TRUE
4	TRUE	TRUE	TRUE
5	FALSE	FALSE	FALSE
6	TRUE	FALSE	FALSE

Diagram 4-7: Truth table for managerid=5 AND firstname='Jenny'

In the preceding truth table, the last column shows two TRUE values, which correspond to the two records retrieved by our query.

Now, let's replace the AND operator with an OR operator. The following screenshot (figure 4-15) shows what records were retrieved.

```
SELECT firstname, lastname, dob, managerid
FROM person WHERE managerid=5 OR
firstname='Jenny';
```

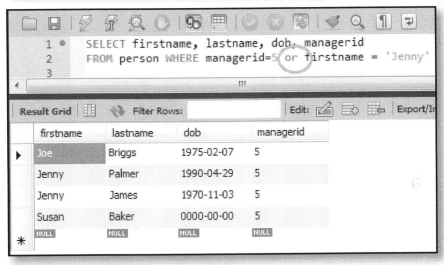

Figure 4-15: The OR logical operator.

The screenshot now shows four records were retrieved just by changing the AND operator in the previous query to the OR operator.

To analyze why these four records were retrieved, the following truth table for the conditions in the predicate of the WHERE clause has been created and completed.

id	managerid=5	firstname='Jenny'	managerid=5 OR firstname='Jenny'	
1	TRUE	FALSE	TRUE	✓
2	FALSE	FALSE	FALSE	
3	TRUE	TRUE	TRUE	✓
4	TRUE	TRUE	TRUE	✓
5	FALSE	FALSE	FALSE	
6	TRUE	FALSE	TRUE	✓

Diagram 4-8: Truth table for managerid=5 OR firstname='Jenny'

In the preceding truth table, the last column shows four TRUE values that correspond to the four records retrieved by our query.

Now, let's try three conditional expressions joined by two AND operators in our predicate as shown in the following screenshot.

```
SELECT id, firstname, lastname, dob,
managerid FROM person WHERE dob > '1970-12-
31' AND managerid=5 AND id>1;
```

Figure 4-16: Three conditional expressions connected by AND.

We then construct a truth table for three conditional expressions connected by two AND logical operators. This table shows that the entire predicate will return TRUE only if the three conditional expressions all return TRUE.

Cond1	Cond2	Cond3	Cond1 AND Cond2 AND Cond3 Returns
TRUE	TRUE	TRUE	TRUE
TRUE	FALSE	FALSE	FALSE
FALSE	TRUE	FALSE	FALSE
FALSE	FALSE	TRUE	FALSE
TRUE	TRUE	FALSE	FALSE
FALSE	TRUE	TRUE	FALSE
FALSE	FALSE	FALSE	FALSE

Diagram 4-9: AND truth table for three conditional expressions.

Thus, in our last query, it is only Jenny Palmer's record that satisfied all three conditions of our predicate.

```
dob > '1970-12-31'
managerid = 5
id > 1
```

In figure 4-17, you can see the records that failed to return TRUE for the entire predicate.

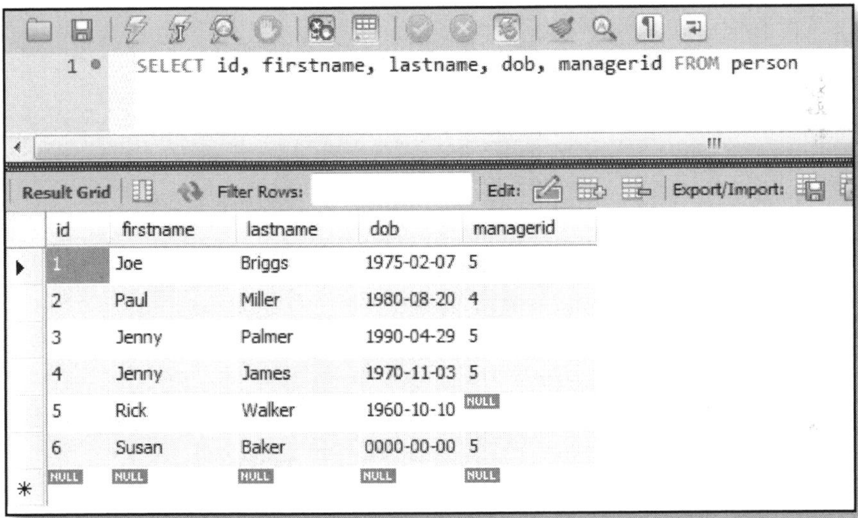

id	firstname	lastname	dob	managerid
1	Joe	Briggs	1975-02-07	5
2	Paul	Miller	1980-08-20	4
3	Jenny	Palmer	1990-04-29	5
4	Jenny	James	1970-11-03	5
5	Rick	Walker	1960-10-10	NULL
6	Susan	Baker	0000-00-00	5
NULL	NULL	NULL	NULL	NULL

Figure 4-17: All records of *person*.

Now, let's replace the two AND operators with the OR operator. Figure 4-18 shows our modified SELECT statement and the results in the result grid.

```
SELECT id, firstname, lastname, dob,
managerid FROM person WHERE dob > '1970-12-
31' OR managerid=5 OR id > 5;
```

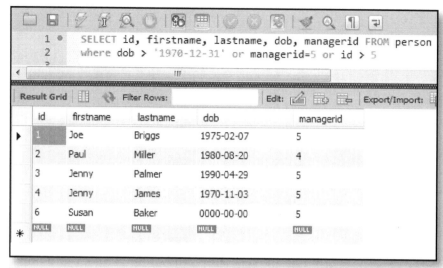

Figure 4-18: dob > '1970-12-31' OR managerid=5 OR id > 5

In the predicate shown in this screenshot, all three conditional expressions are connected entirely by OR operators. This means that for the entire predicate to result in TRUE, only one of the three conditional expressions must evaluate to TRUE.

The entire predicate will result in FALSE only if all three conditional expressions evaluate to FALSE.

Now, let's make things more exciting and complicated. In the next screenshot (figure 4-19), the SELECT statement still has the same three conditional expressions, but this time we have an AND logical operator and an OR logical operator connecting the three conditional expressions.

```
SELECT id, firstname, lastname, dob,
managerid FROM person WHERE (dob > '1970-
12-31' OR managerid=5) AND id > 5;
```

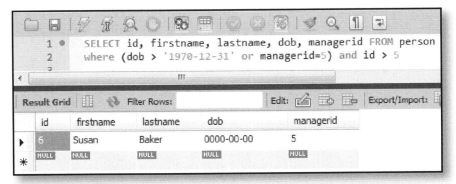

Figure 4-19: (dob > '1970-12-31' OR managerid=5) AND id > 5

Let's take a careful look at our entire predicate.

```
(dob > '1970-12-31' or managerid=5) and id > 5
```

First, take note of the parentheses. This will instruct SQL to evaluate the conditional expression within the parentheses first using the OR truth table.

```
(dob > '1970-12-31' or managerid=5)
```

Then the result of the expression within the parentheses and the third conditional expression, id > 5, will be evaluated using the AND truth tables.

```
(dob > '1970-12-31' or managerid=5) and id > 5
```

RESULT

If you omit the parentheses, the results will not only be unpredictable but incorrect.

> **TIP:** When constructing a predicate that has more than two conditional expressions connected by either AND and OR logical operators, use parentheses to establish an order of evaluation. Otherwise, the results will be erroneous.

To assist us in evaluating the predicate, we construct a modified truth table which is only applicable to our particular predicate.

To help us accurately fill in the table, here we are reproducing the fields *id, dob* and *managerid* and all six records of table *person*

ID	Cond1 dob > '1970-12-31'	Cond2 Managerid = 5	(cond1 or cond2)	Cond3 Id > 5	(cond1 or cond2) and cond3
1	True	True	True	False	False
2	True	False	True	False	False
3	True	True	True	False	False
4	False	True	True	False	False
5	True	False	True	False	False
6	true	True	True	True	True

Diagram 4-10: Truth table for the predicate: (dob > '1970-12-31' or managerid=5) and id > 5.

As we can see in the last column of this truth table, only the record whose *id* is 6 is retrieved by the query.

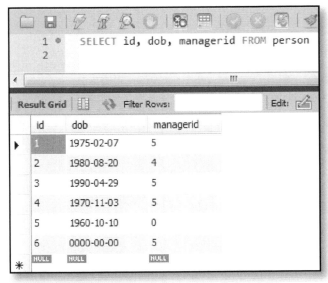

Figure 4-20: The *id*, *dob* and *managerid* for all records of *person*.

QUESTIONS FOR REVIEW

1. Which of the following is an invalid comparison operator?
   a. <
   b. >
   c. !=
   d. ==

2. The only time the OR operator returns FALSE is when the two conditional expressions it operates on are both FALSE.
   a. True.
   b. False.

3. Using parenthesis in a complex predicate is required.
   a. True.
   b. False.

4. What is the main function of a truth table?
   a. It determines the algebraic result of a simple predicate.
   b. It determines the Boolean result of a complex predicate.
   c. It determines the numeric result of a logical expression.
   d. It determines the maximum value of a string function.

The following diagram is a truth table for a complex predicate consisting of three conditional expressions connected by two OR logical operators. Fill in the last column.

Cond1	Cond2	Cond3	Cond1 OR Cond2 OR Cond3 Returns
TRUE	TRUE	TRUE	
TRUE	FALSE	FALSE	
FALSE	TRUE	FALSE	
FALSE	FALSE	TRUE	
TRUE	TRUE	FALSE	
FALSE	TRUE	TRUE	
TRUE	FALSE	TRUE	
FALSE	FALSE	FALSE	

LAB SOLUTION

Cond1	Cond2	Cond3	Cond1 OR Cond2 OR Cond3 Returns
TRUE	TRUE	TRUE	TRUE
TRUE	FALSE	FALSE	TRUE
FALSE	TRUE	FALSE	TRUE
FALSE	FALSE	TRUE	TRUE
TRUE	TRUE	FALSE	TRUE
FALSE	TRUE	TRUE	TRUE
TRUE	FALSE	TRUE	TRUE
FALSE	FALSE	FALSE	FALSE

4.4 Test Operators

We start with the Range Test which uses the BETWEEN operator to check if a data value lies between two specified values—a low value and a high value. The BETWEEN operator is inclusive in nature which means that the low and high values will be included in the resultset.

BETWEEN

Figure 4-21 shows a SELECT statement that will retrieve all rows in *person* whose *id* holds the values beginning from 2 to and 5 inclusive.

```
SELECT * FROM person WHERE id BETWEEN 2 AND 5;
```

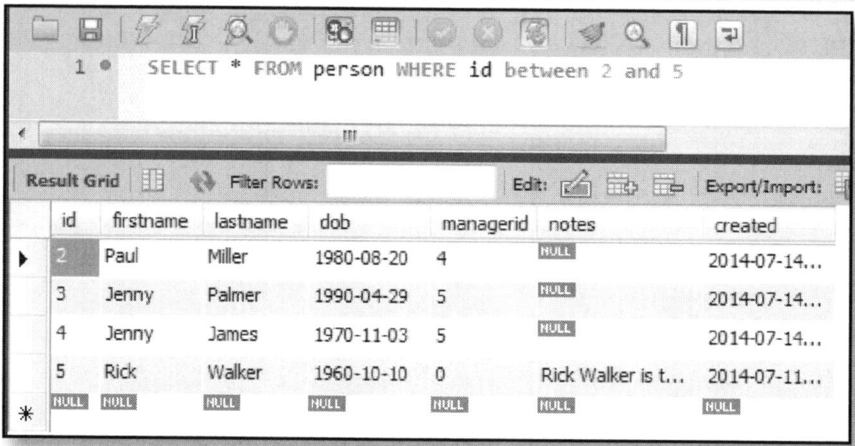

id	firstname	lastname	dob	managerid	notes	created
2	Paul	Miller	1980-08-20	4	NULL	2014-07-14...
3	Jenny	Palmer	1990-04-29	5	NULL	2014-07-14...
4	Jenny	James	1970-11-03	5	NULL	2014-07-14...
5	Rick	Walker	1960-10-10	0	Rick Walker is t...	2014-07-11...
NULL	NULL	NULL	NULL	NULL	NULL	NULL

Figure 4-21: Using the between operator on numeric values.

The data types of the data value to be tested and the lower and upper limits must be compatible. In the previous SELECT statement, *id* is numeric, so the upper and lower values are written as numeric literals.

In figure 4-22, the data value to be tested is a *string* data type and so the upper and lower values are written as *string* literals.

```
SELECT * FROM person WHERE lastname BETWEEN
'Baker' AND 'Miller';
```

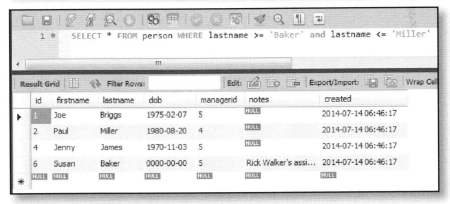

Figure 4-22: Using the *between* operator on string values.

The BETWEEN operator is actually a convenient way of using the >= and <= comparison operators. In the following screenshot, the previous SELECT statement has been rewritten using the >= and <= comparison operators.

```
SELECT * FROM person WHERE lastname >=
'Baker'AND lastname <= 'Miller';
```

Figure 4-23: Using the >= and <= instead of the *between* operator.

As you can see, we get exactly the same results as when we used the BETWEEN operator.

Now, we study the Set Membership Test which uses the IN operator to check whether a data value matches one of a list of target values. In the following screenshot, the data value of *lastname* is being checked to see if it is one of the target values 'Palmer' and/or 'James.'

IN

```
SELECT * FROM person WHERE lastname IN
('Palmer','James');
```

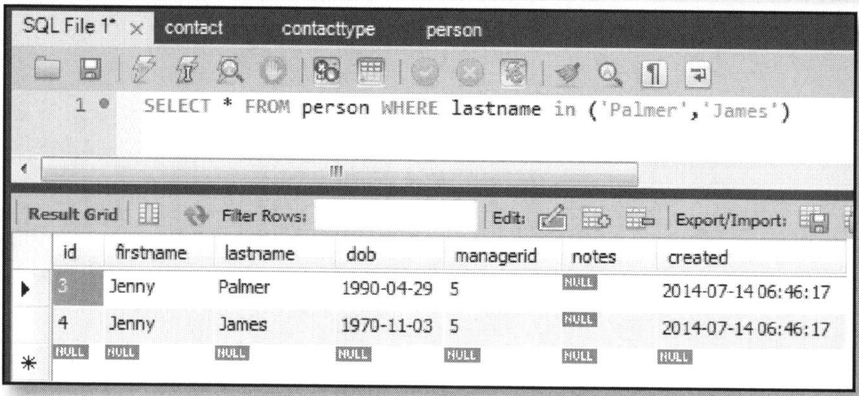

Figure 4-24: Using the Set Member Test operator – the *in* operator.

The IN operator is a convenient way of using multiple OR operators. In figure 4-24, the previous SELECT statement has been rewritten using the logical OR operator.

```
SELECT * FROM person WHERE
lastname='Palmer' OR lastname='James';
```

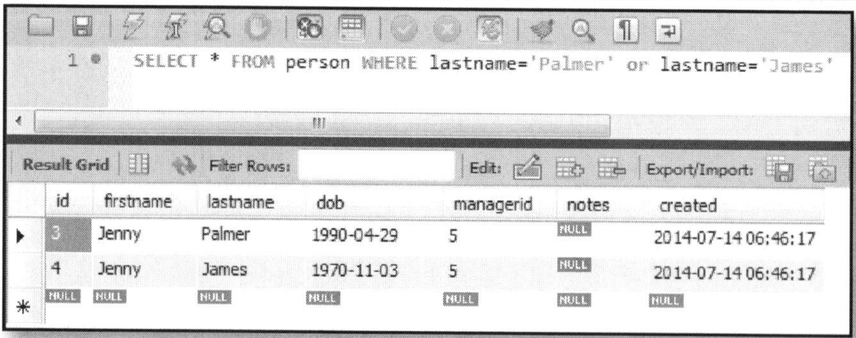

Figure 4-25: Using the OR logical expression instead of the IN operator.

We get exactly the same results as when we used the IN operator.

We now move to what many consider the most powerful and useful test operator, the LIKE operator, which is used in the Pattern Matching Test. With this test you can retrieve string or text values that match a certain pattern string. In this pattern string you use for testing, you usually include one or more of the wildcard characters, % (percent) or _ (underscore) whose functions are summarized in the following table:

LIKE

WILDCARD DIAGRAM

Wildcard	Name	Result
%	Percent	Matches any sequence of zero or more characters.
_	Underscore	Matches any single character.

Diagram 4-11: Examples of wildcard characters

The following diagram also provides examples of pattern strings for study to further your understanding of their effective use.

PATTERN STRING DIAGRAM

Pattern String	Matching Results
235%	Finds values that start with 235.
%abc%	Finds strings that contain the characters abc.
_P	Finds two-character strings whose last character is P.
%.%	Finds strings with any number of characters before and after a period.
W%.doc	Finds strings whose first character is W followed by any number of characters ending in .doc.
7___5	Finds 5-digit numbers that start with 7 and end with 5.
Y_%_%	Finds any string that starts with Y and is at least 3 characters in length.

Diagram 4-12: Examples of wildcard characters

The first wildcard character we will use is the percent sign (%).

In figure 4-26, the SELECT statement will retrieve a row in *person* whose *notes* field contains the characters 'CEO'. Placing the wildcard character (%) before and after the characters 'CEO' in the pattern string indicates that the characters 'CEO' can be located anywhere in the string value of *notes*.

```
SELECT id, firstname, lastname, notes FROM
person WHERE notes LIKE '%CEO%';
```

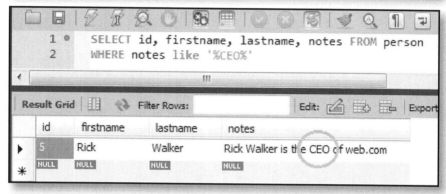

Figure 4-26: Using the % wildcard operator to search for a particular string in a field.

In the following screenshot, we have removed the first '%' character from the pattern string '%CEO%'. This indicates that the characters 'CEO' should be at the beginning of *notes*.

```
SELECT id, firstname, lastname, dob, notes
FROM person WHERE notes LIKE 'CEO%';
```

Figure 4-27: Using the % wildcard operator to search for a particular string in the beginning of a field.

Since no text value of *notes* has 'CEO' at its beginning, we don't retrieve any records.

Figure 4-28 shows a query using the LIKE operator.

```
SELECT * FROM person WHERE notes LIKE
'rick%';
```

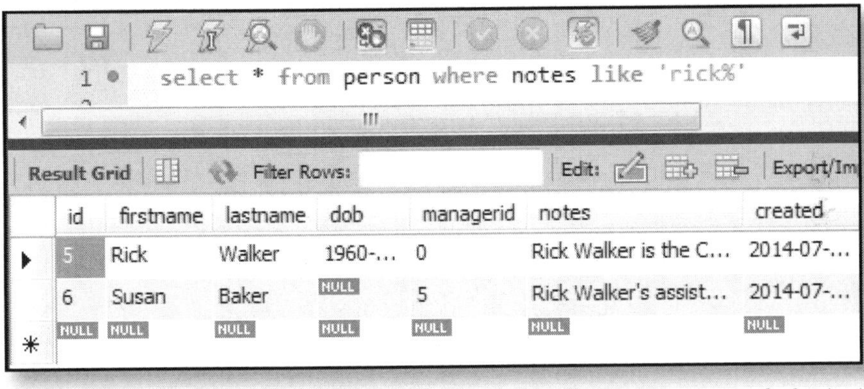

	id	firstname	lastname	dob	managerid	notes	created
▶	5	Rick	Walker	1960-...	0	Rick Walker is the C...	2014-07-...
	6	Susan	Baker	NULL	5	Rick Walker's assist...	2014-07-...
*	NULL	NULL	NULL	NULL	NULL	NULL	NULL

Figure 4-28: Using the % wildcard operator to search for a particular string in the beginning of a field.

In this query, where the characters 'Rick' should be found at the beginning of *notes*, two records were obtained.

In our last example for this section, we use the underscore (_) that matches any single character. In the SELECT statement in figure 4-29, we want to retrieve the records of persons with last names whose second character is the lowercase "a."

```
SELECT id, firstname, lastname, dob, notes
FROM person WHERE lastname LIKE '_a%';
```

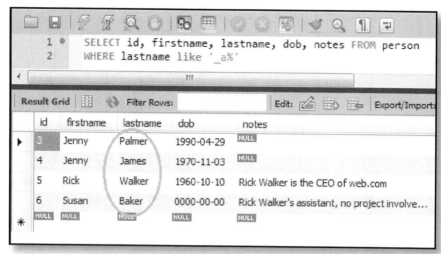

Figure 4-29: Using the _ wildcard operator to search for names with 'a' as their second character.

1. What test operator would you use to determine if a 3-character code is one of a valid list of 3-character codes?
   a. BETWEEN.
   b. LIKE.
   c. DISLIKE.
   d. IN.

2. What test operator would you use to retrieve the records of a person who falls between the ages of 31 and 40?
   a. BETWEEN.
   b. LIKE.
   c. DISLIKE.
   d. IN.

3. What pattern string would retrieve names that start with "A" and whose fifth character is "a"?
   a. A%a___
   b. A__a__
   c. A_%a_
   d. A___a%

4. What pattern string would retrieve records that start with the character "A" and end with the character "z," with any number of characters in between?

   a. A%z

   b. A*z

   c. a%z

   d. BETWEEN (A,z)

LAB ACTIVITY

For this lab activity, refer to the following image displaying all records of table *person:*

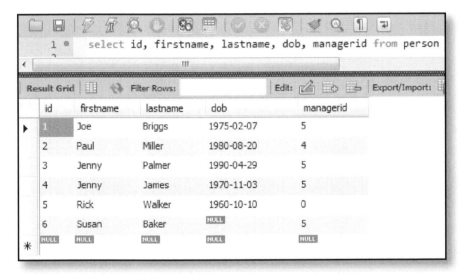

1. Write a query that displays *lastname* in the range of Palmer and Briggs.

2. Write a query that displays all records whose *firstname* starts with J.

3. Write a query that displays all records whose *firstname* starts with P or *lastname* ends with R.

Lab Solution

1.
```
SELECT * FROM person WHERE lastname IN
('Briggs', 'Palmer');
```

2.
```
SELECT * FROM person WHERE firstname LIKE
'j%';
```

3.
```
SELECT * FROM person WHERE firstname LIKE
'P%' OR lastname LIKE '_R%';
```

4.5 NULL VALUES

In the last chapter, we introduced the NULL value, which is an indicator that data is missing, unknown, or just doesn't apply. Sometimes, you will encounter the term "null data" or "null data type." This can sometimes lead to confusion because the NULL value is not a data type in the sense that integer and character values are data types. The NULL value, as stated earlier, is just an indicator that data is missing, unknown, or doesn't apply. Various DBMSs also handle NULL values differently, which can lead to even more confusion.

Let's consider the case of Susan Baker's record in *person*. The following screenshot shows that we had initially set it to the value '0000-00-00' because that piece of data was unavailable when Susan Baker's record was originally created.

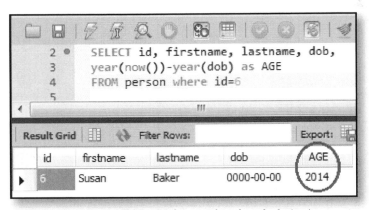

Figure 4-30: An impossible age, of course, but the calculation is correct.

This caused some problems because SQL could still calculate Susan's age based on the date '0000-00-00'. This erroneous calculation of age could go unnoticed and cause problems in later processing.

The proper procedure would be to set Susan Baker's *dob* to the NULL value. Then, SQL would also indicate her age as NULL as the following screenshot (figure 4-31) shows.

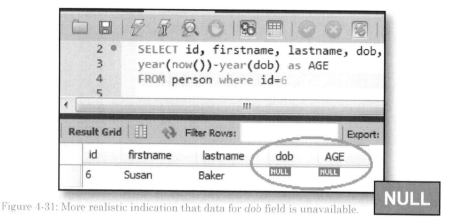

Figure 4-31: More realistic indication that data for *dob* field is unavailable.

Let's study another situation. Suppose there is a new project whose budget has not yet been determined, but persons have to be immediately assigned to it. As figure 4-32 demonstrates, a new record has been added to the *project* table.

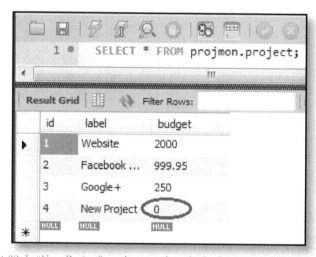

Figure 4-32: Is "New Project" pro-bono, or has the budget not yet been estimated?

Notice that *budget* has been set to zero. A budget of zero could be intended to represent a pro-bono project as opposed to a project with an unknown budget. To avoid confusion, a project with no budget should have its value of *budget* set to the NULL value, as shown in figure 4-33.

Figure 4-33: Here it is clear that budget data is still unavailable for New Project.

If you have to test for a NULL or a non-NULL value in a condition in your predicate, you have to use the IS NULL or IS NOT NULL tests. For example,

```
dob IS NULL
dob IS NOT NULL
```

You cannot use expressions like these:

```
dob = NULL
dob != NULL
```

The NULL keyword isn't really a data value, it is just an indicator or signal that the value is missing, unavailable, or not applicable. Even if the previous two examples were syntactically correct and would most likely execute without error, the results would be unpredictable and erroneous.

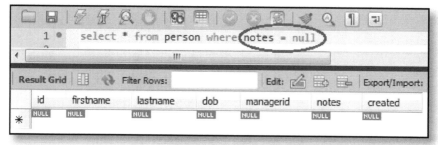

Figure 4-34: This is not the way to test for the NULL value in a conditional expression.

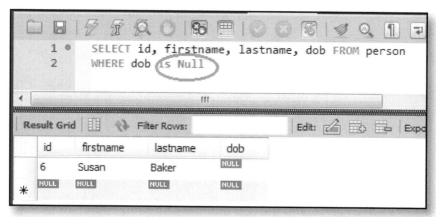

Figure 4-35: Using the IS NULL test operator.

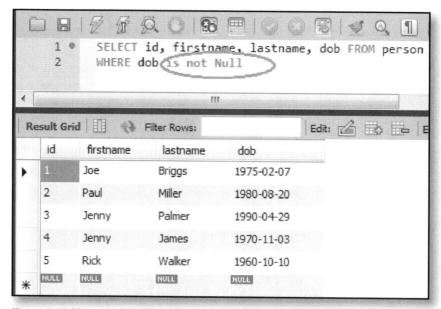

Figure 4-36: Using the IS NOT NULL test operator.

QUESTIONS FOR REVIEW

1. Why can't the equality operator (=) be used to test for NULL values?
   a. The equality operator does not recognize the NULL value.
   b. The NULL value is not a true data type.
   c. The equality operator evaluates the NULL value as true.
   d. The equality operator evaluates the NULL value as false.

2. Which conditional expression is valid for testing non-NULL values in the field *managerid*?
   a. managerid IS NOT = NULL
   b. managerid <> NULL
   c. managerid != NULL
   d. managerid IS NOT NULL

3. The NULL value can be considered to be the Boolean FALSE value in many cases.
   a. True.
   b. False.

4. When an optional field does not have a value, it is best practice to give that field the NULL value.
   a. True.
   b. False.

CHAPTER 4 LAB EXERCISE

1. Write a query returning the name and budget of the project with *id*= 3 in the *project* table.

2. Write a query returning all projects in *project* with the name "Website."

3. Write a query returning the names of all the projects in *project* with *budget* more than 500.

4. Write a query returning all projects in *project* with *budget* between 250 and 1500.

5. Write a query returning all projects in *project* with *budget* below 500 or above 1500.

6. Write a query returning all projects in *project* with *id* above 1 and *budget* above 500.

7. Write a query returning all projects in *project* without a defined *budget*.

8. Write a query returning all roles from *role* whose *title* includes "manager."

9. Write a query returning roles from *role* whose *title* is "Developer" or "Tester."

CHAPTER 4 LAB SOLUTION

1.
```
SELECT label, budget FROM project WHERE
id = 3;
```

2.
```
SELECT * FROM project WHERE label =
"Website";
```

3.
```
SELECT label FROM project WHERE budget >
500;
```

4.
```
SELECT * FROM project WHERE budget BETWEEN
250 AND 1500;
```

5.
```
SELECT * FROM project WHERE budget < 500
OR budget > 1500;
```

6.
```
SELECT * FROM project WHERE id > 1 AND
budget > 500;
```

7.
```
SELECT * FROM project WHERE budget IS
NULL;
```

8.
```
SELECT label FROM role WHERE label LIKE
'%manager%';
```

9.
```
SELECT label FROM role WHERE label =
'Tester' OR 'Developer';
```

CHAPTER SUMMARY

This chapter was devoted entirely to the WHERE clause. You learned how to build conditional expressions for the predicate of the WHERE clause.

You learned how to use comparison operators, logical operators, test operators, the negation operator, and wildcard characters in building various types of conditional expressions for the predicate of the WHERE clause.

We spent some time understanding the NULL value and we saw examples of some situations where it was appropriately used. There are still more aspects in the correct use of the NULL value to be considered, which we will encounter in the next chapters.

In the next chapter we will continue our study of the SELECT statement's powerful capabilities. We will be using all the clauses, operators, built-in functions, data types, constants, and other elements that we have already learned, but this time, instead of retrieving fields and records, we will be using the SELECT statement to provide summaries of our data.

CHAPTER 5

SUMMARY QUERIES

CHAPTER OBJECTIVES

- You will learn the five core ANSI standard aggregate functions: avg(), count(), max(), min(), and sum().
- You will learn how to use aggregate functions in the SELECT clause of a SQL query.
- You will learn how to combine query results with the UNION SQL feature.

5.1 THE COLUMN FUNCTIONS, AN OVERVIEW

In the last two chapters, we have been using the SELECT statement to retrieve individual fields and records of a table in a database. But the SELECT statement can also be used to provide comprehensive summaries of the data in the tables of our databases.

For example, we would like to know:
1. How many records does a table have?
2. How many NULL values are there in a column of data?
3. How many people work in the company?
4. What is the total amount of all the projects the company is working on?
5. How many employees can be contacted by cell phone or by email or by landline?

SQL provides **column** or **aggregate functions** that let you summarize data from a database. The column functions are used in the SELECT clause of the SELECT statement.

> **Column Functions**
>
> **Aggregate Functions**

The following table lists five ANSI standard column functions, which are also the most frequently used. These are the functions we will study in this chapter.

ANSI STANDARD COLUMN FUNCTIONS DIAGRAM

Function Name	Function Title	Description
avg()	Column Average	Computes the average value in a column.
count()	Column Count	Counts the number of values in a column. (NULL values are not counted.)
max()	Maximum Column Value	Finds the largest value in a column.
min()	Minimum Column Value	Finds the smallest value in a column.
sum()	Column Total	Computes the total of a column.

Diagram 5-1: ANSI SQL Column or Aggregate functions.

Each column function takes one argument that can be either a simple column name or a SQL expression.

Let's review the syntax of the SELECT statement.

SELECT { all, distinct } { select-item }
  FROM table-specification
  WHERE search condition
  GROUP BY grouping-column
  HAVING search condition
  ORDER BY sort-specification.

Here is a summary of the SELECT statements we will be using in this chapter:

```
SELECT * FROM person;
SELECT * FROM project;

SELECT count(*) FROM person;
SELECT count(notes) FROM person;
SELECT count(dob) FROM person;

SELECT sum(budget) FROM project;
SELECT avg(budget) FROM project;
SELECT min(budget) FROM project;
SELECT max(budget) FROM project;
SELECT max(label) FROM project;
SELECT min(label) FROM project;
SELECT min(budget) FROM project WHERE id <
3;

SELECT firstname, lastname, managerid FROM
person WHERE LEFT(firstname, 1) = 'J'
UNION
SELECT firstname, lastname, managerid FROM
person WHERE dob > '1980-01-01'
ORDER by lastname ASC;
```

5.2 THE COUNT() FUNCTION

Before we begin learning about our first column function, let's execute two queries to display all fields of all records in *person* and *project*.

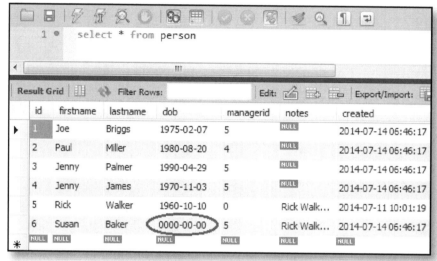

Figure 5-1: All fields of all records of *person*.

Notice that in figure 5-1, Susan Baker's *dob* is set to '0000-00-00' when it should have been set to the NULL value. We'll correct this later on, but for right now let's leave it as is to see the problems that arise from this setting.

The next screenshot shows all the fields and records of *project*.

Again, note carefully *budget* of the record with *id* 4. It has been set to the NULL value, indicating that the value for *budget* has not yet been determined.

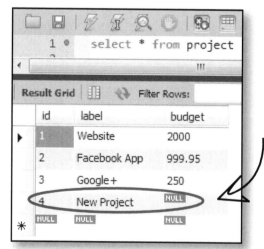

Figure 5-2: All fields of all records of the table *project*.

The first column function we will study is **count()**. The following code shows its simplest form in a SELECT statement.

```
SELECT COUNT(*) FROM person;
```

Figure 5-3 shows you the result of the simple SELECT statement.

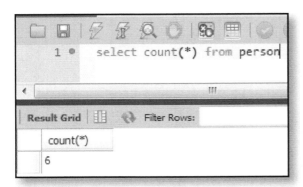

Since we used the asterisk as the argument to the **count()** function, it counted all of the records of *person*.

Figure 5-3: Counting all records of *person*.

In our next SELECT statement we are going to replace the asterisk with "notes," shown in the following code sample.

```
SELECT COUNT(notes) FROM person;
```

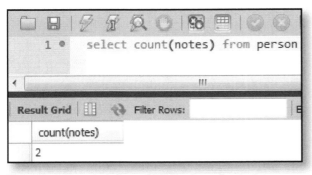

Now, we get only 2 as a result instead of the expected 6 because NULL values are ignored by the column functions. Take a look at the query showing all fields of all records of *person* and focus on the *notes* column. Of the six records, four have NULL values for *notes*.

Figure 5-4: Counting all non-NULL values of *notes* in *person*

> **TIP:** The **avg()**, **count()**, **max()**, **min()**, and **sum()** aggregate functions ignore NULL values in their processing.

Now, let's **count()** on a date field. Run the query in this next screenshot.

```
SELECT COUNT(dob) FROM person;
```

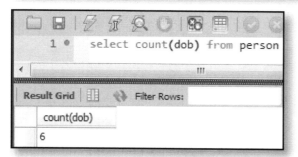

We get 6 even if Susan Baker's *dob* is set to '0000-00-00'. But what if her *dob* is set to the NULL value?

Figure 5-5: Counting all non-NULL values in *dob* with Susan Baker's *dob* field set to '0000-00-00'

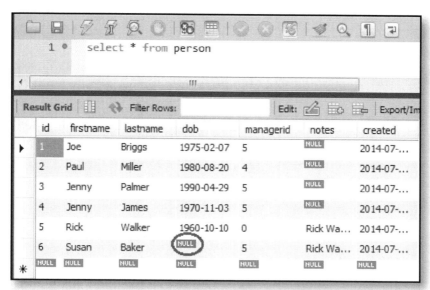

Figure 5-6 All fields of all records of table *person*, where Susan Baker's dob field is set to NULL.

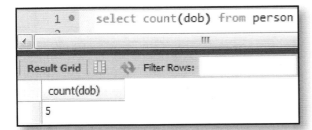

With Susan Baker's *dob* set to the NULL value (as it should be for unavailable data), the query in our next screenshot shows only five records counted.

Figure 5-7: Counting all non-NULL values in *dob*.

The **count()** function ignored the NULL value in the *dob*.

Let's practice conditional counting by adding an ORDER BY clause to our query. In the next screenshot, let's count how many people were born after 1980 in our table *person*.

```
SELECT COUNT(*) FROM person WHERE
dob>='1980-01-01';
```

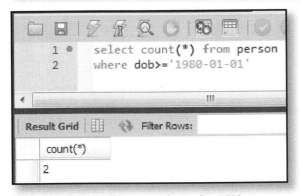

The query returned two. To find out who these two employees are, we execute the query in figure 5-9.

Figure 5-8: Two employees were born after 1980.

```
SELECT id, firstname, lastname, dob FROM
person WHERE dob>='1980-01-01';
```

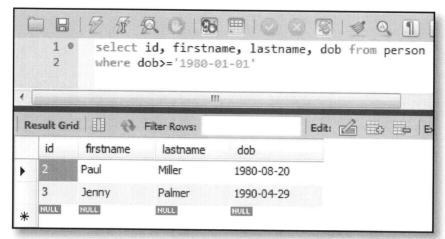

Figure 5-9: These are the two employees born after 1980.

Now, let's count the number of persons born before 1980.

```
SELECT COUNT(dob) FROM person WHERE
dob<'1980-01-01';
```

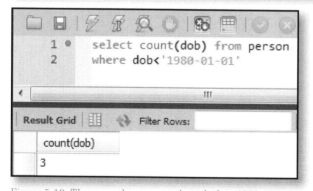

The query returned three. To find out who those three employees are, we execute the query in figure 5-11.

Figure 5-10: Three employees were born before 1980.

```
SELECT id, firstname, lastname, dob FROM
person WHERE dob<'1980-01-01';
```

Figure 5-11: These are the three employees born before 1980.

You will notice that in the last four queries, Susan Baker's record with its *dob* set to the NULL value never appeared. When SQL evaluated these two conditional expressions...

```
dob >= '1980-01-01'
```

```
dob < '1980-01-01'
```

...it completely ignored the NULL value in the *dob* of Susan Baker's record. The ANSI standard rules explain why the value was ignored.

Here are three rules of the ANSI standard, regarding how column or aggregate functions handle NULL values.

1. Any NULL values in a column or field are ignored for the purpose of computing the column function's result.

2. If every data item in the column or field is NULL or the column is empty, then the **count()** function returns zero while the **avg()**, **max()**, **min()** and **sum()** functions return a NULL value.

3. The **count(*)** counts rows regardless of the values in the fields of a record. It will return zero if there are no rows, meaning the table is empty.

1. A query performs **count()** on a column which has 17 NULL values in a table that has 90 rows. What value will the **count()** function return?
   a. 117.
   b. 73.
   c. 17.
   d. 83.

2. A query performs the **max()** and **min()** function on an empty table. What values will be returned by the **max()** and **min()** functions, respectively?
   a. 0 and 0.
   b. NULL and 0.
   c. NULL and NULL.
   d. 0 and NULL.

3. How will a query that performs **count()** on a column with NULL values treat those NULL values?
   a. As though they had the value 0.
   b. They will be included in a query result footnote table.
   c. They will not be included in the **count()** result value.
   d. Using **count()** on a column with NULL values causes an error.

4. Using **count()** on a table will return the number of records in that table.
   a. True.
   b. False.

LAB ACTIVITY

For this lab exercise, we will first execute a script that will create a new table *hourstask* in our *projmon* database and populate *hourstask* with test data.

CODE LISTING:

CREATES TABLE *HOURSTASK* AND ITS TEST DATA

```
CREATE TABLE IF NOT EXISTS hourstask (
  id int(11) NOT NULL AUTO_INCREMENT,
  pid int(11) NOT NULL,
  date_worked date NOT NULL,
  task_type char(3) NOT NULL DEFAULT '010',
  hours_worked decimal(6,2) DEFAULT 0,
  PRIMARY KEY (id),
  KEY fk_hourstask_person_idx (pid),
  CONSTRAINT fk_hourstask_person FOREIGN KEY(pid)
REFERENCES person(id) ON DELETE CASCADE ON UPDATE
CASCADE
) ENGINE=InnoDB DEFAULT CHARSET=utf8;

INSERT INTO hourstask (pid, date_worked, task_type,
hours_worked) VALUES (4, '2014-5-5', '172', 4.);
INSERT INTO hourstask (pid, date_worked, task_type,
hours_worked) VALUES (4, '2014-5-5', '171', 1.5);
INSERT INTO hourstask (pid, date_worked, task_type,
hours_worked) VALUES (4, '2014-5-6', '172', 4);
INSERT INTO hourstask (pid, date_worked, task_type,
hours_worked) VALUES (4, '2014-5-6', '171', 2.5);
INSERT INTO hourstask (pid, date_worked, task_type,
hours_worked) VALUES (4, '2014-5-6', '173', 3.25);

INSERT INTO hourstask (pid, date_worked, task_type,
hours_worked) VALUES (5, '2014-5-5', '172', 8.);
INSERT INTO hourstask (pid, date_worked, task_type,
hours_worked) VALUES (5, '2014-5-5', '171', 3.35);
INSERT INTO hourstask (pid, date_worked, task_type,
hours_worked) VALUES (5, '2014-5-6', '172', 6);
INSERT INTO hourstask (pid, date_worked, task_type,
hours_worked) VALUES (5, '2014-5-7', '171', 5);
INSERT INTO hourstask (pid, date_worked, task_type,
hours_worked) VALUES (5, '2014-5-8', '173', 13.7);

INSERT INTO hourstask (pid, date_worked, task_type,
hours_worked) VALUES (3, '2014-5-5', '171', 2.1);
INSERT INTO hourstask (pid, date_worked, task_type,
hours_worked) VALUES (3, '2014-5-5', '172', 1.35);
INSERT INTO hourstask (pid, date_worked, task_type,
hours_worked) VALUES (3, '2014-5-5', '173', 4.40);
INSERT INTO hourstask (pid, date_worked, task_type,
hours_worked) VALUES (3, '2014-5-7', '171', 5);
INSERT INTO hourstask (pid, date_worked, task_type,
hours_worked) VALUES (3, '2014-5-7', '173', 2.9)
```

Now, enter this code into your Workbench Query Panel.

Creating the table *hourstask* and populating it with data:

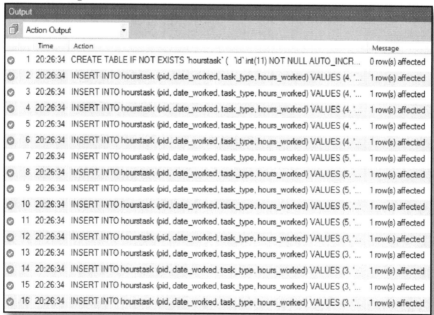

When you execute the code, your Output panel should show white checkmarks on green circular backgrounds.

The output panel that resulted from the creation of the table *hourstask* and its filling of data:

	Time	Action	Message
1	20:26:34	CREATE TABLE IF NOT EXISTS 'hourstask' ('id' int(11) NOT NULL AUTO_INCR...	0 row(s) affected
2	20:26:34	INSERT INTO hourstask (pid, date_worked, task_type, hours_worked) VALUES (4, '...	1 row(s) affected
3	20:26:34	INSERT INTO hourstask (pid, date_worked, task_type, hours_worked) VALUES (4, '...	1 row(s) affected
4	20:26:34	INSERT INTO hourstask (pid, date_worked, task_type, hours_worked) VALUES (4, '...	1 row(s) affected
5	20:26:34	INSERT INTO hourstask (pid, date_worked, task_type, hours_worked) VALUES (4, '...	1 row(s) affected
6	20:26:34	INSERT INTO hourstask (pid, date_worked, task_type, hours_worked) VALUES (4, '...	1 row(s) affected
7	20:26:34	INSERT INTO hourstask (pid, date_worked, task_type, hours_worked) VALUES (5, '...	1 row(s) affected
8	20:26:34	INSERT INTO hourstask (pid, date_worked, task_type, hours_worked) VALUES (5, '...	1 row(s) affected
9	20:26:34	INSERT INTO hourstask (pid, date_worked, task_type, hours_worked) VALUES (5, '...	1 row(s) affected
10	20:26:34	INSERT INTO hourstask (pid, date_worked, task_type, hours_worked) VALUES (5, '...	1 row(s) affected
11	20:26:34	INSERT INTO hourstask (pid, date_worked, task_type, hours_worked) VALUES (5, '...	1 row(s) affected
12	20:26:34	INSERT INTO hourstask (pid, date_worked, task_type, hours_worked) VALUES (3, '...	1 row(s) affected
13	20:26:34	INSERT INTO hourstask (pid, date_worked, task_type, hours_worked) VALUES (3, '...	1 row(s) affected
14	20:26:34	INSERT INTO hourstask (pid, date_worked, task_type, hours_worked) VALUES (3, '...	1 row(s) affected
15	20:26:34	INSERT INTO hourstask (pid, date_worked, task_type, hours_worked) VALUES (3, '...	1 row(s) affected
16	20:26:34	INSERT INTO hourstask (pid, date_worked, task_type, hours_worked) VALUES (3, '...	1 row(s) affected

Now, display all fields of all records of table *hourstask* and the results you get should match the results shown in the following screenshot:

All fields of all records of the table *hourstask:*

```
1 •    SELECT * FROM projmon.hourstask;
```

Result Grid | Filter Rows: | Edit:

id	pid	date_worked	task_type	hours_worked
1	4	2014-05-05	172	4.00
2	4	2014-05-05	171	1.50
3	4	2014-05-06	172	4.00
4	4	2014-05-06	171	2.50
5	4	2014-05-06	173	3.25
6	5	2014-05-05	172	8.00
7	5	2014-05-05	171	3.35
8	5	2014-05-06	172	6.00
9	5	2014-05-07	171	5.00
10	5	2014-05-08	173	13.70
11	3	2014-05-05	171	2.10
12	3	2014-05-05	172	1.35
13	3	2014-05-05	173	4.40
14	3	2014-05-07	171	5.00
15	3	2014-05-07	173	2.90
NULL	NULL	NULL	NULL	NULL

Now, using what you know about the structure of column functions and what you can surmise about the functions mentioned in the screenshot, attempt to write queries to answer the following questions:

1. How many hours did the employee with *pid=5* work on May 5, 2014?
2. Show the individual records in *hourstask* where the employee with *pid=5* worked on May 5, 2014.
3. What is the total number of working hours that employee, *pid=4*?

1. The answer is 11.35. The following screenshot shows the SELECT statement you should have executed and its results.

```
SELECT  SUM(hours_worked)  FROM hourstask
WHERE pid=5 AND date_worked='2014-05-05';
```

The number of hours the employee with *pid=5* worked on May 5, 2014:

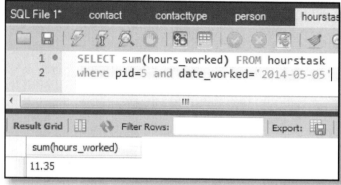

2. The next screenshot shows the breakdown of the 11.35 hours that the employee with *pid=5* worked on May 5, 2014.

```
SELECT  *  FROM hourstask WHERE pid=5 AND
date_worked='2014-05-05';
```

The breakdown of the number of hours the employee with *pid=5* worked on May 5, 2014:

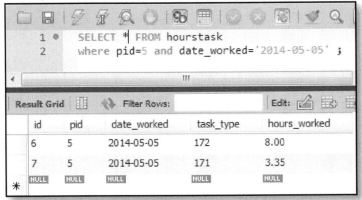

3. The last screenshot shows how many hours employee *pid=4* has worked.

```
SELECT SUM(hours_worked) FROM hourstask
WHERE pid=4;
```

The total number of hours employee *pid=4* has worked:

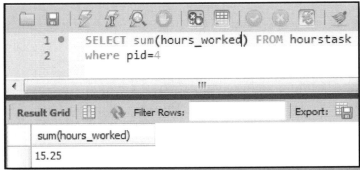

5.3 THE AVG(), MAX(), MIN(), AND SUM() FUNCTIONS

Let's start with **sum()**, which computes the sum of the values in a column of data.

sum()

```
SELECT SUM(budget) FROM project;
```

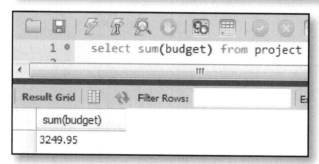

To verify this result, carry out manually the following addition. 2000 + 999.95 + 250. Your answer should be 3249.95.

Figure 5-12: The sum() function.

Now, what is the amount of the biggest budget? To answer that question, the query in figure 5-13 uses **max()**, which finds the largest value in a column.

max()

```
SELECT MAX(budget) FROM project;
```

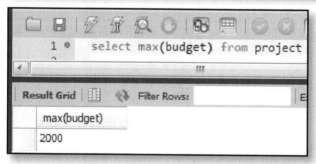

Figure 5-13: The max() function.

What is the amount of the smallest budget? The query in figure 5-14 uses **min()**, which finds the smallest value in a column, to answer our question.

min()

```
SELECT MIN(budget) FROM project;
```

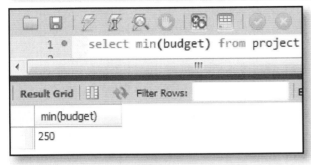

Figure 5-14: The **min()** function.

To find the average amount of the budgets of our projects, we use the query in figure 5-15. The query in the next screenshot uses **avg()** to answer our question.

avg()

```
SELECT AVG(budget) FROM project;
```

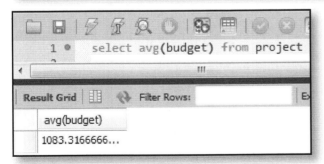

Figure 5-15: The **avg()** function.

avg() used the standard formula for calculating averages. It added all the values in *budget* and divided by the number of records that do not have a NULL *budget* value.

We can use **round()** to refine our result as the next screenshot shows.

```
SELECT ROUND(AVG(budget),2) FROM project;
```

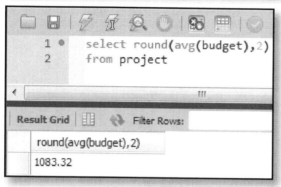

You'll note that **round()** takes a second argument, 2, in our example case. This argument determines the precision that the value will be rounded to. Note also that **round()** is not an aggregate function because it does not work on a column.

Figure 5-16: The **round()** function.

sum() and **avg()** will work only on columns that consist of numeric data types such as integer, decimal, floating point, money, and so on. The numeric results returned by these two functions will be of the same data type as the column values, but the results could have a higher precision. For example, the values in the column may consist of 16-bit integers, but **sum()** and **avg()** would return a 32-bit number.

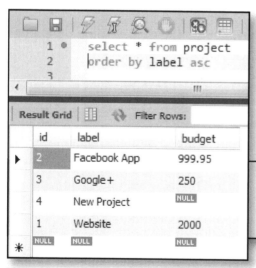

As for **max()** and **min()**, they can also operate on columns with string values. To see how this works, let's first sort the records of *project* by *label* in ascending order. Figure 5-17 shows the query that will do this.

```
SELECT * FROM
project ORDER BY
label ASC;
```

Figure 5-17: The *projects* table sorted on the field *label* in ascending order.

Now, take a look at the query in figure 5-18.

```
SELECT MAX(label) FROM project;
```

This query returned the last record of *project* when sorted by *label*.

Figure 5-18: **max()** used on a column of string values.

```
SELECT MIN(label) FROM project;
```

This query returned the first record of *project* when sorted by *label*.

Figure 5-19: **min()** used on a column of string values.

When **min()** and **max()** are used with string data, the determination of the largest and smallest value depends on the character set being used.

American Standard Code for Information Interchange, or ASCII, is the character set used on personal computers and servers. In ASCII, digits come before letters and uppercase characters come before lowercase characters. Your computer may use Unicode Transformation Format 8-bit, or UTF-8. UTF-8 is a variable-width encoding that can represent every character in the Unicode character set, and is backward compatible with ASCII.

The Extended Binary Coded Decimal Interchange Code, or EBCDIC, character set is used on mainframes. In EBCDIC, the lowercase characters precede the uppercase characters and digits come after the letters.

When it comes to dates, **max()** and **min()** consider earlier dates to be smaller than later dates. To put it another way, older people would come before younger ones. The following two screenshots illustrate this behavior of **max()** and **min()** with dates.

```
SELECT MAX(dob) FROM person;
```

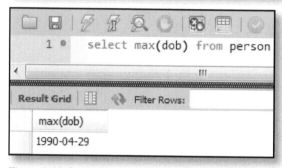

Figure 5-20: Later dates come last.

```
SELECT MIN(dob) FROM person;
```

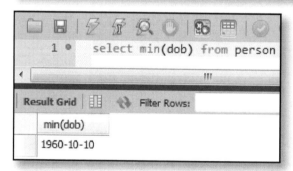

Figure 5-21: Earlier dates come first.

QUESTIONS FOR REVIEW

1. Which of the following is not an aggregate function?
   a. max()
   b. round()
   c. min()
   d. avg()

2. **min()** and **max()** select the smallest and largest values, respectively, in what data types?
   a. Integers.
   b. Decimals.
   c. Floats.
   d. All of the above.

3. Using **min()** on a date will return the earliest date value of a set.
   a. True.
   b. False.

4. Which of the following is NOT a type of text encoding?
   a. ANSI
   b. UTF-8
   c. UFO-16
   d. EBCDIC

LAB ACTIVITY

Let's continue to use our newly created *hourstask* table. Write SELECT statements that will answer the following questions:

1. What is the maximum number of hours an employee worked in one day?
2. Which employee rendered the maximum number of hours worked in one day?
3. What is the average number of hours an employee worked in one day?

LAB SOLUTION

1. `SELECT MAX(hours_worked) FROM hourstask;`

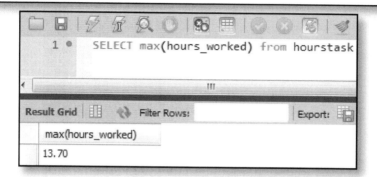

2. `SELECT * FROM hourstask WHERE hours_worked >= 13.70;`

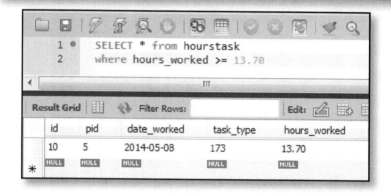

3. `SELECT AVG(hours_worked) FROM hourstask;`

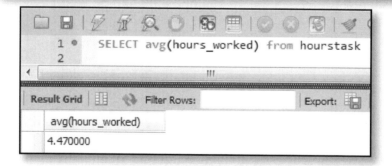

5.4 UNION AND OTHER MULTISET OPERATIONS

Every now and then it becomes necessary to combine several *query results* into one *query result*. The **UNION** feature of the SELECT statement provides this capability.

However, there are restrictions in the use of the UNION operation, namely:

1. The query results that will be combined must have the same number of columns.
2. Not only must the number of columns be the same, but corresponding columns must have the same data type.
3. Neither of the query results to be combined can be sorted by the ORDER BY clause, but the combined query can be sorted.

Now, let's create two queries whose result sets will be combined.

Figure 5-22 shows the first query that we will combine. Type the SELECT statement in your Query Panel and check if your results match the results shown in the screenshot.

```
SELECT firstname, lastname, managerid FROM
person WHERE LEFT(firstname,1) = 'J';
```

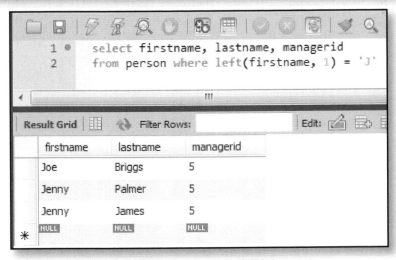

Figure 5-22: The first query for a UNION operation

The second query that we will combine is shown in this screenshot.
Execute the query in your Workbench and check your results against the
results shown in figure 5-23.

```
SELECT firstname, lastname, managerid FROM
person WHERE dob > '1980-01-01';
```

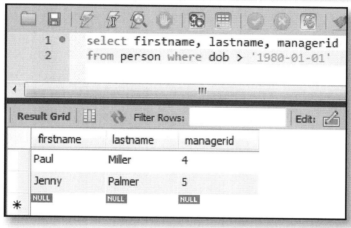

Figure 5-23: The second query for a UNION operation.

Notice how the two queries we will combine have the same number of
columns and corresponding columns have the same data type.

The next screenshot shows the SELECT statement that will merge the two *query results* we created.

```
SELECT firstname, lastname, managerid FROM
person WHERE LEFT(firstname,1) = 'J'
UNION
SELECT firstname, lastname, managerid FROM
person WHERE dob > '1980-01-01';
```

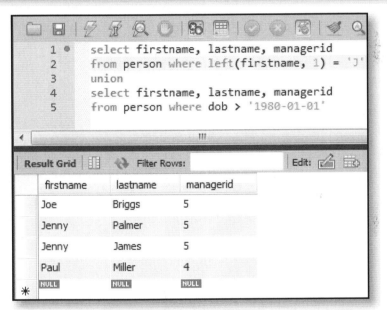

Figure 5-24: The UNION of two queries with duplicates removed.

Notice that our first query had three records and our second query had two records, but when we combined those two queries, we only got four records. That's because duplicate records have been removed.

If for some reason we need to retain the duplicates, then we use the **ALL** keyword after the UNION keyword, as shown in the following screenshot.

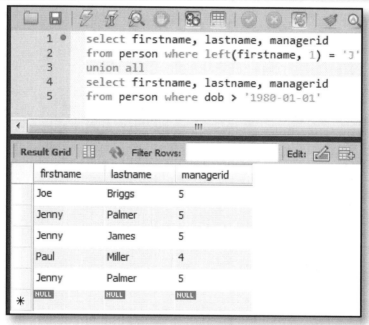

ALL

```
SELECT firstname, lastname, managerid FROM
person WHERE LEFT(firstname,1) = 'J'
UNION ALL
SELECT firstname, lastname, managerid FROM
person WHERE dob > '1980-01-01';
```

Figure 5-25: The UNION ALL keywords retain duplicates in the UNION of two queries.

Now, we see a total of five records and two records for "Jenny Palmer" with a *managerid* of 5.

Now that we have merged the two queries, we can sort the merged rows. This is shown in figure 5-26.

```
SELECT firstname, lastname, managerid FROM
person WHERE LEFT(firstname,1) = 'J'
UNION
SELECT firstname, lastname, managerid FROM
person WHERE dob > '1980-01-01'
ORDER BY lastname ASC;
```

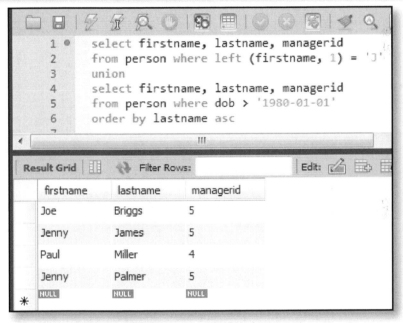

Figure 5-26: Sorting the UNION of two queries.

The two queries we just combined retrieved their data from *person*.

Now, we are going to combine two queries where each query retrieves data from a different table. Figure 5-27 shows the first query which retrieves rows from *role*.

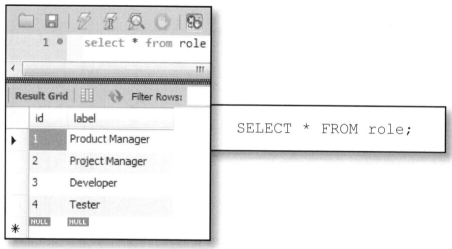

Figure 5-27: The first query to combine.

The next screenshot shows the second query which retrieves data from *contactype*.

Figure 5-28: The second query to combine.

```
SELECT * FROM role
UNION
SELECT * FROM contacttype;
```

Figure 5-29: The UNION of the two queries.

You will notice that the column *id* shows duplicate entries. This is because in the union of two queries, duplicates are allowed for primary key values.

Also, the code formatting that we used is for the sake of human readability and clarity, not any technical reason. You could place any of the statements that we have used in this section on a single line in MySQL Workbench and get the same results.

1. What are the SELECT statement keywords that retain duplicates in the UNION of two queries?
   a. NO DISTINCT.
   b. ALLOW DUPLICATES.
   c. YES DUPLICATES.
   d. UNION ALL.

2. When should a sorting operation using the ORDER BY clause be carried out in a UNION operation?
   a. Just before duplicates are either retained or removed.
   b. As each individual query is being processed.
   c. Immediately
   d. After the queries have been merged.

3. A UNION operation does not require matching data types.
   a. True.
   b. False.

4. A UNION can be used to combine data from multiple tables.
   a. True.
   b. False.

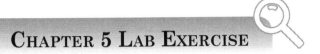

CHAPTER 5 LAB EXERCISE

1. Write a query returning the number of records in the Project table.

2. Write a query returning the number of project names in the Project table.

3. Write a query returning the number of project names in the Project table whose budget is below 1000.

4. Write a query returning the grand total of all project budgets listed in the project table.

5. Write a query returning the average project budget listed in the project table.

6. Write a query returning the lowest project budget listed in the project table.

7. Write a query returning the average length of role names in the role table. Use the SQL length function.

8. Write a query returning a merged list of project names and role titles.

CHAPTER 5 LAB SOLUTION

1.
```
SELECT COUNT(*) FROM project;
```

2.
```
SELECT COUNT(label) FROM project;
```

3.
```
SELECT COUNT(label) FROM project WHERE
budget < 1000;
```

4.
```
SELECT SUM(budget) FROM project;
```

5.
```
SELECT AVG(budget) FROM project;
```

6.
```
SELECT MIN(budget) FROM project;
```

7.
```
SELECT AVG(length(label)) FROM role;
```

8.
```
SELECT label FROM project
UNION
SELECT label FROM role;
```

CHAPTER SUMMARY

In this chapter, you learned about five core ANSI Standard aggregation functions: **avg()**, **count()**, **max()**, **min()**, **sum()** and how to use them in the SELECT statement.

We also tackled the UNION operation of the SELECT statement, which is used to combine the query results of two or more queries. We covered in detail the requirements that should be fulfilled before a successful UNION operation can be carried out.

You will be seeing the aggregation functions and other similar functions in the following chapters as we take a look at more complex forms of the SELECT statement.

SQL Database for Beginners

CHAPTER 6

GROUPING YOUR DATA

CHAPTER OBJECTIVES:

- You will learn how to use the GROUP BY clause
- You will learn how to use the HAVING clause.
- You will learn the difference between the WHERE clause and the HAVING clause.

6.1 THE GROUP BY CLAUSE

Many reports generated by businesses, corporations and government offices have overall or grand totals at the bottom of the last page of the report, but these reports also have subtotals scattered throughout the pages. For example, most reports, such as production, expense, and profit reports, would show subtotals by department, region, or product, in addition to showing the grand totals at the end of the report.

The **GROUP BY** clause sorts and groups retrieved records according to the column names you provide. What's more, you can perform the aggregation functions: **avg()**, **count()**, **max()**, **min()**, and **sum()** on each group. Then, with the **HAVING** clause, you can apply a conditional expression on your groups and that conditional expression can include an aggregation function.

First, as we did in all the past chapters, we review the basic syntax of the SELECT statement.

GROUP BY

HAVING

SELECT { all, distinct } { select-item }
  FROM table-specification
  WHERE search-condition
  GROUP BY grouping-column
  HAVING search condition
  ORDER BY sort-specification.

Now, let's clarify some terminology. A query that uses the GROUP BY clause to group the data from its source tables and to produce summary data for each group is called a **grouped query**. The columns specified in the GROUP BY clause are called the **grouping columns** because they fix the rules which determine how the rows are grouped.

Grouped Query

Grouping Columns

Here is a summary of the SELECT statements in this chapter.

```
SELECT managerid FROM person GROUP BY
managerid;
SELECT distinct managerid FROM person;

SELECT managerid, COUNT(*) FROM person
GROUP BY managerid;
SELECT LEFT(firstname, 1) initial, COUNT(*)
FROM person GROUP BY initial;

SELECT managerid, LEFT(firstname, 1)
initial, COUNT(*) FROM person GROUP BY
managerid, initial;
SELECT managerid, COUNT(*), MIN(dob),
MAX(dob)
FROM person GROUP BY managerid;

SELECT pid, SUM(hours_worked) FROM
hourstask GROUP BY pid;
SELECT pid, date_worked, SUM(hours_worked)
FROM hourstask GROUP BY pid, date-worked;
SELECT pid, date_worked, task_type,
SUM(hours_worked) FROM hourstask GROUP BY
pid, date-worked, task_type;
```

First, let's take a look again at all fields of all records of *person*. This time, all fields with unavailable, incomplete, or not applicable values have been set to the NULL value. If you have been following along, then that should only be *dob* from Susan Baker's record. To ensure that the value is set correctly, enter and run the following code.

```
UPDATE person SET dob=NULL WHERE id=6;
```

```
1 ●    select * from person
2
```

id	firstname	lastname	dob	managerid	notes	created
1	Joe	Briggs	1975-02-07	5	NULL	2014-07-...
2	Paul	Miller	1980-08-20	4	NULL	2014-07-...
3	Jenny	Palmer	1990-04-29	5	NULL	2014-07-...
4	Jenny	James	1970-11-03	5	NULL	2014-07-...
5	Rick	Walker	1960-10-10	NULL	Rick Walker is the CE...	2014-07-...
6	Susan	Baker	NULL	5	Rick Walker's assistan...	2014-07-...
*	NULL	NULL	NULL	NULL	NULL	NULL

Figure 6-1: All fields of all records of the table *person*.

Now, let's execute our first SELECT statement with a GROUP BY clause as shown in the following screenshot.

```
SELECT managerid FROM person GROUP BY
managerid;
```

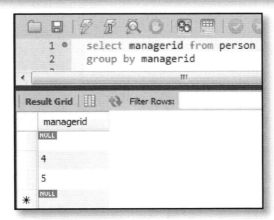

Figure 6-2: Grouping and consolidating the records of *person* in the grouping column *managerid*.

This screenshot shows that *managerid* stores three distinct values: NULL, 4, and 5.

If we execute the query shown in figure 6-3, we get the same result but in a different order.

```
SELECT DISTINCT managerid FROM person;
```

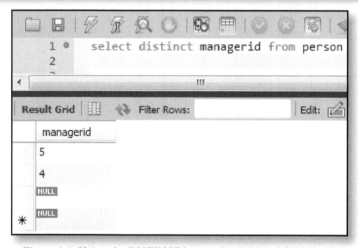

Figure 6-3: Using the DISTINCT keyword to removed duplicates.

So, what is the difference between using GROUP BY and DISTINCT?

First, DISTINCT is a SQL keyword while GROUP BY is a SQL clause.

Second, GROUP BY requires a conditional expression while DISTINCT doesn't.

Third, the GROUP BY clause's main purpose is consolidation or aggregation, while the DISTINCT keyword simply eliminates duplicates.

Let's explore how the GROUP BY clause's consolidation feature works. In particular, we will apply the function **count()** to each group retrieved. Take a look at the SELECT statement in the next screenshot.

```
SELECT managerid, COUNT(*) FROM person
GROUP BY managerid;
```

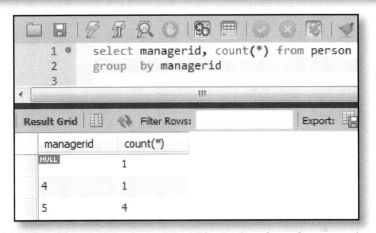

Figure 6-4: Using the **count()** function to return the number of records per grouping column *managerid.*

The query we just executed counted the number of rows or records of each unique value in *managerid* of *person*. The query stated that there is one record with the NULL value, one record with the value '4' in *managerid*, and four records the value '5' in *managerid*. (You can check these results by manually counting the records shown in figure 6-1, as it shows all fields of all records of *person*.)

You cannot obtain those results with the DISTINCT keyword. Instead of just removing duplicates, GROUP BY is consolidating the records according to its grouping column and then acting on the records that exist in that consolidation.

The next screenshot shows another example of the consolidation capabilities of the GROUP BY clause.

```
SELECT LEFT(firstname, 1) initial, COUNT(*)
FROM person GROUP BY initial;
```

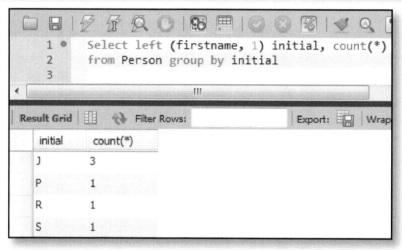

Figure 6-5: Using the **count()** function to return the number of records per grouping column *initial.*

This query reports that there are three people with first names that begin with the letter 'J' and one person each who have first names beginning with either 'P', 'R' or 'S.'

Note that we cannot use a function in the conditional expression of the GROUP BY clause. This is why we used the alias "initial" for the expression "left(firstname,1)."

> **Reminder**: You must only use column names or aliases in the GROUP BY clause. You cannot use functions.

Here is an example of using the aggregation functions **max()** and **min()** with the GROUP BY clause. Take a careful look at the SELECT statement and the results shown in the following screenshot.

```
SELECT managerid, COUNT(*), MIN(dob),
MAX(dob) FROM person GROUP BY managerid;
```

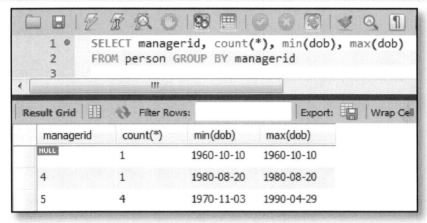

Figure 6-6: Using the **max()** and **min()** functions to return the oldest and youngest person per grouping column *managerid*.

Study the values in the *max(dob)* and *min(dob)* columns of this query and compare the values with the previous screenshot showing all fields of all records in the table *person*. You will realize that **max()** and **min()** functions returned the youngest and oldest employees, respectively, in each *managerid* group.

In the previous chapter, we used the aggregation or column functions to perform various calculations on the rows of a table. We would count all the rows of a table, sum up the values on all the rows, compute the average, and so on.

We can also use the aggregation or column functions to perform those same calculations on each sub-group or grouping level. We can now get separate counts, totals, averages, and so on per each sub-group. That's the power of the GROUP BY clause when used with the aggregation functions.

Now, we are going to show the power of the GROUP BY clause by using it to summarize data on more than one column. This is sometimes referred to as **multi-level grouping**.

For our examples, we will be using data from the *hourstask* table. We first show all fields of all records of the table *hourstask*, as you can see in figure 6-7.

> **Multi-Level Grouping**

```
SELECT * FROM projmon.hourstask;
```

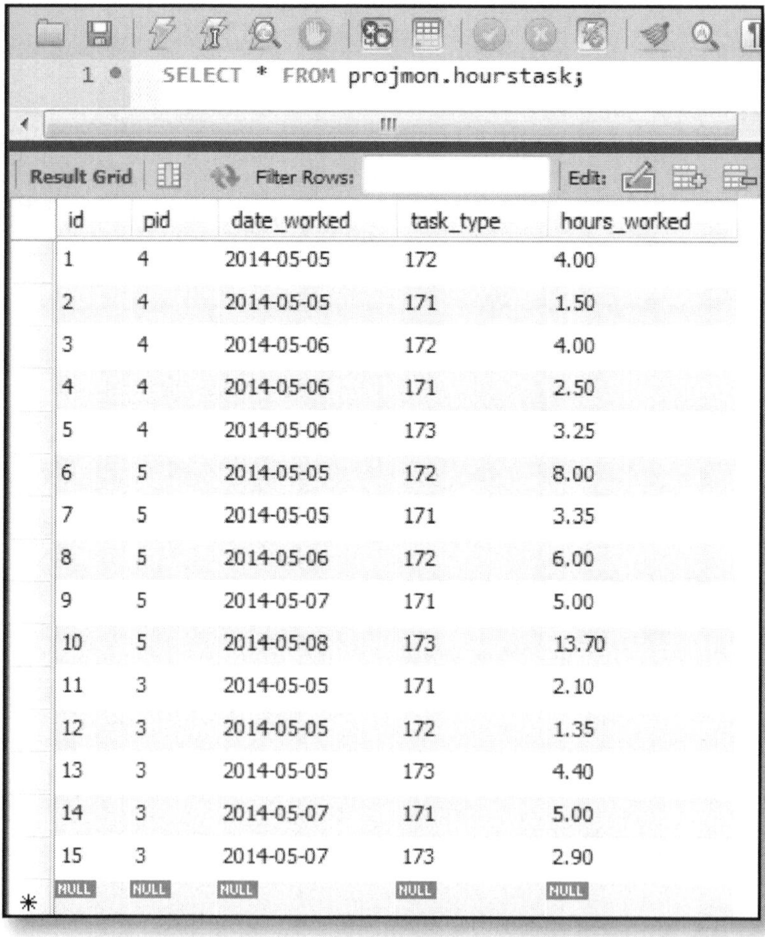

Figure 6-7: All fields of all records of the table *hourstask*

In figure 6-7 you can see that we are computing the total number of hours worked by each employee.

```
SELECT pid, SUM(hours_worked) FROM
hourstask GROUP BY pid;
```

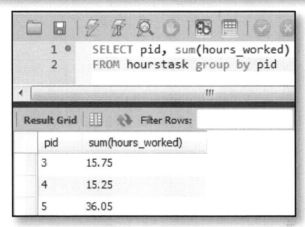

Figure 6-8: The total number of hours worked by each employee.

You can verify these totals by manually adding the value in *hours_ worked* from figure 6-7.

Now, we will add a second level to our GROUP BY clause. We want to break down the hours worked by each employee per day. Figure 6-9 shows the SELECT statement we executed and the results.

```
SELECT pid, date_worked, SUM(hours_worked)
FROM hourstask GROUP BY pid, date_worked;
```

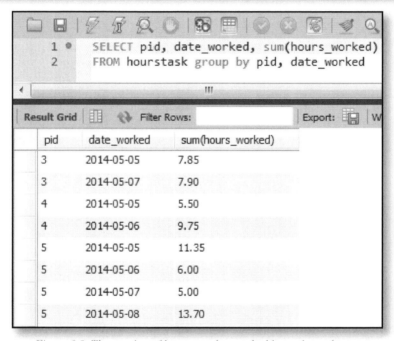

Figure 6-9: The number of hours per day worked by each employee.

Now, for our third and last level, we add *task_type* to our GROUP BY clause.

```
SELECT pid, date_worked, task_type,
SUM(hours_worked) FROM hourstask GROUP BY
pid, date_worked, task_type;
```

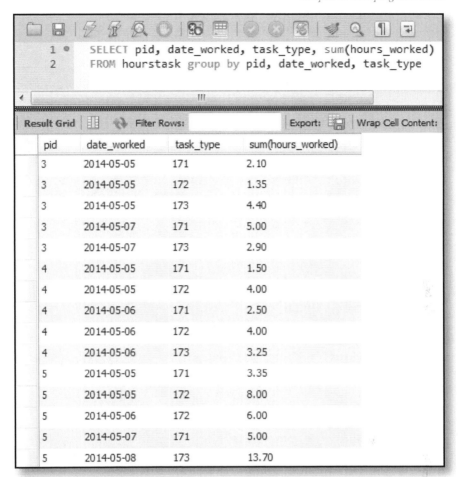

Figure 6-10: The number of hours per day per task type worked by each employee.

Looking at figure 6-10, you might first think that the query results are no different from the query results that were obtained from the select statement:

```
SELECT * FROM hourstask;
```

In fact, you would get the same results if you had executed the query:

```
SELECT * FROM hourstask ORDER BY pid, date-
worked, task_type
```

Now, the reason our most recent GROUP BY query showed all records in *hourstask* is because there are no rows or records to consolidate based on the three grouping columns specified: *pid, date_worked* and *task_type*.

In practical terms, no person did the same task on the same day at different times. For example, take the person with *pid* 3. On 2014-05-05, they worked 2.10 hours on task 171 (the first record in the previous screenshot), then did tasks 172 and 173.

Now, let's say they worked again on task 171 for four hours. Let's add a record to *hourstask* to reflect this.

```
INSERT INTO hourstask (pid, date_worked,
task_type, hours_worked) VALUES (3, '2014-
5-5', '171', 4.);
```

Now, execute the query shown in figure 6-11 and ascertain that you get the same results as we have.

```
SELECT pid, date_worked, task_type, hours_
worked FROM hourstask WHERE pid=3 ORDER BY
date_worked, task_type;
```

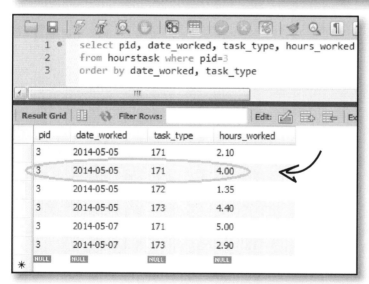

In this screenshot, we can see our newly added record.

Figure 6-11: The new record we added to *hourstask*.

Now, let's try our grouped query again on the three grouping columns specified: *pid, date_worked* and *task_type*. The query is shown in figure 6-12, but note that we have added a WHERE clause which instructs the query to retrieve only the records where *pid* is 3. This speeds up the query's processing time, as there are fewer records to work on.

```
SELECT pid, date_worked, task_type,
SUM(hours_worked) FROM hourstask WHERE
pid=3 GROUP BY pid, date_worked, task_type;
```

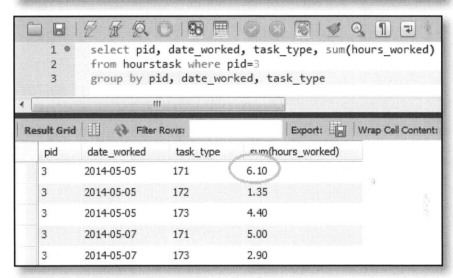

Figure 6-12: Grouping by *pid, date_worked* and *task_type*.

You will note that in figure 6-12 we only have five rows, while in the previous figure we had six rows. This shows that two rows (*pid=3, date_worked*='2014-5-5', task_type='171') were consolidated into one.

1. Which clause of the SELECT statement allows us to sort and retrieve data by groups?
   a. SELECT clause.
   b. FROM clause.
   c. ORDER by clause.
   d. GROUP BY clause.

2. Which of the following aggregation functions can be used as a grouping column of the GROUP BY clause?
   a. sum()
   b. count()
   c. avg()
   d. None of the above.

3. How does the GROUP BY clause differ from the DISTINCT keyword?
   a. They do not differ.
   b. DISTINCT creates distinct selections of records and acts on them, while GROUP BY creates a group by removing duplicate values.
   c. GROUP BY creates a group of records according to a grouping column, while DISTINCT removes duplicate values.
   d. GROUP BY modifies values in the columns, DISTINCT does not.

4. Queries can be grouped according to more than one grouping column.
   a. True.
   b. False.

For this lab exercise, we will access *contact*. Its fields and records are shown in this screenshot.

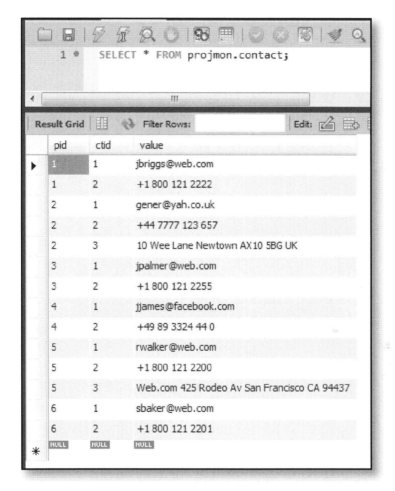

Write queries that will:

1. Summarize the number of people who can be contacted by each contact type.
2. Summarize the contact type per person to find out if anyone has more than one cell phone or more than one email, and so on.

1. `SELECT ctid, COUNT(*) FROM contact GROUP BY ctid;`

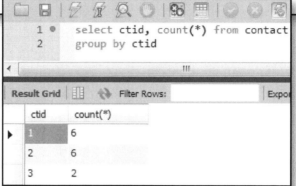

2. `SELECT pid, ctid, COUNT(*) FROM contact GROUP BY pid, ctid;`

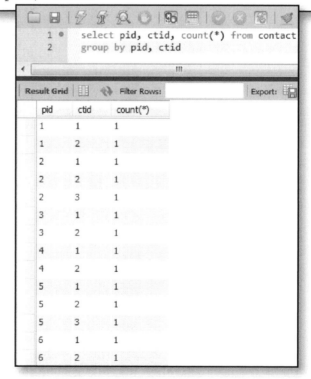

6.2 THE HAVING CLAUSE

As you learned in the last section, we use the WHERE clause with a conditional expression to filter out the rows that we want to retrieve. The conditional expression of the WHERE clause must apply to the individual rows. This expression must be computable for individual rows.

We use the **HAVING** clause with a conditional expression to filter out the groups that we want to retrieve. The conditional expression of the HAVING clause must apply to the group as a whole. This expression must be computable for a group of rows.

Let's emphasize that important difference between the WHERE clause and the HAVING clause: the WHERE clause filters out individual rows, while the HAVING clause filters out groups.

In order to clarify when to use WHERE and when to use HAVING, we will go over the SQL query process again. Keep in mind that HAVING is only useful when used in conjunction with a GROUP BY clause. If you use HAVING but do not have a GROUP BY clause, your query will still execute, but the HAVING clause will add confusion to anyone who reads your code and could potentially increase processing overhead on your server.

THE SQL QUERY PROCESS

1. SQL first determines the table or tables from which the data will be obtained.
2. SQL next determines the fields that will be retrieved.
3. SQL then retrieves the rows based on the search condition provided in the WHERE clause. (This reduces the number of records to be processed in the next steps.)
4. SQL then sorts the retrieved records based on the ORDER BY clause.
5. Grouping and consolidation of retrieved records are then carried out based on the grouping columns of a GROUP BY clause.
6. Retrieved results are then filtered based on the search condition of a HAVING clause.

The important point to be emphasized is that by using the WHERE clause wisely, you can reduce the number of records that have to be sorted and grouped, thus speeding up your queries.

That doesn't mean that using the HAVING clause should be avoided. The nature of the query will determine whether to use the HAVING clause or the WHERE clause, or a combination of the two.

Let's study some examples to shed light on the rules and concepts we just explained. First, look at figure 6-13, which shows a SELECT statement we executed in the last section.

```
SELECT managerid, COUNT(*) FROM person
GROUP BY managerid;
```

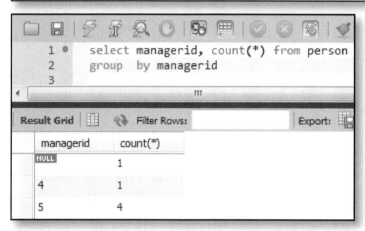

Figure 6-13: Grouping records from *person* by *managerid*.

To refresh your memory, this query shows the number of records per *managerid* value. That is, four people have *managerid* 5, one person has *managerid* 4 and one person has a NULL value for *managerid*.

Now, what if we wanted to take a cost-cutting measure and force the managers handling only one person into early retirement?

Figure 6-14 shows the query to execute and the results we get.

```
SELECT managerid, COUNT(*) FROM person
GROUP BY managerid HAVING COUNT(*)<=1;
```

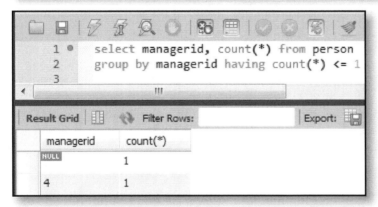

Figure 6-14: Retrieving managers who have only one person under them.

Our search condition, "COUNT(*) <= 1" should be used in a HAVING clause, as that search condition includes an aggregate function and thus would be useless if applied to individual rows.

As the screenshot shows, the query result revealed that the record in *person* with the *managerid* 4 is a possible candidate for early retirement.

The query result also gave some additional information: it identified that there is a person who is not reporting to any manager. Is this a data entry error, or do we really have an unproductive employee who has fallen through the cracks? Whatever our course of action, it was the query that alerted us to this abnormal situation.

For our next example, we will use the *hourstask* table. Let's say we want to analyze the time it takes to accomplish task '171'. First, let's just focus on rows with the value '171' in *task_type*.

```
SELECT pid, date_worked, task_type, hours_
worked FROM hourstask WHERE task_type =
'171';
```

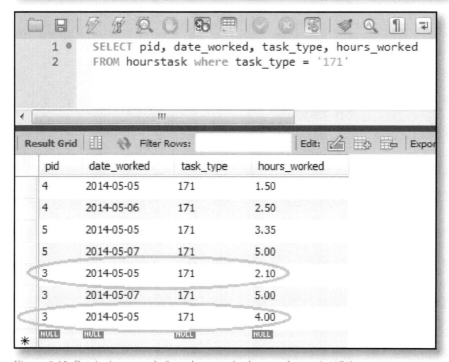

Figure 6-15: Retrieving records from *hourstask* where *task_type* is '171'.

We obtained seven records. Notice also that we have circled two records which will later be consolidated.

Now, let's group these records by *pid*, *date_worked* and *task_type*. The next screenshot shows how we achieved this with a query that uses the GROUP BY clause.

```
SELECT pid, date_worked, task_type,
SUM(hours_worked) FROM hourstask WHERE
task_type='171' GROUP BY pid, date_worked,
task_type;
```

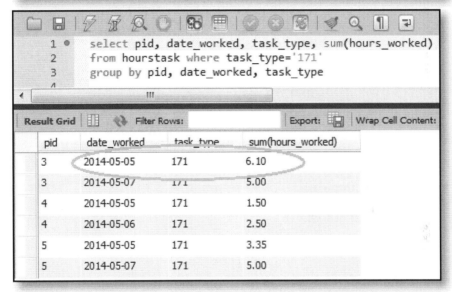

Figure 6-16: Consolidated record where *pid* is 3, *date_worked* is '2014-05-05', and *task_type* is '171'

We obtained six records, meaning two records were consolidated into one, which we have circled in figure 6-16.

Now, we want to extract only those employees who accomplished task '171' in less than 3.50 hours. The next screenshot shows how we carried this out by adding a HAVING clause.

```
SELECT pid, date_worked, task_type,
SUM(hours_worked)
FROM hourstask WHERE task_type='171'
GROUP BY pid, date_worked, task_type
HAVING SUM(hours_worked) < 4;
```

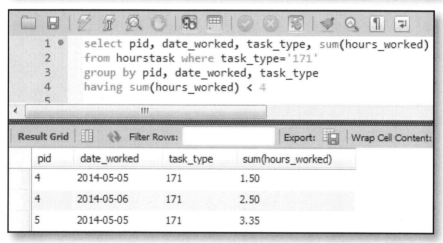

Figure 6-17: Retrieving only records where the total hours worked on project 171 is less than four.

1. Which pair of SELECT statement clauses accept conditional expressions?
   a. WHERE, HAVING.
   b. GROUP BY, ORDER BY.
   c. FROM, WHERE.
   d. HAVING, SELECT.

2. Which SELECT statement clause applies conditional expressions to individual records?
   a. WHERE.
   b. ORDER BY.
   c. FROM.
   d. GROUP BY.

3. Which SELECT statement clause applies conditional expressions to grouped records?
   a. FROM.
   b. HAVING.
   c. SELECT.
   d. WHERE.

4. A HAVING clause in a statement with no GROUP BY clause will produce an error.
   a. True.
   b. False.

For this lab exercise, we will use *projectperson*. The following screenshot shows all fields of all records of *projectperson* ordered by the *pid* and *prid*.

1. Write a query that will list all employees involved in more than one project.

2. Write a query that will list all employees who have assumed more than one role in one project.

LAB SOLUTION

1. First, we group the records by *pid* and *prid* (person id and project id). Then, we count the number of rows per group with the expression "COUNT(pid+prid)". The following shows the query that accomplishes the tasks we just mentioned.

```
SELECT pid, prid, COUNT(pid+prid)
FROM projectperson
GROUP BY pid, prid;
```

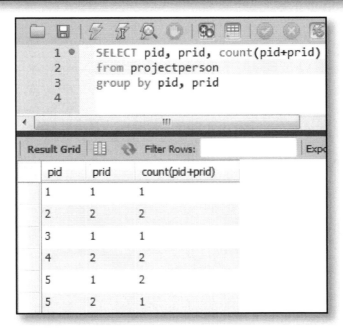

In the last step, we retain only those rows for which "COUNT(pid+prid) > 1" is true.

```
SELECT pid, prid, COUNT(pid+prid)
FROM projectperson
GROUP BY pid, prid
HAVING COUNT(pid + prid) > 1;
```

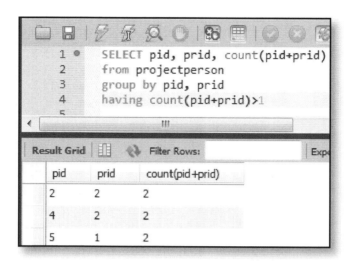

2. This follows the same pattern; we just need to check for *rid* as well as *pid* and *prid*.

```
SELECT pid, prid, rid, COUNT(pid+prid+rid)
FROM projectperson
GROUP BY pid, prid
HAVING COUNT(pid+prid+rid)>1;
```

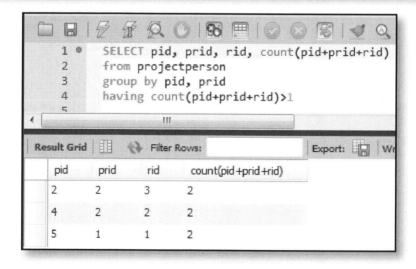

CHAPTER 6 LAB EXERCISE

1. Write a query returning the number of roles per initial of the role title in the role table.

2. Write a query returning all records in the *projectperson* table. The output of this query will allow you to verify the correctness of the results of the following exercise steps.

3. Write a query returning the number of individual staff roles assigned to each project in the *projectperson* table.

4. Write a query returning the number of staff assigned to each role in each project in the *projectperson* table.

5. Write a query returning the number of roles assigned to each person in each project in the *projectperson* table.

6. Modify the query written in step four to only return those projects and roles that have more than one person assigned to them.

7. Modify the query written in step five to only return those persons in each project that are assigned to more than one role.

8. Modify the previous query to return a list of projects in which persons are assigned to more than one role.

1.
```
SELECT LEFT(label,1) initial, COUNT(label)
FROM role GROUP BY initial;
```

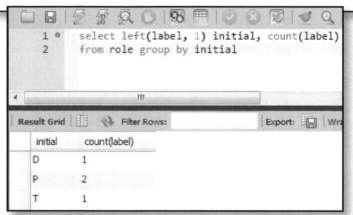

2.
```
SELECT pid, prid, rid FROM projectperson
ORDER BY pid, prid, rid;
```

3.
```
SELECT prid, COUNT(rid) FROM projectperson
GROUP BY prid;
```

4.
```
SELECT prid, rid COUNT(pid) FROM
projectperson GROUP BY prid, rid;
```

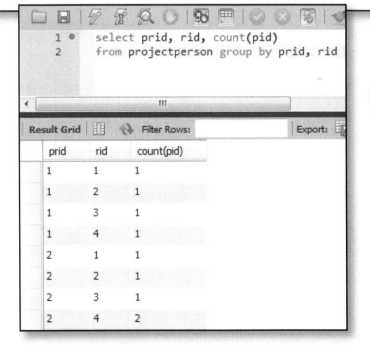

5.
```
SELECT prid, pid COUNT(rid) FROM
projectperson GROUP BY prid, pid;
```

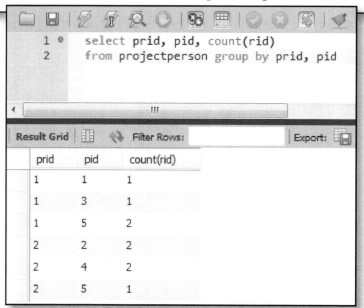

6.
```
SELECT prid, rid, COUNT(pid) FROM
projectperson GROUP BY prid, rid HAVING
COUNT(pid) > 1;
```

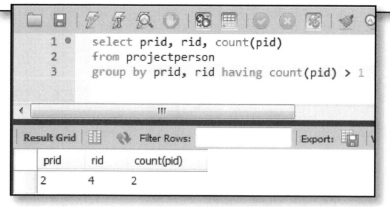

7.
```
SELECT prid, pid, COUNT(rid) FROM
projectperson GROUP BY prid, pid HAVING
COUNT(rid) > 1;
```

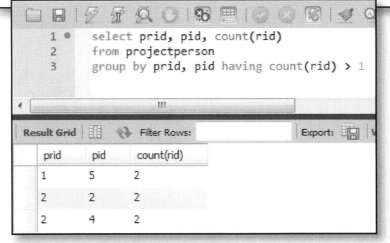

8.
```
SELECT DISTINCT prid FROM projectperson
GROUP BY prid, pid HAVING COUNT(rid) > 1;
```

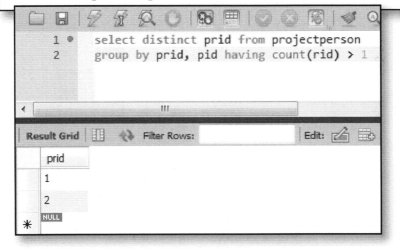

CHAPTER SUMMARY

In this chapter, we studied the GROUP BY clause and the closely related HAVING clause. The HAVING clause is always used in conjunction with the GROUP BY clause

We learned that the GROUP BY clause allows us to use specific grouping columns to organize records into groups. Then, by using the HAVING clause, we can restrict or include these groups from the query results.

More importantly, we can use the aggregation, or column functions, on each group. The aggregation functions can be included in conditional expressions of the HAVING clause.

We discussed the differences between the WHERE clause and the HAVING clause and when to use them.

We have now covered all the main clauses of the SELECT statement, but our queries have been retrieving data from only one table at a time. In the next chapter, you will learn how to retrieve records from two or more tables at a time using a JOIN.

CHAPTER 7

JOINING TABLES

CHAPTER OBJECTIVES:

* You will learn about table aliases and their utility.
* You will understand inner joins and how to use them.
* You will learn how to use left and right joins.
* You will learn how to use self joins.

7.1 INNER JOINS AND TABLE ALIASES

In previous chapters, we have used the SELECT statement to retrieve or summarize data from one table. In this chapter, we are going to execute queries that simultaneously retrieve or summarize data from several tables. Multi-table queries make up the majority of SQL retrieval activities, while single-table queries are a minority.

First, we will again summarize the SELECT statements that we will use in this chapter.

```
SELECT * FROM person, contact WHERE person.id =
contact.pid;

SELECT p.id, p.firstname, p.lastname, p.dob,
p.managerid, c.ctid, c.value FROM person p,
contact c WHERE p.id = c.pid;

SELECT p.id, p.firstname, p.lastname, p.dob,
p.managerid, c.ctid, c.value FROM person p
INNER JOIN contact c ON p.id = c.pid;

SELECT p.id, p.firstname, p.lastname,
p.managerid, prp.prid, prp.rid FROM person p
INNER JOIN projectperson prp ON p.id = prp.pid
ORDER BY lastname, firstname;
```

```sql
SELECT p.id, p.firstname, p.lastname, p.dob,
p.managerid, prj.label FROM person p, INNER
JOIN projectperson prp ON p.id = prp.pid INNER
JOIN project prj ON prp.pid = prj.id ORDER BY
lastname, firstname;

SELECT p.id, p.firstname, p.lastname, p.dob,
p.managerid, prj.label FROM person p INNER
JOIN projectperson prp ON p.id = prp.pid INNER
JOIN project prj ON prp.pid = prj.id WHERE
managerid='5' ORDER BY lastname, firstname;

SELECT p.id, p.firstname, p.lastname, p.dob,
p.managerid, prp.prid, prp.rid FROM person p
LEFT JOIN projectperson prp ON p.id = prp.pid
ORDER BY lastname, firstname;

SELECT prj.id, prj.label, prj.budget, pp.pid,
pp.rid FROM projectperson pp RIGHT JOIN project
prj ON prj.id = pp.prid ORDER BY prj.label;

SELECT prj.id, prj.label, prj.budget,
p.lastname, p.firstname, pp.rid FROM
projectperson pp RIGHT JOIN project prj ON prj.
id = pp.prid LEFT JOIN person p ON pp.pid =
p.id ORDER BY prj.label;

SELECT prj.id, prj.label, prj.budget,
p.lastname, p.firstname, pp.rid FROM
projectperson pp RIGHT JOIN project prj
ON prj.id = pp.prid LEFT JOIN person p ON
pp.pid = p.id ORDER BY prj.label, p.lastname,
p.firstname;

SELECT p.id, p.firstname, p.lastname,
p.managerid, m.firstname, m.lastname FROM person
p, person m WHERE p.managerid = m.id;

SELECT p.id, p.firstname, p.lastname,
p.managerid, m.firstname, m.lastname FROM person
p INNER JOIN person m ON p.managerid = m.id;
```

Let's start with a typical, practical problem. Using our sample *projmon* database, say you have been tasked to generate an alphabetical list of the contact information of all employees. The complete names of all employees are in the table *person,* but contact information is located in a separate table, *contact.* Retrieving the data from both tables involves not only merging the data in both tables, but also matching an employee's record in *person* with his corresponding record or records in *contact.*

To solve this problem, let's first take a look at the entity-relationship diagram of our *projmon* database.

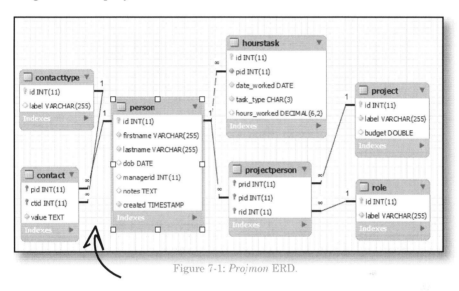

Figure 7-1: *Projmon* ERD.

In this ERD, we see that *person* and *contact* are linked by the former's primary key, *id*, and one of the latter's foreign keys, *pid*. To link the two tables, we are going to match the values in those fields. When the values in those fields are equal, then the record or records in *contact* are the corresponding contact data of an employee in *person.* In database terminology, we are **joining** the two tables over *person.id* (the primary key of *person*).

Joining

> **TIP:** When building multi-table queries, the entity-relationship diagram becomes a vital reference, as it shows how tables are related through primary and foreign key values.

The process of combining tables by matching the contents of a field from one table to the contents of a field from another table is called joining the tables. The combined table (containing records from the two tables whose matching column values are equal) is called a join between the two tables.

A join based on an exact match between two columns is more precisely called an *equi-join* (or a *natural equi-join*). More popularly, it is also called an *inner join,* the term we will use from now on.

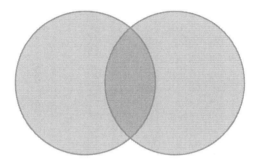

An inner join can be illustrated by the following diagram showing two circles that represent the two tables being joined:

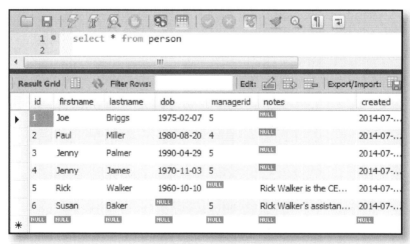

Figure 7-2: Inner Join.

The shaded area, representing the intersection of the two circles, indicates the records whose column values match.

Now, let's take a look at all fields of all six records of *person*.

```
1 •  select * from person
2
```

id	firstname	lastname	dob	managerid	notes	created
1	Joe	Briggs	1975-02-07	5	NULL	2014-07-...
2	Paul	Miller	1980-08-20	4	NULL	2014-07-...
3	Jenny	Palmer	1990-04-29	5	NULL	2014-07-...
4	Jenny	James	1970-11-03	5	NULL	2014-07-...
5	Rick	Walker	1960-10-10	NULL	Rick Walker is the CE...	2014-07-...
6	Susan	Baker	NULL	5	Rick Walker's assistan...	2014-07-...
*	NULL	NULL	NULL	NULL	NULL	NULL

Figure 7-3: All fields of all records of the table *person*.

And here is an overview of all fields of all 14 records of *contact*.

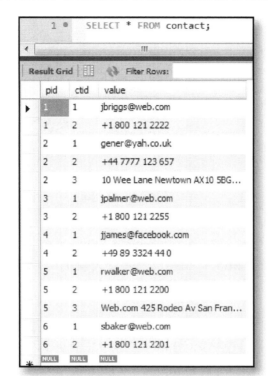

Figure 7-4: All fields of all records of the table *contact*.

If we retrieve records from these two tables to list employees alphabetically and with all their contact information, we should get 14 rows in our query result. As you can see, 14 rows are exactly what figure 7-5 shows.

```
SELECT * FROM person, contact
WHERE person.id = contact.pid;
```

```
1 •    select * from person, contact
2      where person.id = contact.pid
```

	id	firstname	lastname	dob	mana(	notes	created	pid	ctid	value
1	1	Joe	Briggs	1975-...	5	NULL	2014-07-...	1	1	jbriggs...
2	1	Joe	Briggs	1975-...	5	NULL	2014-07-...	1	2	+1 800 ...
3	2	Paul	Miller	1980-...	4	NULL	2014-07-...	2	1	gener@...
4	2	Paul	Miller	1980-...	4	NULL	2014-07-...	2	2	+44 77...
5	2	Paul	Miller	1980-...	4	NULL	2014-07-...	2	3	10 Wee...
6	3	Jenny	Palmer	1990-...	5	NULL	2014-07-...	3	1	jpalmer...
7	3	Jenny	Palmer	1990-...	5	NULL	2014-07-...	3	2	+1 800 ...
8	4	Jenny	James	1970-...	5	NULL	2014-07-...	4	1	jjames...
9	4	Jenny	James	1970-...	5	NULL	2014-07-...	4	2	+49 89 ...
10	5	Rick	Walker	1960-...	NULL	Rick Wa...	2014-07-...	5	1	rwalker...
11	5	Rick	Walker	1960-...	NULL	Rick Wa...	2014-07-...	5	2	+1 800 ...
12	5	Rick	Walker	1960-...	NULL	Rick Wa...	2014-07-...	5	3	Web.co...
13	6	Susan	Baker	NULL	5	Rick Wa...	2014-07-...	6	1	sbaker...
14	6	Susan	Baker	NULL	5	Rick Wa...	2014-07-...	6	2	+1 800 ...

Figure 7-5: All fields of all records from both *person* and *contact*.

Study the SELECT statement in figure 7-5. Note the conditional expression in the WHERE clause.

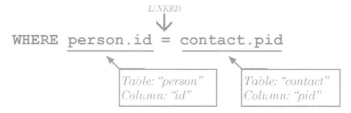

This conditional expression links the value of two columns from two different tables. If the values match, then the rows of both tables are included in the query result.

But we don't want all the fields of both tables, we only want specific fields. So we modify our query, like this:

```
SELECT id, firstname, lastname, dob,
managerid, ctid, value
FROM person, contact WHERE person.id =
contact.pid;
```

This query won't execute because the SQL engine wouldn't know from what tables to obtain the fields we listed. We would get an 'Unknown Column' error as shown in figure 7-6:

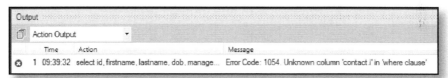

Figure 7-6: Unknown column error.

This is where aliases, particularly **table aliases**, become vital. Recall that aliases are used to temporarily rename a table or a column.

Take a look at the SELECT statement in the following query. Each field that we want to retrieve is preceded by a table alias.

Table Aliases

```
SELECT p.id, p.firstname, p.lastname, p.dob,
p.managerid, c.ctid, c.value
```

The table aliases are defined in the FROM clause. Now, the SELECT statement knows what table to extract the fields from, as you can see in figure 7-7.

```
1 ● select p.id, p.firstname, p.lastname, p.dob, p.managerid,
2   c.ctid, c.value
3   from person p, contact c where p.id = c.pid
4
```

id	firstname	lastname	dob	managerid	ctid	value
1	Joe	Briggs	1975-02-07	5	1	jbriggs@web.com
1	Joe	Briggs	1975-02-07	5	2	+1 800 121 2222
2	Paul	Miller	1980-08-20	4	1	gener@yah.co.uk
2	Paul	Miller	1980-08-20	4	2	+44 7777 123 657
2	Paul	Miller	1980-08-20	4	3	10 Wee Lane Newtow...
3	Jenny	Palmer	1990-04-29	5	1	jpalmer@web.com
3	Jenny	Palmer	1990-04-29	5	2	+1 800 121 2255
4	Jenny	James	1970-11-03	5	1	jjames@facebook.com
4	Jenny	James	1970-11-03	5	2	+49 89 3324 44 0
5	Rick	Walker	1960-10-10	NULL	1	rwalker@web.com
5	Rick	Walker	1960-10-10	NULL	2	+1 800 121 2200
5	Rick	Walker	1960-10-10	NULL	3	Web.com 425 Rodeo ...
6	Susan	Baker	NULL	5	1	sbaker@web.com
6	Susan	Baker	NULL	5	2	+1 800 121 2201

Figure 7-7: Using table aliases.

In the previous screenshot, you will also notice that our original WHERE clause, which was…

```
WHERE person.id = contact.id
```

…is now shortened to:

```
WHERE p.id = c.id.
```

As you construct lengthier queries with many field names and table names, table aliases can reduce typing efforts, minimize errors, and make the query easier to read and maintain.

Now, take a look at the SELECT statement and the query results shown in figure 7-8:

```
SELECT p.id, p.firstname, p.lastname, p.dob,
p.managerid, c.ctid, c.value
FROM person p INNER JOIN contact c
ON p.id = c.pid;
```

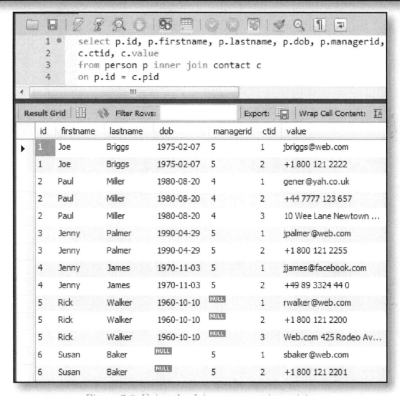

Figure 7-8: Using the Join syntax: an inner join

Firstly, if you compare the query results of this query with that of the previous query, where we introduced table aliases, you will see that the results are identical.

Secondly, in the SELECT statement, you will notice a slightly different syntax with a new clause, INNER JOIN, and a new keyword, ON. This is the SQL join syntax which was implemented in the ANSI Standard revisions of 1992. This syntax is simpler and more flexible than the pre-1992 join syntax.

> **TIP:** Surprisingly, despite the 22 years that have elapsed, not all DBMS vendors fully implement the new join syntax! Be sure to check the specific documentation of the RDBMS you are using.

From now on, we will be using the ANSI Standard join syntax.

Let's write a query that will show what projects our employees are involved in. Figure 7-9 shows this query.

```
SELECT p.id, p.firstname, p.lastname,
p.managerid, prp.prid, prp.rid
FROM person p INNER JOIN projectperson prp
ON p.id = prp.pid
ORDER BY lastname, firstname;
```

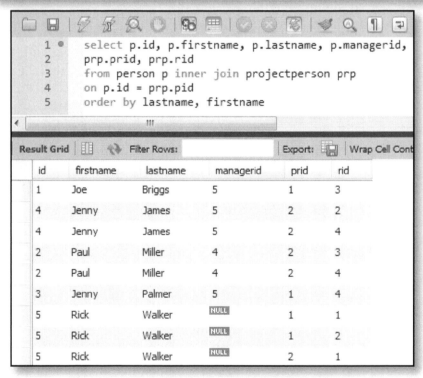

Figure 7-9: An inner join between *person* and *projectperson*.

There are some things to note about this query.

First, we added an ORDER BY clause to sort the records first by *lastname* and then by *firstname*.

Second, only five of the six employees were retrieved by this query. The sixth, Susan Baker, was not retrieved because she has no record in *projectperson*. She hasn't been assigned to a project. This is a screenshot of *projectperson*:

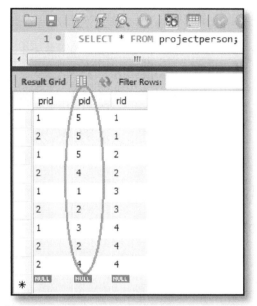

Figure 7-10: All fields of all records of *projectperson*. Employee with *id* 6 is not in the *pid* column of this table.

Third, the query lists the names of five employees (Briggs, James, Miller, Palmer, and Walker) and yet there are nine records in the query result. This is because three of those five employees (James, Miller, and Walker) are involved in more than one project. There is a **parent-child relationship** between *person* (the parent) and *projectperson* (the children).

An inner join will display all matches between records from two tables. Jenny James has one record in *person*, which matched with two records in *projectperson,* so two records for Jenny James were shown in the query result. The same can be said of Paul Miller. Rick Walker has three records in *projectperson* and so three records are displayed in the query result.

Now, what if we wanted this last query to retrieve all employees whether they are assigned to a project or not? If they are assigned to a project, then the project should be listed. If they are not assigned, then a null value should indicate this. We will tackle this in the next section when we discuss **outer joins**.

For now, we will further modify our last query by adding the project name. Notice that the last query retrieved only the field *prid*. How do we get it to retrieve the project name, which is the value of the field *label* in table *project*?

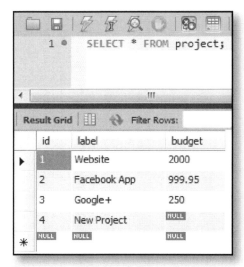

Figure 7-11: All fields of all records of *project*.

To retrieve *label* from *project*, we will have to add *project* to our query that joins *person* and *projectperson*. Figure 7-12 shows the query we used to retrieve data from three tables: *person, projectperson,* and *project.*

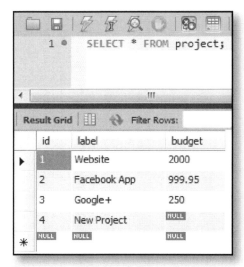

Outer Joins

```
SELECT p.id, p.firstname, p.lastname, p.dob,
p.managerid, prj.label
FROM person p, INNER JOIN projectperson prp
ON p.id = prp.pid
INNER JOIN project prj ON prp.pid = prj.id
ORDER BY lastname, firstname;
```

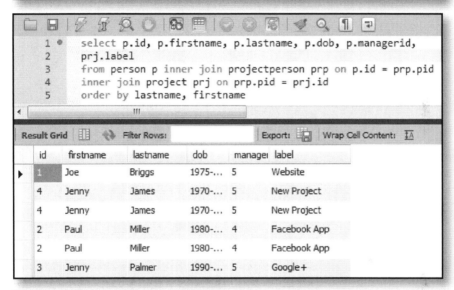

Figure 7-12: Three tables and two inner joins.

Let's compare the two queries. The first query, which is reproduced in the following code, joins the tables *person* and *projectperson*.

```
SELECT p.id, p.firstname, p.lastname,
p.managerid, prp.prid, prp.rid
FROM person p INNER JOIN projectperson prp
ON p.id = prp.pid
ORDER BY lastname, firstname;
```

The second query joins the table *person* and *projectperson,* as in the first query, and then joins a third table, *project,* to the query. The additional join of *project* is accomplished using the foreign keys in *projectperson* to link *person* to *project.*

It's important to understand what is happening when you are joining tables. In the second query, *person* and *projectperson* are joined together to form a new set. That set is a table that contains all of the joined data, but it is not a part of your schema. It can be saved as a new table or used as the basis for a view, which we'll cover later, but it will not persist beyond the query that created it. The key takeaway, though, is that after you do a JOIN you are not working with the original tables that were included, you are working with a new set that is comprised of records from the original tables.

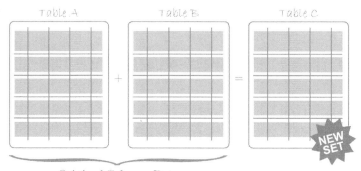

Original Schema Data

Continuing with the second query, when you JOIN *project* you are joining it to the set that was created with the initial JOIN, not to the original tables. This becomes important as you build larger, more complex queries that require multiple joins.

In the following code, this second INNER JOIN with the third table, *project,* is created by the fifth line.

```
SELECT p.id, p.firstname, p.lastname,
p.managerid, prj.label
FROM person p INNER JOIN projectperson prp
ON p.id = prp.pid
INNER JOIN project prj ON prp.pid = prj.id
ORDER BY lastname, firstname
```

It may also help to write the query in the following format:

```
SELECT p.id, p.firstname, p.lastname, p.dob,
p.managerid, prj.label
FROM person p
INNER JOIN projectperson prp
    ON p.id = prp.pid
INNER JOIN project prj
    ON prp.pid = prj.id
ORDER BY lastname, firstname;
```

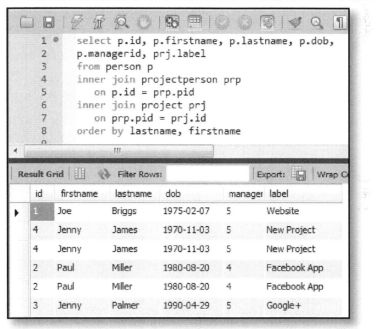

Figure 7-13: Improved format for multi-table queries.

In a query, there is no limit to the number of tables from which you can retrieve data. These tables have to be linked by JOINs. You can JOIN tables using different JOIN methods. In the next sections we will study OUTER JOINs.

Now, for a final flourish before we close this section, let's modify our last query to show only those employees who are under *managerid* 5. This is our modified query:

```
SELECT p.id, p.firstname, p.lastname, p.dob,
p.managerid, prj.label
FROM person p
INNER JOIN projectperson prp
   ON p.id = prp.pid
INNER JOIN project prj
   ON prp.pid = prj.id
WHERE managerid='5'
ORDER BY lastname, firstname;
```

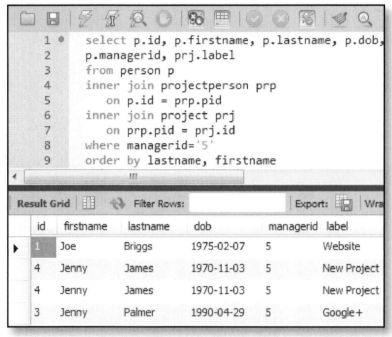

Figure 7-14: WHERE clause added.

You can see that the WHERE clause functions normally with the joined tables.

1. What do you call the process of linking two tables together on the basis of matching the value of a field in one table to the value of the field in the other table?
    a. Connecting.
    b. Uniting.
    c. Linking.
    d. Joining.

2. What SQL tool or mechanism allows us to substitute a shorter label to replace a table's name in a query?
    a. Disguises.
    b. Aliases.
    c. Avatar.
    d. Pseudonyms.

3. What do you call a join that is based on an exact match between two columns?
    a. Exu-join.
    b. Stri-join.
    c. Preci-join.
    d. Equi-join.

4. What happens when three tables are joined in a single query?
    a. The first two tables are joined into a set and the third table is joined to that set.
    b. All three tables are joined immediately.
    c. The second two tables are joined into a set and the first table is joined to that set.
    d. The first and last table are joined into a set and the middle table is joined to that set.

1. Write a query that will display complete contact information of all employees. The output should be sorted by *lastname* and *firstname,* arranged in ascending order. The query should show the following fields (in the order listed) from these three tables.

a. person – id, lastname, firstname

b. contacttype – label (This column should show the full description of the contact type, not just the code. For example, email should be the string "email" and not the id value 1.)

c. contact - value

LAB SOLUTION

This query retrieves data from three tables, (*person, contact* and *contacttype*) and uses two inner joins to link the three tables.

```
SELECT p.id, p.lastname, p.firstname,
ct.label, c.value
FROM person p
INNER JOIN contact c
   ON p.id = c.pid
INNER JOIN contacttype ct
   ON c.ctid = ct.id
ORDER BY lastname, firstname;
```

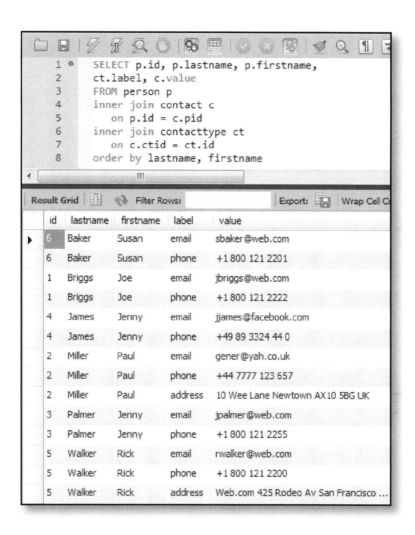

```
1 ● SELECT p.id, p.lastname, p.firstname,
2   ct.label, c.value
3   FROM person p
4   inner join contact c
5      on p.id = c.pid
6   inner join contacttype ct
7      on c.ctid = ct.id
8   order by lastname, firstname
```

id	lastname	firstname	label	value
6	Baker	Susan	email	sbaker@web.com
6	Baker	Susan	phone	+1 800 121 2201
1	Briggs	Joe	email	jbriggs@web.com
1	Briggs	Joe	phone	+1 800 121 2222
4	James	Jenny	email	jjames@facebook.com
4	James	Jenny	phone	+49 89 3324 44 0
2	Miller	Paul	email	gener@yah.co.uk
2	Miller	Paul	phone	+44 7777 123 657
2	Miller	Paul	address	10 Wee Lane Newtown AX10 5BG UK
3	Palmer	Jenny	email	jpalmer@web.com
3	Palmer	Jenny	phone	+1 800 121 2255
5	Walker	Rick	email	rwalker@web.com
5	Walker	Rick	phone	+1 800 121 2200
5	Walker	Rick	address	Web.com 425 Rodeo Av San Francisco ...

7.2 LEFT AND RIGHT JOINS

In the last section, we discussed an INNER JOIN query that listed all employees and the projects that they were involved in. Figure 7-15 shows that query's SELECT statement and its query result.

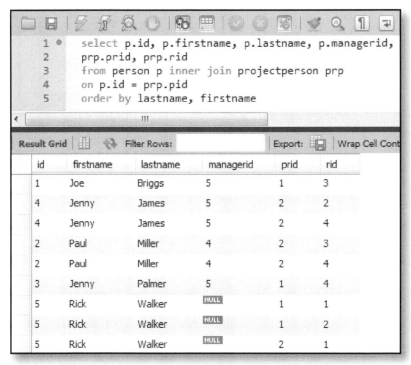

Figure 7-15: Employees and their projects. Notice that Susan Baker is not in the query result. Why is that?

We also pointed out in the last section that Susan Baker is not in this query result because she has not been assigned to any project and therefore has no matching record in the *projectperson* table. How do we modify our query so that it will list all employees, whether they have projects or not?

Figure 7-16 shows our solution.

```
SELECT p.id, p.firstname, p.lastname, p.dob,
p.managerid, prp.prid, prp.rid
FROM person p
LEFT JOIN projectperson prp
    ON p.id = prp.pid
ORDER BY lastname, firstname;
```

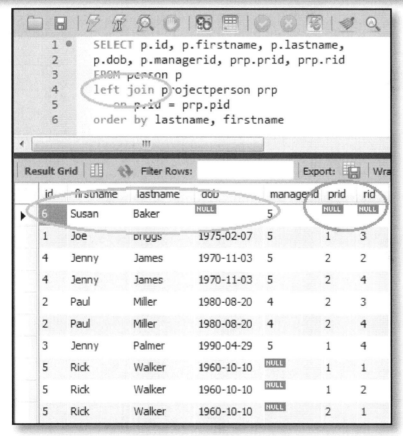

Figure 7-16: A left join query

In figure 7-16, all employees are listed and you can see that Susan Baker is present.

As for the query, the only major change is the use of LEFT JOIN instead of INNER JOIN. So what is a **left join**?

A left join (or **left outer join**) returns every record of the first table for the specified relationship, whether or not it matches a record in the second table. The first table is often referred to as the left table, that is, the table to the left of the LEFT JOIN phrase, as in:

Left Join

```
FROM person p LEFT JOIN projectperson prop
```

Thus, in the previous snippet of SQL code, *person* is the left table while *projectperson* is the right table. We can use the terms "left" and "right" because joins are always done in pairs.

The graphics in figure 7-17 can help you understand the difference between an inner join and a left join. The tables in the joins are represented by circles.

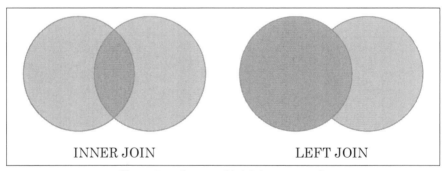

INNER JOIN   LEFT JOIN

Figure 7-17: Inner and left joins compared.

As was stated previously, in an inner join the shaded area at the intersection of the two circles represents the records that satisfy the conditional expression in the ON clause.

```
FROM person p
INNER JOIN projectperson prp
    ON p.id = c.id
```

In an outer join, the entire left circle, representing the left table, is shaded, signifying that all records of the left table become part of the query set. If the record of the left table has no matching record in the right table, then the fields in the query result of the right table record are set to NULL.

A left join is very useful in determining gaps or imparities in a database, as it did in our example of employees not assigned to a project. It could also show you a customer who has not placed an order within a month, a product that has not moved, and so on. Inner joins show us only those records in which all elements are present. Left or right joins show you incomplete records.

It is also important to be careful of the order in which the tables are named in the FROM clause. In our LEFT JOIN query, the left table is *person* while *projectperson* is the right table. But what if we had accidentally swapped the table names? Figure 7-18 shows that *projectperson* is now the left table while *person* is the right table.

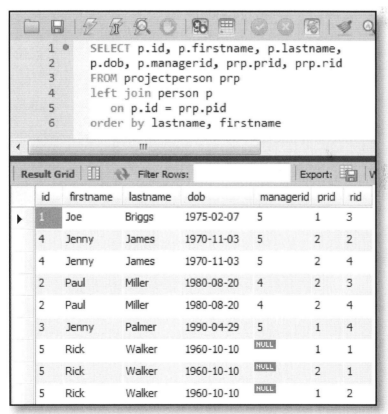

Figure 7-18: Table names swapped. *projectperson* is now the left table while *person* is the right table.

As you can see, the query results are different. In an INNER JOIN, it doesn't matter which table is the left or the right table because we are retrieving records from both tables if they match the conditional expression in the ON clause. But in a LEFT JOIN, the query will automatically retrieve all records from the first table listed, which the query sees as the left table.

Before we discuss the RIGHT JOIN, take a good look at the graphics in figure 7-19.

Right Join

| INNER JOIN | LEFT JOIN | RIGHT JOIN |

Figure 7-19: Inner, left and right joins compared.

As you can see, the RIGHT JOIN is exactly the opposite of the LEFT JOIN. The RIGHT JOIN selects every record of the table on the right and fetches only the matching records from the left table. Let's dive immediately into an example where *projectperson* is the left table while *project* is the right table.

The *projectperson* table shows employees and what projects they are involved in as well as what roles they play in those projects. Figure 7-20 shows all fields of all records of *projectperson*.

Figure 7-21 shows all fields of all records of *project,* which lists all projects and their budgets.

```
1 •    SELECT * FROM projectperson;
```

Result Grid   Filter Rows:

prid	pid	rid
1	5	1
2	5	1
1	5	2
2	4	2
1	1	3
2	2	3
1	3	4
2	2	4
2	4	4
NULL	NULL	NULL

Figure 7-20: All fields of all records of *projectperson.*

We are now going to use a RIGHT JOIN to list all projects and the employees involved in those projects. The next screenshot shows that query and its query results.

```
SELECT prj.id, prj.
label, prj.budget,
pp.pid, pp.rid
FROM projectperson pp
RIGHT JOIN project prj
 ON prj.id = pp.prid
ORDER BY prj.label;
```

Figure 7-21: All fields of all records of *project*.

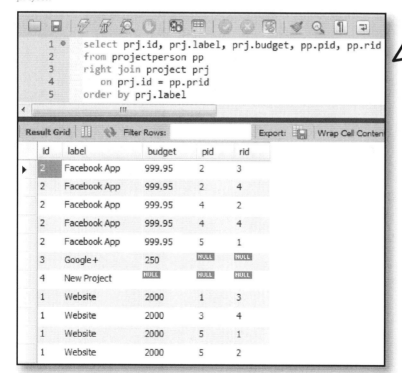

Figure 7-22: Right join of *projectperson* and *project*.

As expected, all records of *project* are listed and we can see that no employees have been assigned to the projects "Google" and "New Project."

It would be more useful to see the name of the employee instead of the value of *pid*. To do this, we'll need to join a third table, *person*. Figure 7-23 shows our modified query.

```
SELECT prj.id, prj.label, prj.budget,
p.lastname, p.firstname, pp.rid
FROM projectperson pp
RIGHT JOIN project prj
   ON prj.id = pp.prid
LEFT JOIN person p
   ON pp.pid = p.id
ORDER BY prj.label;
```

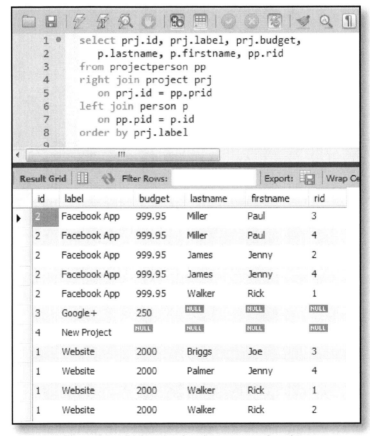

Figure 7-23: Right join of *projectperson* and *project*.

You will notice in the SELECT statement of the previous screenshot that a RIGHT JOIN was used to link *projectperson* and *project*. A LEFT JOIN was used to link the set that resulted from that initial RIGHT JOIN to *person*.

In one SELECT statement, we have mixed a RIGHT JOIN and a LEFT JOIN. There is nothing wrong with that, as long as we get the results we need.

Now, to make our query a little more user-friendly, we will also sort by *lastname* and *firstname* within each project. What if we had 30 or 100 people per project? Then listing the names alphabetically within each project would make the query easier to use.

Figure 7-24 shows the adjustment that was made to the ORDER BY clause to achieve our desired sorting.

```
SELECT prj.id, prj.label, prj.budget,
p.lastname, p.firstname, pp.rid
FROM projectperson pp
RIGHT JOIN project prj
    ON prj.id = pp.prid
LEFT JOIN person p
    ON pp.pid = p.id
ORDER BY prj.label, p.lastname, p.firstname;
```

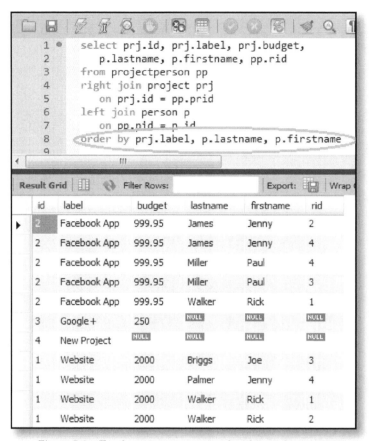

```
1 ● select prj.id, prj.label, prj.budget,
2       p.lastname, p.firstname, pp.rid
3   from projectperson pp
4   right join project prj
5     on prj.id = pp.prid
6   left join person p
7     on pp.nid = n.id
8   order by prj.label, p.lastname, p.firstname
9
```

id	label	budget	lastname	firstname	rid
2	Facebook App	999.95	James	Jenny	2
2	Facebook App	999.95	James	Jenny	4
2	Facebook App	999.95	Miller	Paul	4
2	Facebook App	999.95	Miller	Paul	3
2	Facebook App	999.95	Walker	Rick	1
3	Google+	250	NULL	NULL	NULL
4	New Project	NULL	NULL	NULL	NULL
1	Website	2000	Briggs	Joe	3
1	Website	2000	Palmer	Jenny	4
1	Website	2000	Walker	Rick	1
1	Website	2000	Walker	Rick	2

Figure 7-24: Employee names are sorted within each project.

Before we end this section, let's summarize a few points.

You can mix INNER, LEFT, and RIGHT joins in one query. When to use each of these joins depends on what result you want to achieve.
All joins must occur between pairs of tables, so you will always need one less join than you have tables. For example, to query eight tables you will need seven joins.

If you intend to JOIN more than two tables, every subsequent JOIN happens between the set returned from the initial JOIN and the table being added to the JOIN.

It is good practice to build complex JOIN queries sequentially, testing each JOIN clause to ensure that it returns the appropriate set before adding the next JOIN clause.

The order in which you list the table names is important in a LEFT or RIGHT JOIN. The order doesn't matter in an INNER JOIN.

You have probably noticed that the functionality of a RIGHT JOIN can be replicated by using a LEFT JOIN and modifying the order of the joined tables. Some programmers choose to develop in this way and only ever use INNER and LEFT JOIN clauses. This is personal preference, but whatever technique you choose, be sure that it makes logical sense and that it is easy to understand now and will be easy to understand if you revisit it a year from now.

QUESTIONS FOR REVIEW

1. In which type of join is the query result unaffected by the listing order of the tables?
   a. LEFT.
   b. INNER.
   c. OUTER.
   d. RIGHT.

2. Why would you use a LEFT or RIGHT JOIN in a query that accesses two tables?
   a. To find matching records in both tables.
   b. To find records with incomplete fields.
   c. To find records with null fields.
   d. To find records in one table with no matching records in the other table.

3. A table with 20 records is linked by a LEFT JOIN to a table with 12 records. How many records will appear in the query result?
   a. 240.
   b. 2400.
   c. 32.
   d. 20.

4. The functionality of a RIGHT JOIN can be replicated by using a LEFT JOIN and modifying the order of the joined tables.
   a. True.
   b. False.

The following SQL code is the SELECT statement of the last query of this section. As you can see from the following screenshot, the role of an employee in a project is simply displayed as the role's code, the field *rid*. What changes would you make to the query to replace the display of *rid* with the *label*? For your convenience, this screenshot includes all fields of all records of the table *Role*.

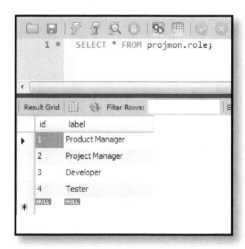

LAB SOLUTION

```
SELECT prj.id, prj.label "Project", prj.
budget, p.lastname, p.firstname, r.label
"Role"
FROM projectperson pp
RIGHT JOIN project prj
   ON prj.id = pp.prid
LEFT JOIN person p
   ON pp.pid = p.id
LEFT JOIN role r
ON pp.pid = p.id
LEFT JOIN role r
   ON pp.rid = r.id
ORDER BY prj.label, p.lastname, p.firstname;
```

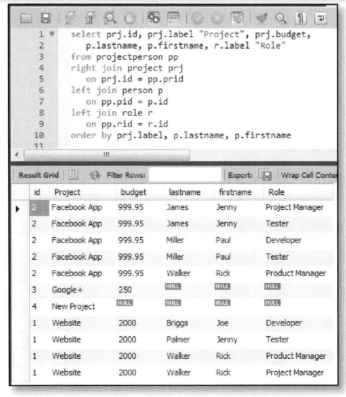

7.3 SELF JOINS

In this section on **self joins,** our primary example will be the table *person*. Here again are all fields of all records of *person*.

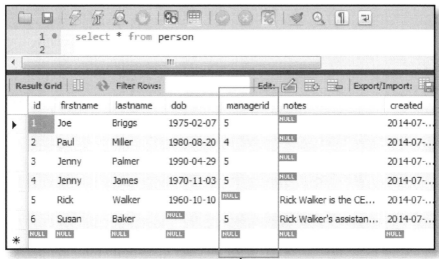

Figure 7-25: All fields of all records of the table *person*.

Let's focus on *managerid*.

In the first record, the record of Joe Briggs, we can see from his record's *managerid* that he reports directly to Rick Walker, the CEO. So do Jenny Palmer, Jenny James, and Susan Baker. Furthermore, Paul Miller's manager is Jenny James and Rick Walker doesn't report to anyone because he is the CEO.

Now, suppose you have been asked to generate a query that will list all employees alphabetically and the names of the managers they report to. If there had been a separate table of managers, then your query would simply join *person* with that table of managers. But in this situation, *person* is also the managers' table.

This is where a self join comes in. A table will be joined with itself by using a table alias.

Take a look at the query and its result in figure 7-26.

```
SELECT p.id, p.firstname, p.lastname,
p.managerid, m.firstname, m.lastname
FROM person p, person m
WHERE p.managerid = m.id;
```

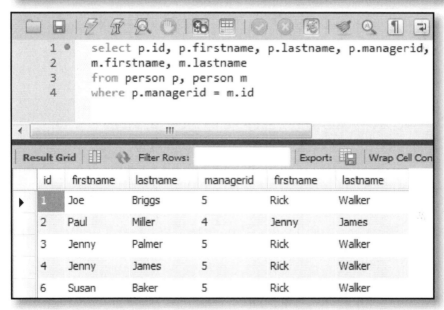

Figure 7-26: Using table aliases in a self join.

Note that the table aliases 'm' and 'p' are used for the same table, *person*. Such aliases for table names are known as **correlation names**.

Correlation Names

Here in figure 7-27, we have rewritten our previous query using JOIN syntax.

```
SELECT p.id, p.firstname, p.lastname,
p.managerid, m.firstname, m.lastname
FROM person p INNER JOIN person m
ON p.managerid = m.id;
```

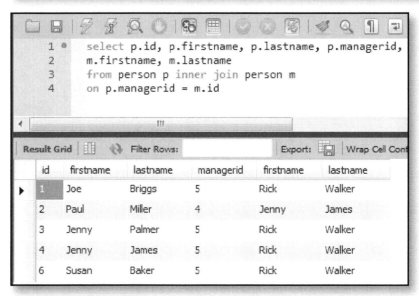

Figure 7-27: Using JOIN syntax to achieve a self join.

But, in the query result of the previous screenshot, we get only five records. To get all six records, we change our INNER JOIN to a LEFT JOIN.

```
SELECT p.id, p.firstname, p.lastname,
p.managerid, m.firstname, m.lastname
FROM person p LEFT JOIN person m
ON p.managerid = m.id;
```

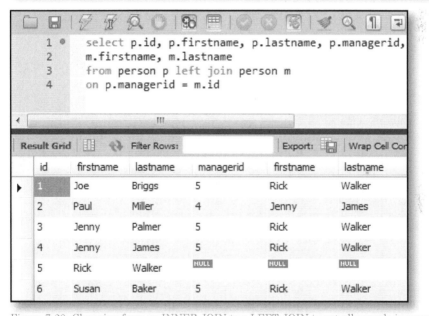

Figure 7-28: Changing from an INNER JOIN to a LEFT JOIN to get all records in *person*.

1. In a query, what type of join do you use to link a table to itself?
a. OUTER JOIN.
b. SELF JOIN.
c. MIDDLE JOIN.
d. LEFT JOIN.

2. What SQL tool or mechanism lets SQL think that a self-join on one table is a join between two tables?
a. Correlation coefficient.
b. Correlation constant.
c. Correlation name.
d. Correlation parameter.

3. When joining a table to itself, you are restricted to using an INNER JOIN.
a. True.
b. False.

4. Self joins can be done using the WHERE clause instead of a JOIN clause.
a. True.
b. False.

LAB ACTIVITY

1. Write a query that will list alphabetically all employees and their respective managers. The report will also show the cell phone numbers of both employees and managers. The columns of the query are:

employee id
employee lastname
employee firstname
employee cell phone number
manager id
manager name (in the format: first initial, followed by a comma and
    space and then last name, for example, "R. Walker")
manager cell phone number.

LAB SOLUTION

In order to solve this lab we will need to make extensive use of LEFT JOIN.

First consider what table you want to start building your query from. We are primarily interested in employees, so we will begin our query with *person*. We are going to use the wildcard selection to ensure that we are getting the information that we need.

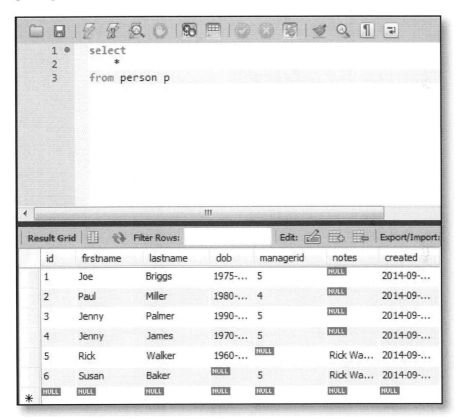

We have formatted it as seen in the screenshot and begin with an alias for *person* because we know that we will have a complex query statement.

Next, we will use LEFT JOIN to
get the contact information for our
employees.

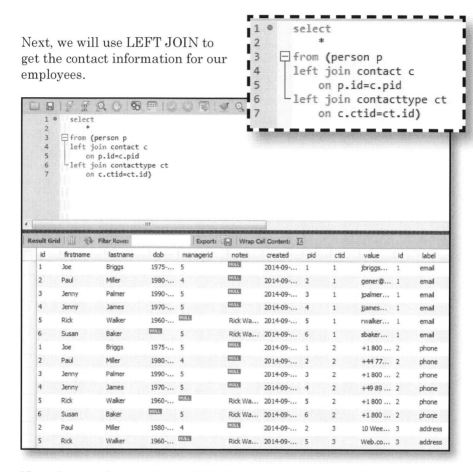

```
1 ●   select
2           *
3     ⊟ from (person p
4         left join contact c
5             on p.id=c.pid
6       └ left join contacttype ct
7             on c.ctid=ct.id)
```

id	firstname	lastname	dob	managerid	notes	created	pid	ctid	value	id	label
1	Joe	Briggs	1975-...	5	NULL	2014-09-...	1	1	jbriggs...	1	email
2	Paul	Miller	1980-...	4	NULL	2014-09-...	2	1	gener@...	1	email
3	Jenny	Palmer	1990-...	5	NULL	2014-09-...	3	1	jpalmer...	1	email
4	Jenny	James	1970-...	5	NULL	2014-09-...	4	1	jjames...	1	email
5	Rick	Walker	1960-...	NULL	Rick Wa...	2014-09-...	5	1	rwalker...	1	email
6	Susan	Baker	NULL	5	Rick Wa...	2014-09-...	6	1	sbaker...	1	email
1	Joe	Briggs	1975-...	5	NULL	2014-09-...	1	2	+1 800 ...	2	phone
2	Paul	Miller	1980-...	4	NULL	2014-09-...	2	2	+44 77...	2	phone
3	Jenny	Palmer	1990-...	5	NULL	2014-09-...	3	2	+1 800 ...	2	phone
4	Jenny	James	1970-...	5	NULL	2014-09-...	4	2	+49 89 ...	2	phone
5	Rick	Walker	1960-...	NULL	Rick Wa...	2014-09-...	5	2	+1 800 ...	2	phone
6	Susan	Baker	NULL	5	Rick Wa...	2014-09-...	6	2	+1 800 ...	2	phone
2	Paul	Miller	1980-...	4	NULL	2014-09-...	2	3	10 Wee...	3	address
5	Rick	Walker	1960-...	NULL	Rick Wa...	2014-09-...	5	3	Web.co...	3	address

Note the use of parentheses. SQL does not require them, but we are
using them in order to make our script easier to understand. We are only
concerned with phone numbers, so we can narrow this data set down
immediately with a WHERE clause.

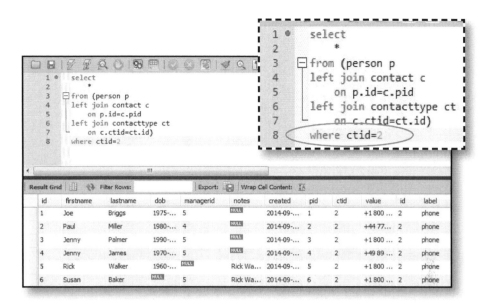

This result set is much more manageable. Now that we have employee names and phone numbers, we want to include employee manager information in the query results. For that, we will use a self LEFT JOIN.

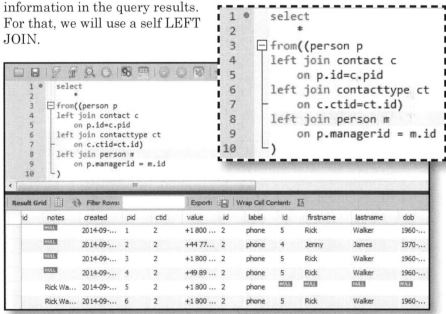

We now have every employee listed along with their phone number and the name of their manager. We will use the same technique to add the manager's phone numbers as we did to add employee phone numbers.

```
1  ● select
2         *
3     ⊟from (((person p
4         left join contact c
5             on p.id=c.pid
6         left join contacttype ct
7             on c.ctid=ct.id)
8         left join person m
9             on p.managerid = m.id)
10        left join contact mc
11            on m.id=mc.pid
12        left join contacttype mct
13            on mc.ctid=mct.id)
14        where c.ctid=2
```

```
1  ● select
2         *
3     ⊟from (((person p
4         left join contact c
5             on p.id=c.pid
6         left join contacttype ct
7             on c.ctid=ct.id)
8         left join person m
9             on p.managerid = m.id)
10        left join contact mc
11            on m.id=mc.pid
12        left join contacttype mct
13            on mc.ctid=mct.id)
14        where c.ctid=2
```

| Result Grid | | | | | | | | | | |
id	firstname	lastname	dob	managerid	notes	created	pid	ctid	value	id
1	Joe	Briggs	1975-...	5	NULL	2014-09-...	1	2	+1 800 ...	2
2	Paul	Miller	1980-...	4	NULL	2014-09-...	2	2	+44 77...	2
3	Jenny	Palmer	1990-...	5	NULL	2014-09-...	3	2	+1 800 ...	2
4	Jenny	James	1970-...	5	NULL	2014-09-...	4	2	+49 89 ...	2
6	Susan	Baker	NULL	5	Rick Wa...	2014-09-...	6	2	+1 800 ...	2
1	Joe	Briggs	1975-...	5	NULL	2014-09-...	1	2	+1 800 ...	2
2	Paul	Miller	1980-...	4	NULL	2014-09-...	2	2	+44 77...	2
3	Jenny	Palmer	1990-...	5	NULL	2014-09-...	3	2	+1 800 ...	2
4	Jenny	James	1970-...	5	NULL	2014-09-...	4	2	+49 89 ...	2
6	Susan	Baker	NULL	5	Rick Wa...	2014-09-...	6	2	+1 800 ...	2
1	Joe	Briggs	1975-...	5	NULL	2014-09-...	1	2	+1 800 ...	2
3	Jenny	Palmer	1990-...	5	NULL	2014-09-...	3	2	+1 800 ...	2

We now have a table which contains employee names and phone numbers, as well as the name of their manager and that manager's contact information. We are only interested in manager phone numbers, so we can narrow this data set by adding to our WHERE clause.

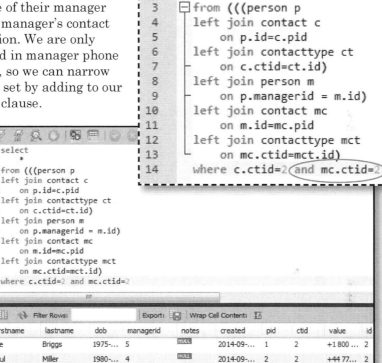

```
1  ●   select
2          *
3      ⊟ from (((person p
4          left join contact c
5              on p.id=c.pid
6          left join contacttype ct
7        ─     on c.ctid=ct.id)
8          left join person m
9        ─     on p.managerid = m.id)
10         left join contact mc
11             on m.id=mc.pid
12         left join contacttype mct
13       ─     on mc.ctid=mct.id)
14         where c.ctid=2 and mc.ctid=2
```

id	firstname	lastname	dob	managerid	notes	created	pid	ctid	value	id
1	Joe	Briggs	1975-...	5	NULL	2014-09-...	1	2	+1 800 ...	2
2	Paul	Miller	1980-...	4	NULL	2014-09-...	2	2	+44 77...	2
3	Jenny	Palmer	1990-...	5	NULL	2014-09-...	3	2	+1 800 ...	2
4	Jenny	James	1970-...	5	NULL	2014-09-...	4	2	+49 89 ...	2
6	Susan	Baker	NULL	5	Rick Wa...	2014-09-...	6	2	+1 800 ...	2

That is a more manageable data set, but we have lost Rick Walker. He does not have a manager and so his manager phone number is NULL. We can fix this problem by further modifying our WHERE clause to look for scenarios where the contact is either "phone" or NULL.

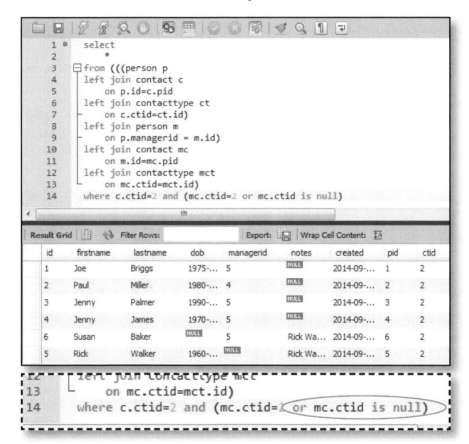

Now that we have all of the information that we need, our final step is formatting the data appropriately. Using column aliases and formatting, you will get the following solution:

```
SELECT
p.id 'ID Number', p.lastname 'Last Name',
p.firstname 'First Name', c.value 'Phone
Number', p.managerid 'Manager ID', CONCAT_
WS(". ", LEFT(m.firstname,1), m.lastname)
'Manager Name', mc.value 'Manager Phone
```

```
Number'
FROM ((( person p
LEFT JOIN contact c
   ON p.id = c.pid
LEFT JOIN contacttype ct
   ON c.ctid = ct.id)
LEFT JOIN person m
   ON p.managerid = m.id)
LEFT JOIN contact mc
   ON m.id = mc.pid
LEFT JOIN contacttype mct
   ON mc.ctid = mct.id)
WHERE c.ctid = 2
AND (mc.ctid = 2 OR mc.ctid IS NULL)
ORDER BY p.lastname, p.firstname;
```

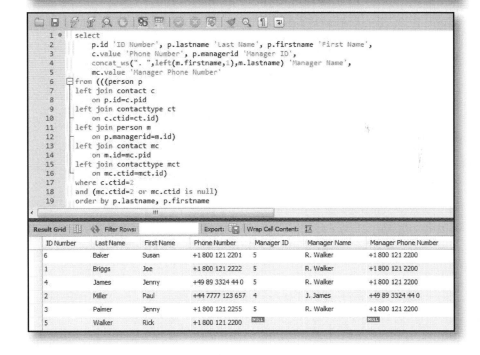

CHAPTER 7 LAB EXERCISE

1. Write a query that retrieves all fields of all matching records of the *person* and *projectperson* tables.

2. Write a query that lists all employees per project.

3. Improve the output of the previous query by sorting and removing duplicates.

4. Extend the previous query to include the project name.

5. Extend the previous query to also output the role of each person within the respective project.

6. Extend the previous query to also output the name of the manager of each person in the respective project.

7. Write a query returning a list of persons including their respective managers, if they are assigned one.

CHAPTER 7 LAB SOLUTION

1.
```
SELECT * FROM projectperson pp, person p
WHERE pp.pid=p.id;
```

2.
```
SELECT pp.prid, p.firstname,p.lastname
FROM ProjectPerson pp, Person p
WHERE pp.pid=p.id
ORDER BY pp.prid, p.lastname,
p.firstname;
```

3.
```
SELECT DISTINCT pp.prid, p.firstname,
p.lastname
FROM ProjectPerson pp, Person p
WHERE pp.pid=p.id ORDER BY pp.prid ASC;
```

4.
```
SELECT DISTINCT pr.label, p.firstname,
p.lastname
FROM Project pr, ProjectPerson pp,
Person p
WHERE pr.id=pp.prid AND pp.pid=p.id
ORDER BY pp.prid ASC;
```

5.
```
SELECT DISTINCT pr.label, r.label,
p.firstname, p.lastname
FROM Project pr, Role r, ProjectPerson
pp, Person p
WHERE pr.id=pp.prid AND r.id=pp.rid AND
pp.pid=p.id ORDER BY pp.prid ASC;
```

6.
```
SELECT DISTINCT pr.label, r.label,
p.firstname, p.lastname, m.firstname,
m.lastname
FROM Project pr, Role r, ProjectPerson
pp, Person p, Person m
WHERE pr.id=pp.prid AND r.id=pp.rid AND
pp.pid=p.id AND p.managerid=m.id
ORDER BY pp.prid ASC;
```

7.
```
SELECT p,firstname, p.lastname,
m.firstname, m.lastname
FROM person p
LEFT JOIN person m
ON p.managerid=m.id;
```

CHAPTER SUMMARY

In this chapter, we focused on the INNER, LEFT, RIGHT, and SELF joins and explained both their use and their utility.

In the next chapter we are going to look at using subqueries and we'll explain their similarities with and differences from joins. We will also look at the use of derived tables in queries.

To summarize this chapter, here is a table of the joins defined by the ANSI SQL standard.

STANDARD SQL JOINS DIAGRAM

Join	Description
Cross Join	Returns all rows from the first table in which each row from the first table is combined with all rows from the second table.
Natural Join	A join that compares, for equality, all the columns in the first table with corresponding columns that have the same name in the second table.
Inner Join	A join that uses a comparison operator to match rows from two tables based on the values in common columns from each table. Inner joins are the most common type of join.
Left Outer Join	Returns *all* the rows from the left table, not just the ones in which the joined columns match. If a row in the left table has no matching rows in the right table, the associated result row contains nulls for all SELECT-clause columns coming from the right table.
Right Outer Join	The reverse of a left outer join. All rows from the right table are returned. Nulls are returned for the left table if a right-table row has no matching left-table row.
Full Outer Join	Returns all rows in both the left and right tables. If a row has no match in the other table, the SELECT-clause columns from the other table contain nulls. If there is a match between the tables, the entire result row contains values from both tables.
Self-Join	A join of a table to itself.

CHAPTER 8

SUBQUERIES

CHAPTER OBJECTIVES:

- You will learn how to use subqueries to filter query results.
- You will understand how the IN clause works.
- You will use the EXISTS clause in subqueries.
- You will learn the difference between using subqueries and using joins.
- You will understand and use derived tables in queries.

8.1 FILTERING USING SUBQUERIES

In this chapter we'll be going over subqueries, the difference between a subquery and a JOIN, and derived tables. The following SELECT statements summarize what you will be using during the examples in this chapter.

Subquery

```
SELECT * FROM person WHERE dob=(SELECT
MAX(dob) FROM person);

SELECT * FROM person WHERE dob>(SELECT
AVG(dob) FROM person);

SELECT * FROM person WHERE id IN ( SELECT
pid FROM projectperson WHERE rid=4 );

SELECT * FROM person p WHERE EXISTS (
SELECT * FROM projectperson pp WHERE
pp.pid=p.id );

SELECT * FROM person p WHERE NOT EXISTS
( SELECT * FROM projectperson pp WHERE
pp.pid=p.id );
```

```
SELECT * FROM person p WHERE EXISTS (
SELECT * FROM projectperson pp WHERE
pp.pid=p.id AND pp.rid=4 )

SELECT MAX(directreports) FROM ( SELECT
managerid, count(*) directreports FROM
person GROUP BY managerid ) counts;
```

A **subquery** is a second query built into a
main query and is used for filtering query
results. A subquery has to be a valid query
in its own right. A subquery is sometimes
called an **inner query** or **nested query**.

Inner Query

Nested Query

Usually a subquery is used in a WHERE clause in order to test against a
dynamically created value.

Let's say that we want to know who the oldest or youngest employee
in our database is. We can easily determine that using a simple select
statement.

```
SELECT MAX(dob) FROM person;
```

The problem is that we only return the data of birth, not the person
with that date of birth. A subquery will allow us to use the dynamically
generated date of birth value in a WHERE clause to return the person
from our database.

We are returning a scalar value, so we can use the standard comparison operators. Enter the following code:

```
SELECT * FROM person
WHERE dob=(SELECT MAX(dob) FROM person);
```

The code selects from person only the entry with the maximum date of birth, which would be the youngest employee. Figure 8-1 shows this.

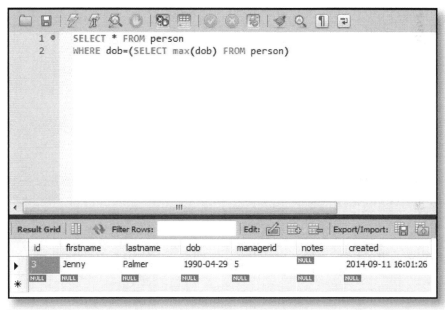

Figure 8-1: Using a subquery to return only the youngest employee record.

If we wanted to return only those employees younger than the average age, we could do that by modifying our subquery to select the average age instead of the max age.

```
SELECT * FROM person
WHERE dob>(SELECT AVG(dob) FROM person);
```

Note that we also need to modify our WHERE clause in order to return records where employees have a date of birth greater than the average.

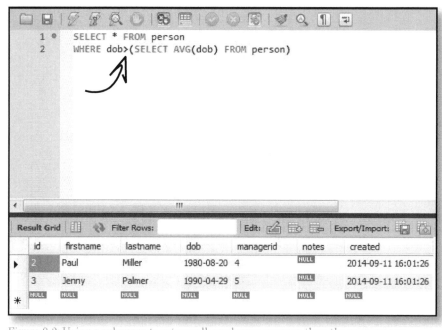

Figure 8-2: Using a subquery to return all employees younger than the average age.

The WHERE clause can again be modified to show all employees older than the average.

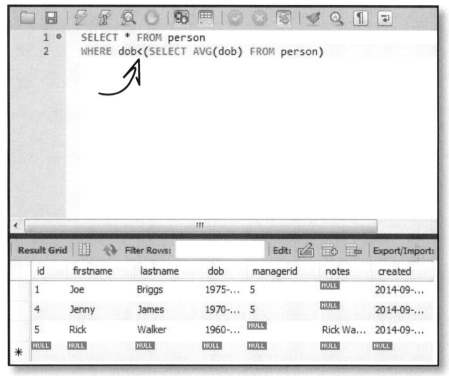

Figure 8-3: All employees older than the average are shown.

Note that these two queries only returned five employees, even though we know that there are six records. This is because one of our employees does not have a date of birth entered into *person*.

When we are using subqueries we have to be aware of what data type the WHERE clause is expecting. In our examples the WHERE clause tests against a date of birth and so we need to ensure that our subquery returns a valid date data type. If we were instead testing against an integer value, then we would need to construct a subquery that would return an integer.

This method of using subqueries works for scalar values, but if we are looking to return records from a range of values we can use the IN clause.

The IN clause returns records that match any value contained in a list. Because the IN clause uses a list, we need to ensure that the subquery returns a single column table. If our subquery returns a multi-column table, we will get an error. To test using the IN clause with a subquery, we will return a list of all the employees who are assigned a certain role.

We know that we have a table, *projectperson*, which links an employee to a role. It uses the *id* field from *person* as a foreign key named *pid* and the *id* field from *role* as a foreign key named *rid*.

Let's look for every employee who is a "Tester." We know from our *role* table that "Tester" is associated with the key value 4, so we can create a SELECT statement that selects all of the records from *projectperson* with that role id using the following code.

```
SELECT * FROM projectperson WHERE rid=4;
```

We cannot use this SELECT statement in our subquery, though, because it does not return a single column table. In order to return a single column table, we need to specify what value we are looking for. We want all of the employees with a certain role, so we would select only *pid* from *projectperson*.

```
SELECT pid FROM projectperson WHERE rid=4;
```

That returns a single column table of id values that we can use as our subquery. Create the complete query with subquery using the following code:

```
SELECT * FROM person
WHERE id IN (
    SELECT pid FROM projectperson WHERE
rid=4
);
```

Our IN clause used the single column table from our subquery to select only those employees who are assigned the role of "Tester" as defined in our *role* table. Figure 8-4 shows the expected output.

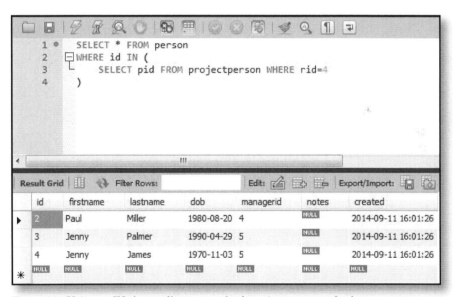

Figure 8-4: Using an IN clause allows us to check against a range of values.

The scalar and the single-column IN clause are the most common types of subqueries.

1. What is a subquery?
   a. A query that is placed below another query.
   b. A query from an external script that is called.
   c. A second query that is built into the main query.
   d. A query that only selects from a subtable.

2. A subquery has to be a valid query in its own right.
   a. True.
   b. False.

3. What does the IN clause allow a user to check against?
   a. A multi-column table.
   b. A range of values.
   c. A scalar value.
   d. A range of columns.

4. The WHERE clause expects a certain data type.
   a. True.
   b. False.

LAB ACTIVITY

1. Display the details of projects from *project* with a budget value greater than the average budget.

2. Display the details of the project from *project* with the largest budget value.

3. Display the details of the project from *project* with the smallest budget value.

4. Display the details of projects from *project* with a budget value smaller than the average budget.

LAB SOLUTION

1.
```
SELECT * FROM project
WHERE budget>(
    SELECT AVG(budget) FROM project
);
```

2.
```
SELECT * FROM project
WHERE budget=(
    SELECT MAX(budget) FROM project
);
```

3.
```
SELECT * FROM project
WHERE budget=(
    SELECT MIN(budget) FROM project
);
```

4.
```
SELECT * FROM project
WHERE budget<(
    SELECT AVG(budget) FROM project
);
```

8.2 The **EXISTS** Clause

The **EXISTS** clause is another means of filtering results based on a subquery. The EXISTS clause tests each record from a SELECT statement and displays the record if the EXISTS clause is true. The EXISTS clause is true if its subquery returns any rows. We will continue looking at the relationships between employees and projects in order to demonstrate the EXISTS clause.

EXISTS

First, we will use the EXISTS clause as a filter to display only those employees who are assigned to a project. Enter the following code.

```
SELECT * FROM person p
WHERE EXISTS
(
    SELECT * FROM projectperson pp
    WHERE pp.pid=p.id
);
```

The code example uses a subquery in the EXISTS clause to select a record from *projectperson* where the foreign key *pid* matches the primary key, *id*, from *person*. If an employee is not assigned to a project, then *projectperson* will not have a record of their *pid* and so the EXISTS clause subquery will not return any rows. If the EXISTS clause is false, then that record will not appear in the results. Figure 8-5 shows the expected results.

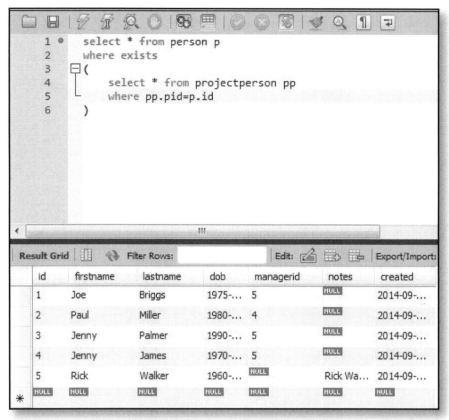

Figure 8-5: The result of using the EXISTS clause to filter only those employees assigned to a project.

We can display those employees who are not assigned to a project using the **NOT** keyword with the EXISTS clause.

NOT

```
SELECT * FROM person p
WHERE NOT EXISTS
(
    SELECT * FROM projectperson pp
    WHERE pp.pid=p.id
);
```

Figure 8-6 displays the result of this query. When the subquery within the EXISTS clause does not return any rows, the record is displayed.

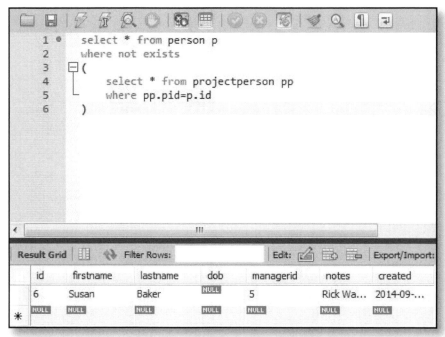

id	firstname	lastname	dob	managerid	notes	created
6	Susan	Baker	NULL	5	Rick Wa...	2014-09-...
NULL	NULL	NULL	NULL	NULL	NULL	NULL

Figure 8-6: Using NOT EXISTS and subqueries to display only employees not assigned to a project.

As we did in section 8.1 we are going to list only those employees who are assigned the "Tester" role. We know that *projectperson* contains a foreign key from *role* and so we can use that key in a subquery with the EXISTS clause to further filter our query results. The foreign key in *projectperson* that links to *role* is *rid* and the value of "Tester" is 4. Use the following code for your query:

```
SELECT * FROM person p
WHERE EXISTS
(
    SELECT * FROM projectperson pp
    WHERE pp.pid=p.id
    AND pp.rid=4
)
```

By checking for a specific *rid* value within *projectperson* as part of the subquery, we filter out any employee who is not assigned to a "Tester" role on a project, as shown in figure 8-7.

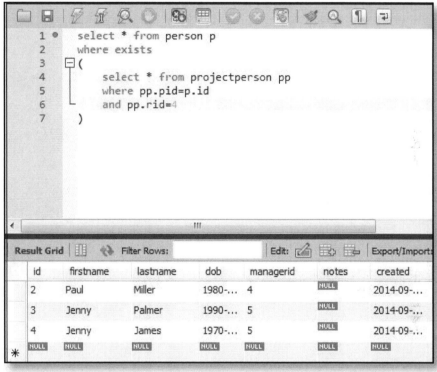

Figure 8-7: Building a more complex subquery with the EXISTS clause allows us to filter for more conditions.

Subqueries can be used as alternatives to JOIN and that's something we'll discuss in the next section.

1. What is returned by the statement in a false EXISTS clause?
   a. A table of NULL values.
   b. A table of "false" Boolean values.
   c. A table that does not contain any rows.
   d. A single "false" Boolean value.

2. An EXISTS clause can be modified with NOT.
   a. True.
   b. False.

3. What is the proper syntax for the EXISTS clause?
   a. SELECT * FROM persons WHERE (subquery) EXISTS
   b. SELECT * FROM persons WHERE EXIST (subquery)
   c. SELECT * FROM persons WHERE EXISTS (subquery)
   d. WHERE EXISTS (subquery) SELECT * FROM persons

4. Each record from the SELECT statement's table is tested against the WHERE clause.
   a. True.
   b. False.

LAB ACTIVITY

1) Using the EXISTS clause, display the employees from *person* that are managers.

2) Using the EXISTS clause, display the records from *contact* that are email addresses.

3) Use NOT EXISTS to show employees who are not managers and records that are not email addresses.

Lab Solution

1.
```
SELECT * FROM person p
WHERE EXISTS (
    SELECT * FROM projectperson pp
    WHERE p.id=pp.pid
    AND rid=2
);
```

2.
```
SELECT * FROM contact c
WHERE EXISTS (
    SELECT * FROM contacttype ct
    WHERE ct.id=c.ctid
    AND ct.id=1
);
```

3.
```
SELECT * FROM person p
WHERE NOT EXISTS (
    SELECT * FROM projectperson pp
    WHERE p.id=pp.pid
    AND rid=2
);
```

4.
```
SELECT * FROM contact c
WHERE EXISTS (
    SELECT * FROM contacttype ct
    WHERE ct.id=c.ctid
    AND ct.id=1
);
```

8.3 Subqueries as Alternatives to Joins

In this chapter, our examples have focused on determining which employees are assigned to a certain role in a project. We have used this problem to explain the usage of subqueries in SQL, but astute readers have probably discovered how the problem can be solved using JOIN. The question of whether a JOIN or a subquery is better is the subject of much debate.

Enter the following code:

```
SELECT * FROM person p, projectperson pp
WHERE p.id=pp.pid
AND pp.rid=4;
```

First, we are using an INNER JOIN between *person* and *projectperson* and only displaying those records that are assigned to *rid* 4, which is the role "Tester" from *role*.

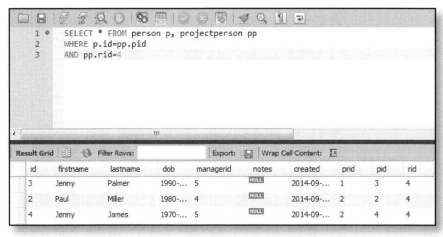

Figure 8-8: Listing employees with a specific role using an INNER JOIN..

Next, enter the following code:

```
SELECT * FROM person p
WHERE id IN (
    SELECT pid
    FROM projectperson
    WHERE rid=4
);
```

Here we are using a subquery with the IN clause to display only those records from *person* where their *id* matches a list of *pid* values from *projectperson* that are linked to the *rid* value 4.

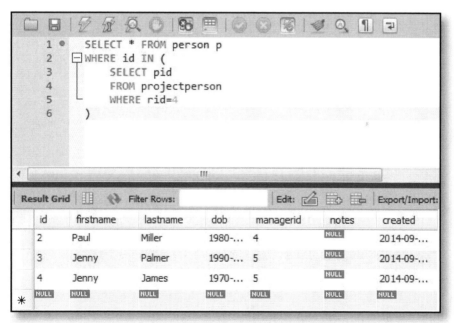

Figure 8-9: Using a subquery with the IN clause to display employees with a certain role.

Finally, enter the following code:

```
SELECT * FROM person p
WHERE EXISTS (
    SELECT * FROM projectperson
    WHERE pid=p.id
    AND rid=4
);
```

This example uses a subquery with the EXISTS clause to display records from *person,* but only when their *id* matches a *pid* value in *projectperson* which also has an *rid* value of 4.

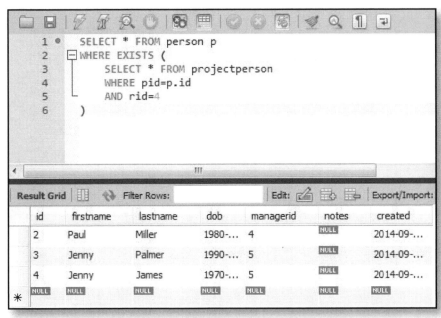

Figure 8-10: A subquery with the EXISTS clause also displays the records that are assigned a certain role.

You can see that all three techniques result in a list containing Paul Miller, Jenny Palmer, and Jenny James. The INNER JOIN also includes the data from *projectperson* while the subqueries do not.

Modern DBMSs are optimized enough to trivialize the performance differences in these query techniques, leaving the choice of subquery versus INNER JOIN to the developer's preference. That said, there may be circumstances when one technique would be preferred, though in order to make that determination, performance testing on a specific database would be needed.

Best practice is to write a query that works correctly in a manner that you logically understand, then to consider optimizations if the need arises.

QUESTIONS FOR REVIEW

1. Joins are always more efficient than subqueries.
   a. True.
   b. False.

2. DBMS optimizations are always correct.
   a. True.
   b. False.

3. What is a difference between using a join and using a subquery?
   a. Joins will return all of the fields from multiple tables.
   b. Subqueries are substantially faster.
   c. Joins use less system resources.
   d. Subqueries are always more processer intensive.

4. What is a good method of preparing your queries?
   a. Determine whether or join or a subquery would be fastest, and use that.
   b. Always use a subquery.
   c. Always use a join.
   d. Determine what works correctly and what you logically understand and optimize later as necessary.

LAB ACTIVITY

You need to find out the details of people who have an email address. Use both JOIN queries and subqueries to achieve your purpose. Display the output.

1.
```
SELECT * FROM person p, contact c
WHERE p.id=c.pid AND c.ctid=1;

SELECT * FROM person p
WHERE id IN (
    SELECT pid FROM contact
    WHERE ctid=1
);
```

2.
```
SELECT * FROM person p
WHERE EXISTS (
    SELECT * FROM contact
    WHERE p.id=pid AND ctid=1
);
```

8.4 Derived Tables

Derived tables are similar to subqueries but have a more specific application. A derived table is a named, temporary table that is created using a SELECT statement in the FROM clause.

Derived tables are an effective way of

> **Derived Tables**

consolidating data to be used in a query. To show how derived tables can be used we will create a query to get the largest number of employees reporting to one manager.

First, display all of the data from *person*.

```
SELECT * FROM person;
```

	id	firstname	lastname	dob	managerid	notes	created
	1	Joe	Briggs	1975-...	5	NULL	2014-09-...
	2	Paul	Miller	1980-...	4	NULL	2014-09-...
	3	Jenny	Palmer	1990-...	5	NULL	2014-09-...
	4	Jenny	James	1970-...	5	NULL	2014-09-...
	5	Rick	Walker	1960-...	NULL	Rick Wa...	2014-09-...
	6	Susan	Baker	NULL	5	Rick Wa...	2014-09-...
*	NULL	NULL	NULL	NULL	NULL	NULL	NULL

Figure 8-11: All of the data from *person*.

Looking at figure 8-11 we can see that Rick Walker, *id* 5, manages the most employees. There are four employees with a *managerid* of 5, so 4 is going to be the desired result from our exercise.

Use the following code to create a simple query that lists *managerid* and the number of employees managed:

```
SELECT managerid, count(*) directreports
FROM person
GROUP BY managerid;
```

Using the GROUP BY clause and **count()** gives us the number of employees who directly report to any given manager. The table that results from this query is going to be our derived table. Figure 8-12 displays the current results.

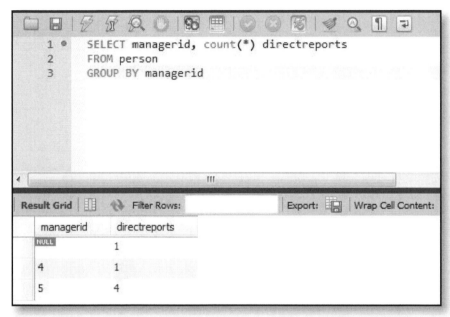

Figure 8-12: First, we create a SELECT statement that will give us the table that will become our derived table.

Now that we have a table that lists the numbers of employees who report to any given manager, we will use it in a query to return the largest number of employees reporting to any one manager. Build your query according to the following code:

```
SELECT MAX(directreports)
FROM
(
    SELECT managerid, count(*) directreports
    FROM person
    GROUP BY managerid
) counts;
```

The two key differences between this derived table and the subqueries
that we have been using are that this table is part of the FROM clause
and that it is given an alias, "counts." Derived tables must be given an
alias. The results are shown in figure 8-13.

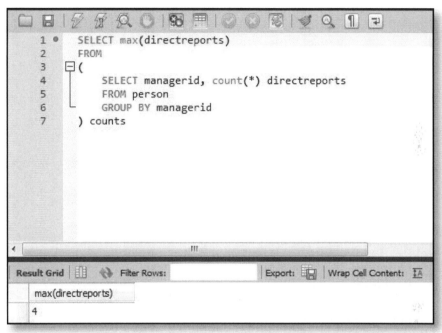

Figure 8-13: Using derived tables to obtain and display the largest number of employees
managed by an individual.

When using derived tables with large databases it is important to be very
aware of how much data you are accessing and how large the tables are.
Derived tables are only temporary, but they still need to exist in memory,
so if they are too large they can cause performance issues.

1. A derived table is a permanent new table in your database.
   a. True.
   b. False.

2. You can use a subquery interchangeably with a derived table.
   a. True.
   b. False.

3. What is the proper syntax to create a derived table?
   a. SELECT * FROM (derived table)
   b. SELECT * FROM (derived table) tablename
   c. SELECT (derived table) *
   d. (derived table) tablename SELECT * FROM tablename

4. A derived table requires a name.
   a. True.
   b. False.

LAB ACTIVITY

Create a derived table containing employee personal and project data and use that in a query to display an employee's last name, the name of the project they are working on, and their role in that project.

LAB SOLUTION

```
SELECT nameProject.lastname 'Last Name',
pr.label 'Project Name' r.label 'Project
Role' FROM
    ( SELECT * FROM person p, projectperson
pp
    WHERE p.id=pp.pid) nameProject, role r,
project pr
WHERE nameProject.rid=r.id AND nameProject.
prid=pr.id
```

CHAPTER 8 LAB EXERCISE

1) Write a query returning the projects with a budget larger than the average of all project budgets.

2) Write a query returning all projects in *project* and their percentage of the total budget.

3) Format the previous query by adding appropriate headings and rounding the budget percentage to three digits.

4) Write a query returning any employee assigned the "Project Manager" role for any project.

5) Write a query returning all projects in *project* that have no staff assigned.

6) Write a query returning all records in *person* that have an "address" listed in *contact*.

7) Write a query returning a table with all contact information from *contact* and the associated type from *contacttype*.

8) Use the previous query as a derived table in a query returning all persons in the Person table with their contact details.

9) Write a query returning how often the most used contact type in *contact* is used.

1.
```
SELECT * FROM project
WHERE budget>(SELECT AVG(budget) FROM
project)
```

2.
```
SELECT label, budget, budget/(SELECT
SUM(budget) FROM Project) FROM Project
```

3.
```
SELECT
label 'Project Name',
budget 'Budget',
CONCAT(100*(ROUND (budget/(SELECT
SUM(budget) FROM project),3)),'%')
'Budget Share'
FROM project
```

4.
```
SELECT * FROM person
WHERE id IN (SELECT pid FROM
projectperson WHERE rid=2)
```

5.
```
SELECT * FROM project pr
WHERE NOT EXISTS(SELECT * FROM
projectperson WHERE prid=pr.id)
```

6.
```
SELECT * FROM person p
WHERE EXISTS (SELECT * FROM CONTACT
    WHERE pid=p.id AND ctid=(
        SELECT id FROM contacttype
WHERE label='address')
    )
```

7.

```
SELECT * FROM contact c, contacttype ct
WHERE c.ctid=ct.id
```

8.

```
SELECT * FROM person p,
    (SELECT * FROM contact c,
contacttype ct
    WHERE c.ctid=ct.id) cinfo
WHERE p.id=cinfo.pid
```

9.

```
SELECT MAX(uses) FROM
(SELECT ctid, COUNT(*) uses FROM
contact c GROUP BY ctid) u
```

CHAPTER SUMMARY

In this chapter we have learned what subqueries are and how to use them to filter query results. We learned how to use the EXISTS clause with subqueries and we also learned how derived tables are created and utilized. The alternative use of JOIN instead of subqueries was discussed, and we noted some best practices for determining which method to use.

In the next chapter, we will look at the data manipulation statements INSERT, UPDATE, and DELETE and we will discuss best practices when using those statements to work with your data.

CHAPTER 9

MANIPULATING YOUR DATA

CHAPTER OBJECTIVES:

- You will learn how to use the INSERT statement to add new records.
- You will learn how to use the UPDATE statement to modify database records.
- You will learn how to safely use the DELETE statement to remove records.
- You will utilize best practices to safely modify your database.

9.1 THE INSERT STATEMENT

The SELECT statement that we have been using is one part of the data manipulation language (DML). The data manipulation language is used to modify the data contained in a database rather than the database schema itself. The other data manipulation elements we will be looking at are the INSERT, UPDATE, and DELETE statements.

The following SQL statements summarize the examples that we will work through in this chapter. The INSERT, UPDATE, and DELETE statements will actually affect the data in the database, unlike the SELECT statement, so do not run these statements until the appropriate point in the text.

```
INSERT INTO person VALUES
(7,'Martin','Holzke','1980-05-
05',5,'xxx',now());

INSERT INTO person
(firstname,lastname,managerid,dob) VALUES
('Martin','Holzke',5,'1970-05-05');

INSERT INTO person
(lastname,firstname,managerid,dob) VALUES
('Martin','Holzke',5,'1960-05-05'),
```

```
('Fred','Flintstone',5,'0070-05-05');

INSERT INTO person (firstname, lastname,
managerid, dob) SELECT concat('copy of
',firstname),lastname,managerid,dob FROM
person WHERE id>=9;

UPDATE person SET dob='1990-01-01';

UPDATE person SET dob='1990-01-01' WHERE
id=7;

UPDATE person SET dob='1990-01-01',
firstname='Mike' WHERE id=7;

UPDATE person SET firstname='Mike' WHERE
firstname='Martin';

UPDATE project SET budget=budget*1.2;

DELETE FROM person WHERE id=9;

DELETE FROM person WHERE firstname
LIKE('copy%');
```

The SQL **INSERT** statement is used to add new records to a database. Although it is called an INSERT statement, it does not actually insert a record at a particular position.

INSERT

Functionally, INSERT is more like an append statement because it adds a new record to the end of the database. The database will take care of indexing and managing the location of the data you insert.

Before we attempt an example INSERT, it is important to note that any record inserted into a database has to satisfy the rules of the table that it is inserted into. Fields that require a value through the NOT_NULL flag and that are not set to AUTO_INCREMENT are mandatory when inserting new data. Fields that do not have the NOT_NULL flag can be omitted.

NOT_NULL

AUTO_INCREMENT

To understand this in detail, let's consider the *person* table.

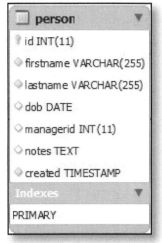

Figure 9-1: Our *person* table. showing the fields that can be included in the INSERT statement.

The *id* field has the AUTO_INCREMENT flag and is set as the table's primary key, so it is managed by the database. The *firstname* and *lastname* fields have the NOT_NULL flag set, so they must be included in an INSERT statement. *dob, managerid,* and *notes* do not have the NOT_NULL flag, and so are optional fields. If data is entered for those fields it must match the data type expected, but if data is not entered they will be given NULL values. The *timestamp* field has a NOT_NULL flag set but it was also set with DEFAULT CURRENT_ TIMESTAMP. This flag means that if the field is not explicitly set by the INSERT statement it will be given a default value of the current time.

We can only INSERT values into one table at a time, but we can INSERT more than one record at a time. First, we will use INSERT to create a single new record in *person*. Enter the following code:

```
INSERT INTO person
VALUES (7,'Martin','Holzke','1980-05-
05',5,'xxx',now());
```

When you execute that query you will create a new record in *person*. This is what is called an implicit INSERT because we are not stating what columns we want the values to be inserted into. Look at the syntax. INSERT INTO is followed by the name of the database to which we want to add a record. VALUES is followed by a comma-separated list of values that we want our new record to contain. Each value is of the appropriate type for the field we are adding it to. The *created* field expects a timestamp, so we use **now()** to get the current timestamp.

CURRENT TIMESTAMP

INSERT INTO

VALUES

It is important to note that when you use an implicit INSERT, your statement must include values for all of the fields in the table.

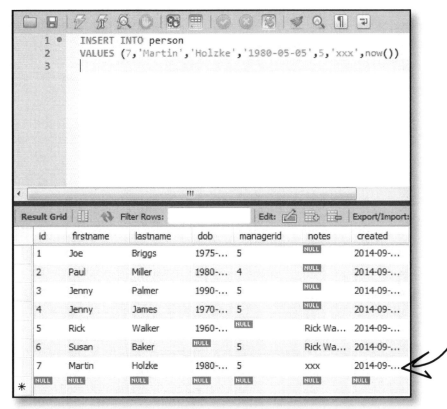

Figure 9-2: The INSERT statement and the result of the record being inserted into *person*.

When doing an INSERT, it is more usefull to explicitly instruct SQL which fields you want to insert data into. Enter the following code:

```
INSERT INTO person
(firstname,lastname,managerid,dob)
VALUES ('Martin','Holzke',5,'1970-05-05');
```

In the example code we declare what fields from *person* we intend to insert values into with a comma-separated list after the database name. We know that *firstname* and *lastname* are required, so we include data for those fields. We choose to include data for *managerid* and *dob* even though those fields can be NULL. Note that we did not include values for *id* or *created* because those fields both have default values. *id* is the primary key, so it is managed by the DBMS and *created* is given the default value of CURRENT_TIMESTAMP.

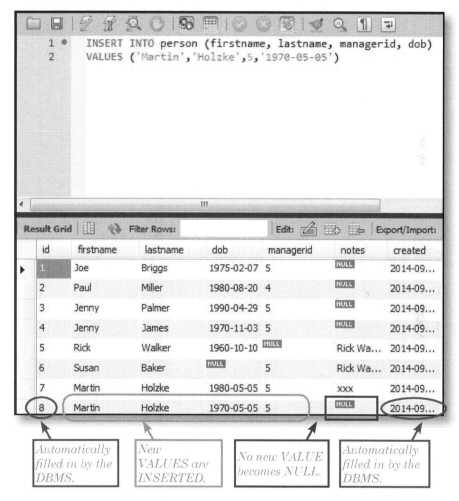

Figure 9-3: Using an explicit INSERT only enters data into the fields we specify. Note that fields with default values are populated by the DBMS.

Multiple records can be inserted into a table with a single statement. Enter the following code:

```sql
INSERT INTO person
(lastname,firstname,managerid,dob)
VALUES  ('Martin','Holzke',5,'1960-05-05'),
    ('Fred','Flintstone',5,'0070-05-05');
```

We are still using an explicit INSERT statement and the values are in the same parenthetical comma-separated list, but we include additional records using a comma-separated list of record values. View the output of your *person* table; it should look like figure 9-4.

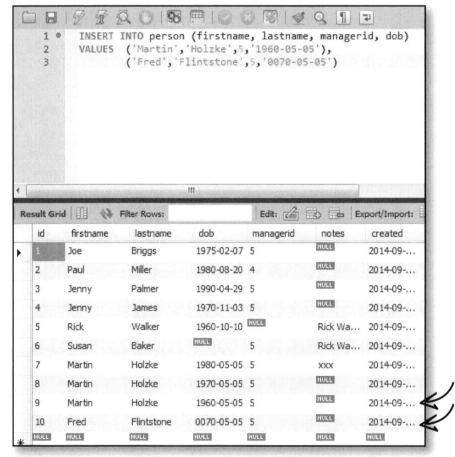

Figure 9-4: Multiple records can be added using a single INSERT statement.

So far we have been inserting records using input values but an INSERT statement can create records in a table using the results of a SELECT statement. The following code demonstrates this:

```
INSERT INTO person (firstname, lastname,
managerid, dob)
SELECT concat('copy of
',firstname),lastname,managerid,dob
FROM person
WHERE id>=9;
```

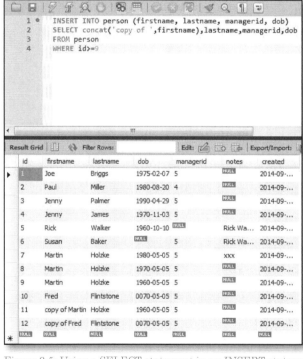

This INSERT statement is using the results of a SELECT statement to populate new records. Note that we use **concat()** with the string 'copy of' to confirm that we have created copies of existing table data. Figure 9-5 shows the expected results.

Figure 9-5: Using a SELECT statement in an INSERT statement we have copied multiple records from *person*.

As long as the result of the SELECT statement matches the data types that the table expects from an INSERT statement, you can use any possible SELECT statement to generate the values you intend to add.

In our examples we have used INSERT to create records in *person*, a table that does not have any foreign keys. When using INSERT it's important to remember any of those foreign key dependencies that may exist. For example, a *person* cannot be inserted into a *project* through *projectperson* if that *project* does not exist. Similarly, a *project* cannot have a *person* assigned to it if that *person* does not exist.

 QUESTIONS FOR REVIEW

1. When using an INSERT statement, which of the following fields is required?
   a. The primary key.
   b. Any field with a DEFAULT flag set.
   c. Any field with a NOT_NULL flag set.
   d. Every field is required.

2. The INSERT statement allows you to insert a new record at any point in the database.
   a. True.
   b. False.

3. INSERT statements must be explicit.
   a. True.
   b. False.

4. What is the correct syntax for INSERT?
   a. INSERT (field) INTO table VALUES (value)
   b. INSERT INTO table VALUES (field) (value)
   c. INSERT (value) INTO (field) table
   d. INSERT INTO table (field) VALUES (value)

LAB ACTIVITY

1. Create a new record for "Barney Rubble" in *person*.

2. Create a new means of contact into *contacttype* called "Dinosaur Mail."

3. Create records in *contact* that link "Fred Flintstone" and "Barney Rubble" from *person* with "Dinosaur Mail" from *contact* using the values "123 Rock Street" and "456 Rock Street."

LAB SOLUTION

1.
```
INSERT INTO person (firstname,lastname)
VALUES ('Barney','Rubble')
```

2.
```
INSERT INTO contacttype (label)
VALUES ('Dinosaur Mail')
```

3.
```
INSERT INTO contact (pid,ctid,value)
VALUES
    (10,5,'123 Rock Street'),
    (14,5,'456 Rock Street')
```

Ensure that you verify the *id* value for Fred and Barney before you add them to *contact*.

9.2 THE UPDATE STATEMENT

The second DML tool we are going to learn about is the **UPDATE** statement. The UPDATE statement modifies existing records in a table without creating new records.

UPDATE

As with the INSERT statement, when using UPDATE you need to be aware of any table constraints. Data types need to be respected and fields that cannot be NULL must not be modified to a NULL value. We must also keep in mind relational constraints between tables.

Depending on how the UPDATE statement is constructed, an UPDATE will affect a set of records rather than an individual record. To demonstrate the syntax of the UPDATE statement we will work on the *person* table.

Display the current contents of *person* before we begin. Figure 9-6 shows what your *person* table should look like:

id	firstname	lastname	dob	managerid	notes	created
1	Joe	Briggs	1975-...	5	NULL	2014-09-...
2	Paul	Miller	1980-...	4	NULL	2014-09-...
3	Jenny	Palmer	1990-...	5	NULL	2014-09-...
4	Jenny	James	1970-...	5	NULL	2014-09-...
5	Rick	Walker	1960-...	NULL	Rick Wa...	2014-09-...
6	Susan	Baker	NULL	5	Rick Wa...	2014-09-...
7	Martin	Holzke	1980-...	5	xxx	2014-09-...
8	Martin	Holzke	1970-...	5	NULL	2014-09-...
9	Martin	Holzke	1960-...	5	NULL	2014-09-...
10	Fred	Flintstone	0070-...	5	NULL	2014-09-...
11	copy of Martin	Holzke	1960-...	5	NULL	2014-09-...
12	copy of Fred	Flintstone	0070-...	5	NULL	2014-09-...
14	Barney	Rubble	NULL	NULL	NULL	2014-09-...
*	NULL	NULL	NULL	NULL	NULL	NULL

Figure 9-6: The current *person* table. Yours may be different if you practiced more with INSERT.

We will change the date of birth of the first instance of "Martin Holzke" to January 01, 1990. Enter the following code, but do not run it:

```
UPDATE person
SET dob='1990-01-01';
```

This code example demonstrates how easy it is to cause problems for yourself with UPDATE. As written, that example will update the value of *dob* in every record in *person*. This is not what we want. As a general rule, the shorter your UPDATE statement is, the more records you are going to affect.

In order to specify exactly what we want to update, we will use a WHERE clause. Before we do an UPDATE we should validate the WHERE clause that we intend to use. To validate the WHERE clause we will build a SELECT statement to find the records we want to modify and then use that SELECT statement to create our UPDATE statement's WHERE clause.

We have said that we want to modify the first instance of "Martin Holzke." Looking at our *person* table from figure 9-6 we can see that the *id* of the record we want to modify is 7. The primary key is the simplest way to specify a record to modify. Enter and run the following code to verify that you have the correct record:

```
SELECT * FROM person
WHERE id=7;
```

Figure 9-7: This SELECT statement validates the WHERE clause we will use for our UPDATE statement.

The SELECT statement returns the correct record so we can safely use its WHERE clause in our UPDATE. Modify the UPDATE statement from the prior code example to match the following:

```
UPDATE person
SET dob='1990-01-01'
WHERE id=7;
```

Once you've run the UPDATE statement, display the record again in order to verify that the date of birth updated correctly. Figure 9-8 shows the updated record.

Figure 9-8: Using an UPDATE statement with a specific WHERE clause, the record is appropriately modified.

Multiple fields can be updated in a single UPDATE statement. Modify the example code so that it matches the following, and run it:

```
UPDATE person
SET dob='1990-01-01', firstname='Mike'
WHERE id=7;
```

The SET clause of the UPDATE statement has a comma-separated list of fields to update. Figure 9-9 displays the resulting record after the UPDATE.

SET

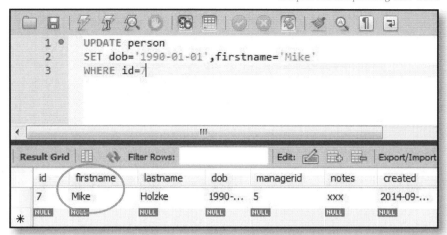

Figure 9-9: UPDATE can modify multiple fields in a single statement.

As we discussed above, UPDATE will modify every record in a table if a WHERE clause is not provided. If the WHERE clause results in multiple records, UPDATE will modify all of them. We will demonstrate this by modifying every record from *person* with the first name of "Martin" and change that name to "Mike."

The first step when using UPDATE is always to create a SELECT statement with a WHERE clause that correctly returns the records to be updated. For our example, use the following code:

```
SELECT * FROM person
WHERE firstname='Martin';
```

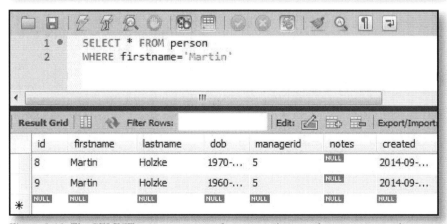

Figure 9-10: The SELECT statement correctly returns the records we want to update.

The SELECT statement returns two records that we want to update. Once we verify that they are correct we can use the WHERE clause in our UPDATE.

```
UPDATE person
SET firstname='Mike'
WHERE firstname='Martin';
```

Use a SELECT statement to display all of the records with a first name of "Mike." Figure 9-11 displays the result.

> **Tip:** You may see an error in MySQL Workbench when attempting an UPDATE using *firstname* in your WHERE clause. This is due to a safety setting implemented to keep you from accidentally modifying large swaths of your database. Turn this feature off by going to Edit->Preferences and selecting the "SQL Queries" tab. Uncheck the box for "Safe Updates."

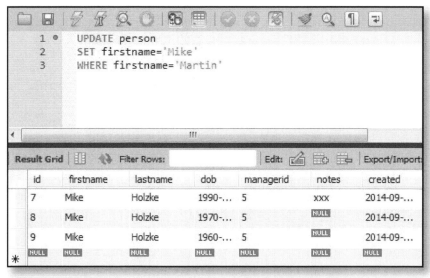

Figure 9-11: UPDATE has changed every instance of "Martin" to "Mike."

UPDATE can also be used to create calculated values. To demonstrate this we will use the *project* table instead of *person*. Currently, *project* should match figure 9-12.

	id	label	budget
▶	1	Website	2000
	2	Facebook App	999.95
	3	Google+	250
✳	NULL	NULL	NULL

Figure 9-12: The current records and values of *project*

We are going to assume that a windfall has allowed us to increase the budgets of all of our projects by 20%. We do not need a WHERE clause because we are updating every record in the table. Enter and run the following script:

```
UPDATE project
SET budget=budget*1.2;
```

The modified value of *budget* is set to the result of a calculation, as opposed to a specific input. Figure 9-13 shows the newly expanded project budgets.

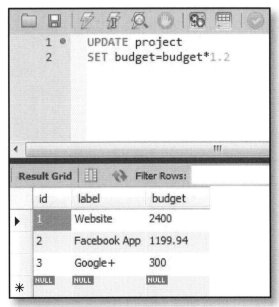

In the *project* example we modified every record in a table, but this is an unlikely scenario. The WHERE clause in an UPDATE statement is very important. The best way to ensure that you are modifying the record you intend to modify is to build your WHERE clause from the validated result of a SELECT statement.

Figure 9-13: The values of every *budget* in *project* has been increased by 20%.

1. Do we need to keep table constraints in mind when using UPDATE?
   a. Yes.
   b. No.

2. In order to safely use UPDATE, what should your first step be when building the query?
   a. Run the UPDATE without a WHERE clause.
   b. Create an UPDATE statement with a WHERE clause that looks right.
   c. Create a new test database to make sure that the UPDATE statement doesn't cause any problems.
   d. Create a SELECT statement to verify that the WHERE clause of your UPDATE affects the correct values.

3. The UPDATE statement can only be used when its WHERE clause checks for a primary key.
   a. True.
   b. False.

4. It is possible to use UPDATE to modify multiple records at once.
   a. True.
   b. False.

LAB ACTIVITY

1. Change all of the instances of "Mike" from the examples back to "Martin."

2. Unfortunately, the deal that granted the extra money for projects fell through. Return the value of *budget* for all records in *project* to their original state using UPDATE.

3. Fred and Barney have moved. Update their addresses so they both live at 1175 Broken Stone Way.

LAB SOLUTIONS

1.
```
UPDATE person
SET firstname='Martin'
WHERE firstname='Mike'
```

2.
```
UPDATE project
SET budget=budget/1.2
```

3.
```
UPDATE contact
SET value='1175 Broken Stone Way'
WHERE pid=10 OR pid=14
```

9.3 THE DELETE STATEMENT

The final DML tool that we will discuss is the **DELETE** statement. The DELETE statement completely deletes one or more records from a table. It does not delete content from an individual column. In order to delete individual column content, an UPDATE statement would have to be used.

DELETE

As with all other DML statements, it's important to remember that there is no undo capability in a DBMS. Once a DELETE occurs, it is permanent.

When using the DELETE statement you cannot violate table or relationship constraints. If an employee is assigned to a project, then that employee's record cannot be removed from *person* until the relationship constraint is first resolved.

Like UPDATE, the DELETE statement without a WHERE clause will affect every record in a table. The following code will show you the basic DELETE syntax. Do not run the following code!

```
DELETE FROM person;
```

DON'T RUN THIS CODE!

The example code would remove every record from *person*. We do not want to do that, so we will use a WHERE clause. SELECT all from *person* so that we can choose which record we want to delete.

id	firstname	lastname	dob	managerid	notes	created
1	Joe	Briggs	1975-...	5	NULL	2014-09-...
2	Paul	Miller	1980-...	4	NULL	2014-09-...
3	Jenny	Palmer	1990-...	5	NULL	2014-09-...
4	Jenny	James	1970-...	5	NULL	2014-09-...
5	Rick	Walker	1960-...	NULL	Rick Wa...	2014-09-...
6	Susan	Baker	NULL	5	Rick Wa...	2014-09-...
7	Martin	Holzke	1990-...	5	xxx	2014-09-...
8	Martin	Holzke	1970-...	5	NULL	2014-09-...
9	Martin	Holzke	1960-...	5	NULL	2014-09-...
10	Fred	Flintstone	0070-...	5	NULL	2014-09-...
11	copy of Martin	Holzke	1960-...	5	NULL	2014-09-...
12	copy of Fred	Flintstone	0070-...	5	NULL	2014-09-...
14	Barney	Rubble	NULL	NULL	NULL	2014-09-...
*	NULL	NULL	NULL	NULL	NULL	NULL	NULL

Figure 9-14: The contents of *person*.

We will delete the third instance of "Martin Holzke." As with UPDATE, we will use a SELECT statement to create a WHERE clause that only returns the record we are concerned with. In this case we can use the primary key *id* as follows:

```
SELECT * FROM person
WHERE id=9;
```

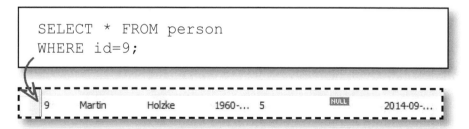

This correctly returns a single record that we want to delete, so we can safely use the WHERE clause in our DELETE statement.

```
DELETE FROM person
WHERE id=9;
```

Once that query is complete, *person* should match figure 9-15.

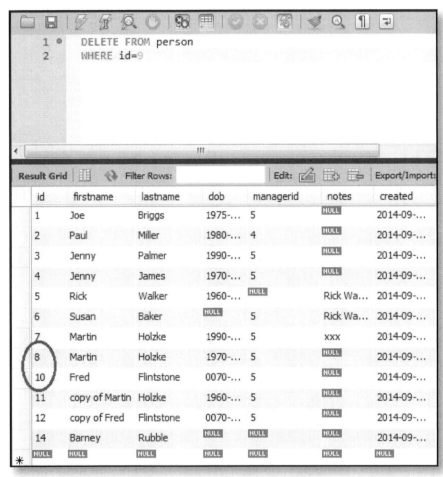

Figure 9-15: The record with *id* 9 has been removed with DELETE.

We will now use DELETE to remove multiple records from *person*. We do not need the two copied records, so we will remove both of them with a single DELETE statement. First, verify the WHERE clause using a SELECT statement.

```
SELECT * FROM person
WHERE firstname LIKE('copy%');
```

| 11 | copy of Martin | Holzke | 1960-... | 5 | NULL | 2014-09-... |
| 12 | copy of Fred | Flintstone | 0070-... | 5 | NULL | 2014-09-... |

Here we have used **like()** to find only those records that begin with the word "copy." The result is the two records that we intend to delete, so use this WHERE clause in our DELETE statement.

```
DELETE FROM person
WHERE firstname LIKE('copy%');
```

Once that query is run and *person* is displayed, the results should match figure 9-16.

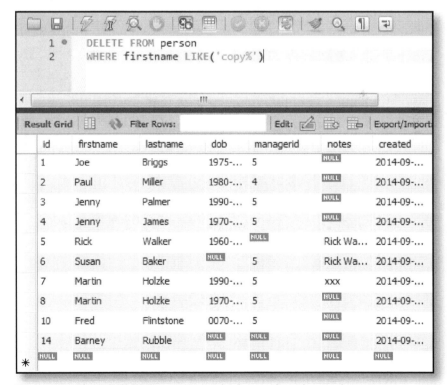

Figure 9-16: Using DELETE to remove multiple records with a single statement.

The WHERE clause in the DELETE statement can be built like any other WHERE clause in an UPDATE or SELECT statement; however, DELETE cannot remove records from multiple tables. It is important to validate any WHERE clause you use with a DELETE statement to ensure that only the correct records are being removed.

 QUESTIONS FOR REVIEW

1. DELETE statements can easily be reversed with an UNDO command.
   a. True.
   b. False.

2. What is the proper method to remove a value from an individual field?
   a. You must specify the field within the record when you construct your DELETE statement.
   b. You must use INSERT to create a copy of the record that contains every field except the one you want to delete, and then use DELETE to remove the original record.
   c. You cannot remove a value from an individual field. You must remove the entire record.
   d. You cannot use DELETE for this, you must instead use UPDATE.

3. What is the proper syntax for the DELETE command?
   a. DELETE FROM table WHERE field=value
   b. DELETE field=value FROM table
   c. DELETE FROM table (field) VALUES (value)
   d. DELETE table WHERE field=value

4. It is good to verify the WHERE clause of a DELETE statement before you execute your DELETE statement.
   a. True.
   b. False.

LAB ACTIVITY

1. Fred Flintstone and Barney Rubble are not going to remain as employees, so delete them from the database. Remember to remove their reference from *contact* before you remove them from *person!*

2. It's not likely that Dinosaur Mail will be useful with Fred and Barney, so clean up *contacttype* by removing that record.

LAB SOLUTIONS

1.
```
DELETE FROM contact
WHERE pid=10 OR pid=14;
DELETE FROM person
WHERE id=10 OR id=14;
```

2.
```
DELETE FROM contacttype
WHERE id=5
```

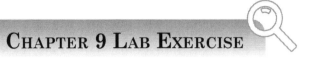

CHAPTER 9 LAB EXERCISE

1. Using a single INSERT statement, create five new employees.

2. Use a single UPDATE statement to modify all of the new employees so that their *lastname* field begins with "TEMP " followed by their actual last name.

3. Use a single DELETE statement to remove all of the temporary employees from *person*.

CHAPTER 9 LAB SOLUTION

1. First you will create an explicit INSERT statement with a comma-separated list of values for the five new employees.

```
INSERT INTO person (firstname,lastname)
VALUES
('Smith','John'),('Donalds','Rachel'),
('Rozanski','Carol'),('Fuller','Kristof'),
('McDonalds','Esther')
```

2. Next, use **concat()**, UPDATE, and a carefully crafted WHERE clause to modify only those records you've just added.

```
UPDATE person SET lastname=CONCAT('TEMP
',lastname)
WHERE id>=9
```

In our case, the first new employee added had the primary key *id* value of 9. Depending on the state of your database, the primary key *id* in *person* may be a different value. Ensure that you are only modifying the records you've just created and remember, you cannot "undo" in SQL.

3. Now that we know that each new employee has "TEMP " preceding their last name, we can use that to only delete temporary employees if we implement the **like()** function.

```
DELETE FROM person
WHERE lastname LIKE('TEMP%')
```

Chapter Summary

In this chapter you learned how to use the DML statements INSERT, UPDATE, and DELETE. You were shown how to craft both an implicit and explicit INSERT statement. You utilized best practices to create safe UPDATE and DELETE statements by validating WHERE clauses with a SELECT statement. Finally, you learned that SQL does not have any undo function, so you know that any change that you make to your database is permanent.

In the next chapter, you will learn about transactions in SQL. You will learn why transactions are important, how and when you can use them and you will implement transactions in MySQL using MySQL Workbench.

CHAPTER 10

TRANSACTION CONTROL

CHAPTER OBJECTIVES:

- You will learn what transactions are and why they are useful.
- You will be able to identify situations where transactions are important.
- You will learn the proper syntax to initiate a transaction.
- You will learn how to either COMMIT or ROLLBACK a transaction, as necessary.

10.1 WHAT ARE TRANSACTIONS?

Transactions in database management are blocks of statements that are executed together in order to provide reliable units of work and to isolate multiple users accessing a database concurrently.

Transactions

In a transaction, multiple statements will be run, but the changes that those statements would make to the database do not take effect until every transaction statement succeeds. In this way, transactions maintain database reliability and consistency. Transactions are most useful with INSERT, UPDATE, and DELETE statements.

To better understand transactions, consider a bank money transfer. When money is being transferred by a bank it must be removed from one account and then added to another account. With two separate UPDATE statements, there is the chance that one UPDATE will succeed and the other will fail. The bank may remove the money from the sending account but fail to add the money to the receiving account, for example.

In order to keep such an error from happening, a transaction would be used. The UPDATE statement would temporarily remove the money from the first account and then the next UPDATE statement would temporarily add the money to the second account. Only when it was verified by the DBMS that both statements succeeded would the actual changes be made. When transaction changes are made, they are said to be **committed**. If either or both of the

Committed

Rolled Back

transactions fail, then they are **rolled back**, returning the database values to their original state.

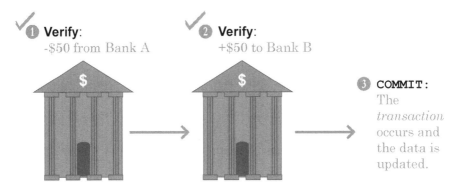

1 **Verify**:
-$50 from Bank A

2 **Verify**:
+$50 to Bank B

3 **COMMIT**:
The *transaction* occurs and the data is updated.

SQL Transaction Metaphor

Another feature of transactions is **isolation**. Isolation keeps multiple users from modifying the same data at the same time. Isolation levels vary according to database platforms, but the purpose is the same. Isolation ensures that while a transaction is occurring, other users cannot utilize the data being modified until the transaction is complete.

Isolation

Different database platforms will handle isolation differently. Certain platforms will lock blocks of records around the record being affected by the transaction, while others will lock the entire table that contains the affected record. Still other platforms will keep the entire table from being readable at all during a transaction. In those cases, any query against the table will wait until the transaction is either committed or rolled back.

You can understand that transactions that could lock up a multi-user database would need to be as succinct and efficient as possible. When creating transactions it's very important to keep statements short and efficient so that the database performance doesn't suffer.

QUESTIONS FOR REVIEW

1. What is a good reason to use transactions?
   a. To ensure database reliability and consistency.
   b. To increase database script readability.
   c. To validate WHERE clauses for UPDATE statements.
   d. There is no good reason to use transactions.

2. A transaction will only commit if every statement succeeds.
   a. True.
   b. False.

3. You cannot stop a transaction from changing values once it has been started.
   a. True.
   b. False.

4. What is a good way to mitigate performance issues in a multi-user database where transactions lock database records due to isolation levels?
   a. Don't use transactions.
   b. Keep transactions short and efficient.
   c. Purchase faster hardware.
   d. Reduce the number of active users.

LAB ACTIVITY

With what you have already learned about databases and DBMS, consider circumstances where transactions would be useful. Note three distinct situations where a transaction would be useful.

LAB SOLUTION

Transactions in databases are very useful in many situations. In fact, there is a growing consensus that unless you have an explicit reason to not use transactions, you should always use transactions. Some example situations are:
- Updating personal information for a user.
- Editing the settings on a blog site.
- Purchasing virtual items in a game.
- Managing a website's comment section.
- Updating purchase order status.

10.2 IMPLEMENTING TRANSACTIONS

In order to utilize transactions you must define when the transaction begins, create the transaction statements, and then either COMMIT or ROLLBACK the transaction. We will use two instances of MySQL Workbench to simulate multiple users and explain how transactions are implemented.

First, open a second instance of MySQL Workbench. Do this by opening your database as usual, then return to your home screen, and finally select to open your database again. This will launch a second instance of your database connection in a separate tab in MySQL Workbench. Figures 10-1 and 10-2 show you how this will look.

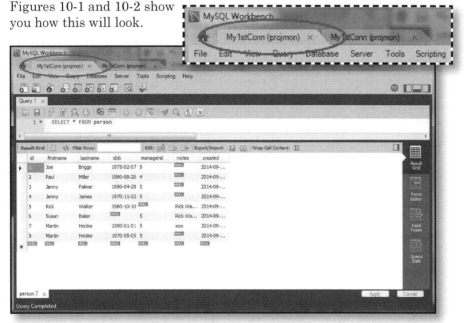

Figure 10-1: The first instance of MySQL Workbench. Note that it is the leftmost tab, circled.

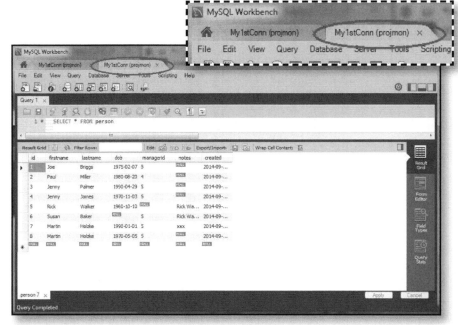

Figure 10-2: The second instance of MySQL Workbench. Note that it is the rightmost tab, circled.

Once two instances are open, display the contents of *person*. We have already done this in figures 10-1 and 10-2. The value of Susan Baker's date of birth is still NULL. We want her to have a correct date of birth, so we will modify that field using a transaction.

| 6 | Susan | Baker | NULL |

Enter the following code in the first instance of your database:

```
START TRANSACTION;

UPDATE person SET dob='1967-08-09'
WHERE id=6;

SELECT * FROM person;
```

The preceding code begins with the START TRANSACTION command. This instructs MySQL to begin a transaction. Note that because we are using multiple statements we need to terminate each statement with a semicolon.

START TRANSACTION

Once the transaction has been started we execute our UPDATE statement. From our table output we know that Susan Baker's primary key *id* is 6, so we use that in our WHERE clause.

Once this is complete, we display our table output again. Figure 10-3 shows you the expected results.

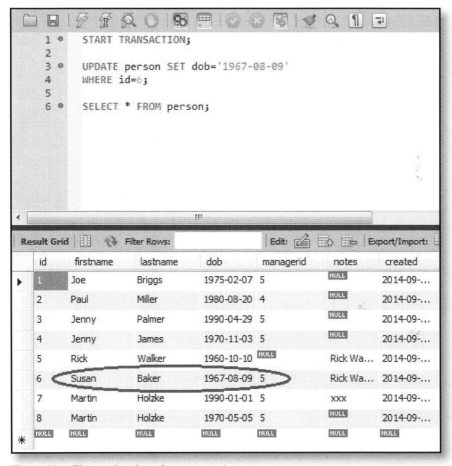

Figure 10-3: The results of our first transaction.

You'll see that Susan Baker's *dob* field has updated even though we have not committed the transaction. This is because the instance that we are working in has been isolated and is showing us the temporary results of our pending transaction. Go to your second instance and display the current *person* table data. It should match figure 10-4.

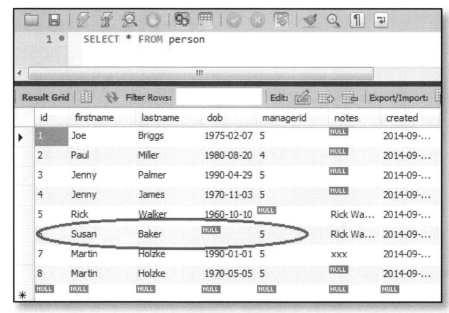

Figure 10-4: The transaction has not yet been committed.

Circled here you can see that Susan Baker's *dob* field is still NULL. The transaction has been isolated by the DBMS and so the changes will not appear to a different user until they have been committed.

Before we demonstrate COMMIT we will demonstrate ROLLBACK. ROLLBACK cancels the changes that the transaction was going to make. In your first instance, with the START TRANSACTION command, modify the code you entered earlier so that it matches the following:

```
START TRANSACTION;

UPDATE person SET dob='1967-08-09'
WHERE id=6;

ROLLBACK;

SELECT * FROM person;
```

When you execute that script you will have the results displayed in figure 10-5. ROLLBACK cancelled the pending UPDATE statement and reverted the value of Susan Baker's *dob* field to NULL.

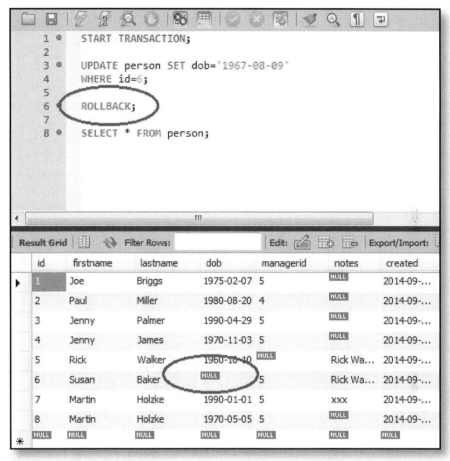

Figure 10-5: The ROLLBACK command reverted back the changes that the transaction would have made.

If you check the second instance you will see that Susan Baker's date of birth is still listed as NULL.

Now, remove the ROLLBACK command and instead enter the COMMIT command.

```
START TRANSACTION;

UPDATE person SET dob='1967-08-09'
WHERE id=6;

COMMIT;

SELECT * FROM person;
```

In the preceding code you have used the COMMIT command to permanently save the changes from your transaction to the database.

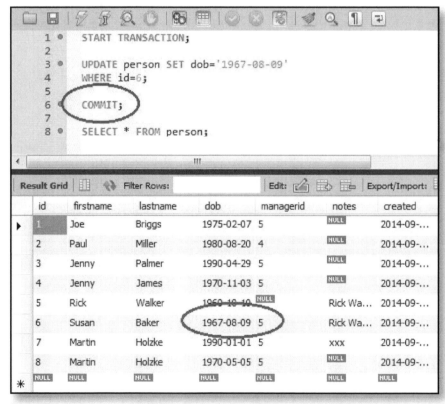

Figure 10-6: After using COMMIT, the transaction changes are permanently made.

As you can see in figure 10-6, the changes have been made to the database. Return to the second instance of your database and select all records from *person*. You will see a result as in figure 10-7 that verifies that the change has been made.

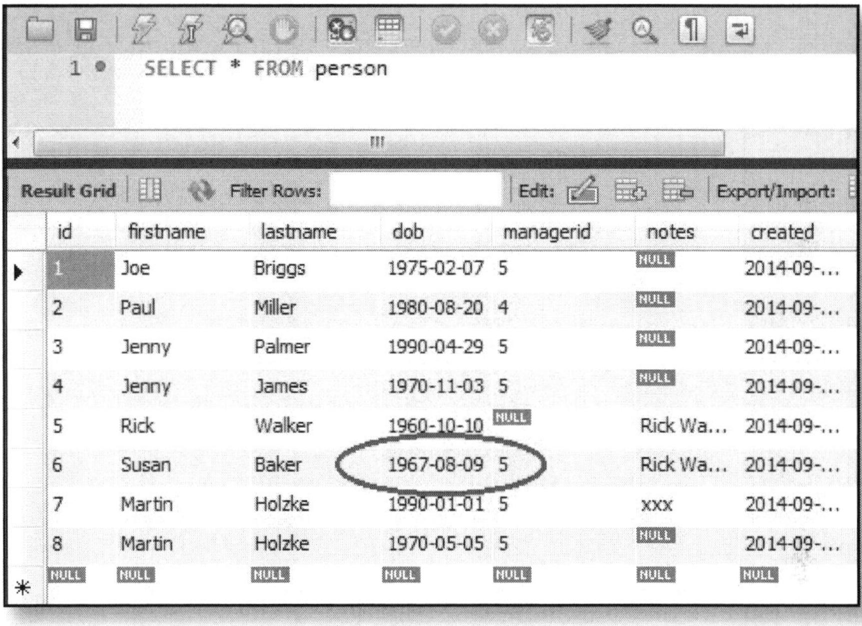
1 SELECT * FROM person
Result Grid
Filter Rows:
Edit:
Export/Import:
id firstname lastname dob managerid notes created
1 Joe Briggs 1975-02-07 5 NULL 2014-09-...
2 Paul Miller 1980-08-20 4 NULL 2014-09-...
3 Jenny Palmer 1990-04-29 5 NULL 2014-09-...
4 Jenny James 1970-11-03 5 NULL 2014-09-...
5 Rick Walker 1960-10-10 NULL Rick Wa... 2014-09-...
6 Susan Baker 1967-08-09 5 Rick Wa... 2014-09-...
7 Martin Holzke 1990-01-01 5 xxx 2014-09-...
8 Martin Holzke 1970-05-05 5 NULL 2014-09-...
NULL NULL NULL NULL NULL NULL NULL
Figure 10-7: The COMMIT from the transaction done by a different user has permanently altered the database.

Once a transaction is started it is important to remember to COMMIT the changes, otherwise they will not take effect. Using transactions carefully allows you to create a safer, more consistent, and reliable database.

1. What is the proper technique for making the transaction statement's changes permanent?
   - a. COMMIT;
   - b. COMMIT
   - c. START TRANSACTION;
   - d. COMET;

2. What is the proper technique for reversing the transaction statement's changes?
   - a. ROLL BACK;
   - b. REVERSE;
   - c. UNDO;
   - d. ROLLBACK;

3. A second user will not see any changes a transaction will make until the COMMIT command is used.
   - a. True.
   - b. False.

4. ROLLBACK can be used after a COMMIT command has executed.
   - a. True.
   - b. False.

LAB ACTIVITY

To test your knowledge of transactions, create a transaction that will change Susan Baker's email address and phone number from their original value to their value plus the string "I CAN TRANSACT!" Verify that the temporary changes are made in your first instance and that they have not been made in your second instance. Finally, rollback the changes.

LAB SOLUTION

In your first instance:

```
START TRANSACTION;
UPDATE contact SET value=CONCAT(value, ' I
CAN TRANSACT!') WHERE pid=6;

SELECT * FROM contact WHERE pid=6;
```

In your second instance:

```
SELECT * FROM contact WHERE pid=6;
```

Verify that the changes exist in the first instance, but do not exist in the second instance. Once completed, in your first instance:

```
ROLLBACK;
```

CHAPTER 10 LAB EXERCISE

In order to more fully understand how transactions work, recreate "Fred Flintstone" and "Barney Rubble" using transactions. First, create each new record in *person* individually, and then set the *note* field of both to "A modern Stone Age family." Finally, remove both of their records. Verify that your transactions are working properly by using a second database instance as a second user.

Chapter 10 Lab Solution

Your script may differ from what is presented, but ensure that you have tested transactions and isolation by using both COMMIT and ROLLBACK commands.

```
START TRANSACTION;

INSERT INTO person (lastname,firstname)
VALUES ('Fred','Flintstone');

COMMIT;

START TRANSACTION;

INSERT INTO person (lastname,firstname)
VALUES ('Barney','Rubble');

COMMIT;

START TRANSACTION;

UPDATE person SET notes='A modern stone age
family'
WHERE id=10 OR id=11;

COMMIT;

START TRANSACTION;

DELETE FROM person
WHERE id=10 OR id=11;

COMMIT;
```

CHAPTER SUMMARY

In this chapter we have learned about the value and utility of transactions. As databases grow in size and importance and DBMS become increasingly complex, using transactions allows you to maintain control and consistency in your projects. This chapter taught us the correct syntax for using transactions, including START TRANSACTION, COMMIT, and ROLLBACK.

In the next chapter we will explain table creation in MySQL in more depth, also taking a look at more advanced database features, specifically as they are implemented in MySQL. These features include stored procedures, views, and triggers.

CHAPTER 11

CREATING DATABASE OBJECTS AND ADDING BUSINESS LOGIC

CHAPTER OBJECTIVES:

- You will learn how to create tables and table constraints.
- You will understand what a view is, why it is important, and how to implement views in your own databases.
- You will be exposed to stored procedures and learn about their impressive utility for database administration.
- You will utilize a trigger and learn when and why they are used.

11.1 CREATING TABLES

In chapter one we created the tables that we have been using throughout the book, but we didn't go into a tremendous amount of detail about the mechanics of the table creation process. In this section we will reexamine table creation, recreate a few of our tables using standard SQL syntax, and then recreate them again using MySQL platform-specific options.

Creating a table is done with the Data Description Language (DDL) rather than the Data Manipulation Language. DDL shares many syntactical elements with DML but serves a very different purpose. Data description creates the structure of the database and describes the relationships between elements.

The SQL standard contains commands that will work in any standards-compliant DBMS. Using only the standard commands, we will recreate our *person* table. Enter the following code:

```
CREATE TABLE myperson
(

);
```

That shell specifies a table. The **CREATE TABLE** command creates a table with the name specified, in this case *myperson*, and the information within the opening and closing parenthesis defines the table structure. Table definition ends with a semicolon.

Modify your code to resemble the following:

CREATE TABLE

```
CREATE TABLE myperson
(
id INT(11) NOT NULL,
firstname VARCHAR(255) NOT NULL,
lastname VARCHAR(255) NOT NULL,
dob DATE,
managerid INT(11),
notes TEXT,
created TIMESTAMP NOT NULL,
PRIMARY KEY (id)
);
```

You'll notice that this is somewhat simpler than what we used to create *person* in chapter one. We have created *myperson* using only standard SQL commands, but the basic structure remains the same.

Each column in our table is defined and named, starting with *id*. We have used a 32-bit integer for *id* with the INT(11) data type and we have established that it is a required value with NOT NULL.

lastname and *firstname* are both also set to NOT NULL, but they have been given the VARCHAR(255) data type. VARCHAR(255), if you remember, represents a set of characters that can be any length up to 255.

Our *dob* field expects a standard SQL date data type but can be NULL, and our *managerid* expects a 32-bit integer and can also be NULL.

notes is of the TEXT data type, which has some similarities with VARCHAR. TEXT data types will be variably sized, like VARCHAR, but can be extremely large and are good options for text entry that may be of unknown length.

Next, we require a TIMESTAMP named *created*. If you recall we assigned a default value of CURRENT_TIMESTAMP when we created *person*. Since that flag is not used here, we need to ensure that every INSERT into *myperson* sets the timestamp correctly.

Finally, we use **primary key()** to define *id* as this table's primary key. Note that we did not set *id* to AUTO_INCREMENT, so when using *myperson* you will need to ensure that *id* is managed correctly.

Once you have defined *myperson,* execute the script to create the table. You can then use SELECT to display the contents and your results should match figure 11-1.

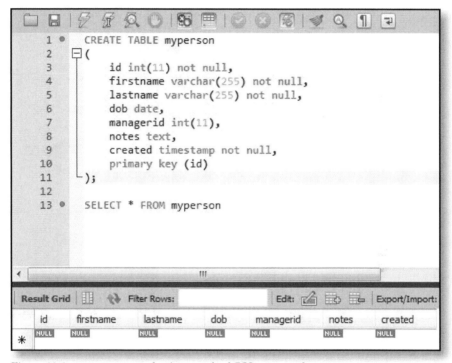

Figure 11-1: *myperson* created using standard SQL commands.

Now that we've created this table and understand how we define it using standard SQL, let's remove it from our schema. In order to remove a table from a database, you use the **DROP TABLE** command. Enter the following code, ensuring that you use the correct table name, *myperson*.

DROP TABLE

```
DROP TABLE myperson;
```

Once you execute that command, the *myperson* table you have just created will be permanently removed from the database. As with the DML tools we discussed, DROP TABLE is permanent, so use it with caution.

Now that you have removed *myperson* we will rebuild it using some MySQL-specific options to show how the platform you choose affects the utility of your database.

After you have removed *myperson*, enter the following code to create the shell of a MySQL-specific *myperson* table.

```
CREATE TABLE IF NOT EXISTS myperson
(

) ENGINE=InnoDB DEFAULT CHARSET=latin1;
```

You can see that the basic structure is the same but there are additional options. **IF NOT EXISTS** modifies CREATE TABLE, a change that instructs MySQL to only create this table if it doesn't already exist in the schema. We then have the familiar table name, *myperson*, and the parenthesis that will define our table structure. After the parenthesis, though, we have a defined **ENGINE** and a defined **DEFAULT CHARSET**. The first option selects the storage engine we want to use. We have selected InnoDB, although if you're using MySQL 5.5 or newer, InnoDB is set as the default. The second option selects the default character set that we want to use, "latin1."

IF NOT EXISTS

ENGINE

DEFAULT CHARSET

In the body of the table, define its columns with the following code:

```
CREATE TABLE IF NOT EXISTS myperson
(
id INT(11) NOT NULL AUTO_INCREMENT,
firstname VARCHAR(255) NOT NULL,
lastname VARCHAR(255) NOT NULL,
dob DATE DEFAULT NULL,
managerid INT(11) DEFAULT NULL,
```

```
notes TEXT,
created TIMESTAMP NOT NULL DEFAULT CURRENT_
TIMESTAMP,
PRIMARY KEY(id)
) ENGINE=InnoDB DEFAULT CHARSET=latin1;
```

The two table creation syntaxes are quite similar, but MySQL includes some additional options. In *id* we include AUTO_INCREMENT to allow the DBMS to manage the value of *id*. In other SQL implementations the AUTO_INCREMENT idea is represented using different techniques. For example, MSSQL uses IDENTITY.

We have added the DEFAULT clause to *dob, managerid,* and *created.* This clause is not MySQL specific. We have further set the default value for *created* to CURRENT_TIMESTAMP. CURRENT_TIMESTAMP is also a part of standard SQL.

Figure 11-2 will demonstrate what your new, more functional, version of *myperson* should look like.

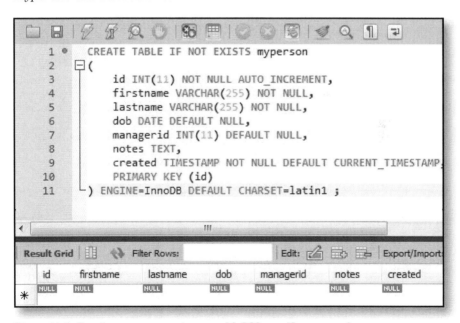

Figure 11-2: Creating *myperson* using some MySQL specific commands.

We now have a *myperson* table that basically mirrors the *person* table we have been working with, though it does not contain any data. Now, we will recreate our *contact* table as *mycontact*. Use the following MySQL specific code to create *mycontact*.

```
CREATE TABLE IF NOT EXISTS mycontact
(
    pid INT(11) NOT NULL,
    ctid INT(11) NOT NULL,
    value TEXT NOT NULL,
    PRIMARY KEY (pid, ctid),
    KEY ctid(ctid)
) ENGINE=InnoDB DEFAULT CHARSET=latin1;

ALTER TABLE mycontact
    ADD CONSTRAINT contact_ibfk_1 FOREIGN
KEY (pid) REFERENCES myperson(id),
    ADD CONSTRAINT contact_ibfk_2 FOREIGN
KEY (ctid) REFERENCES contacttype(id);
```

Everything in this table definition is familiar until the assignment of the keys. The primary key is a composite primary key. Recall from chapter one that a composite primary key is a primary key that is uses the combination of multiple columns that may not be unique to create a primary key that is unique. If a record's *pid* value is 01 and its *ctid* value is 75, the composite primary key value would be 0175. *ctid* is then set as a KEY, which is synonymous with an index in this circumstance.

The ALTER TABLE statement creates the foreign key constraints that we want *mycontact* to have. Like *contact*, *mycontact* would be linked to an employee and a type of contact.

ALTER TABLE is the command that we use when we need to modify the table's attributes. The ADD CONSTRAINT clause adds a new constraint to the table. We use a clear naming convention for each constraint that we want to add. The FOREIGN KEY syntax takes the name of the local column that we want to link our foreign key from followed by the REFERENCES key word and the foreign table and column that our foreign key will link to.

ALTER TABLE

FOREIGN KEY

ADD CONSTRAINT

REFERENCES

Now that we have our two tables—*myperson* and *mycontact*—built, lets verify them using another MySQL-specific command. Enter the following code:

```
DESCRIBE myperson;
```

The DESCRIBE command displays information about a table, as you can see in figure 11-3.

DESCRIBE

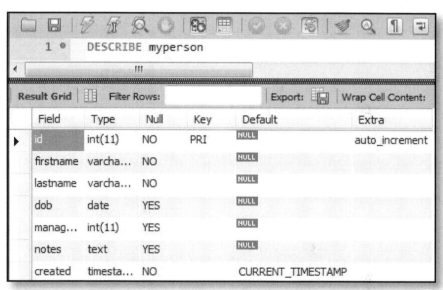

Figure 11-3: DESCRIBE shows details about a table.

Use the same technique to display information about *mycontact*.

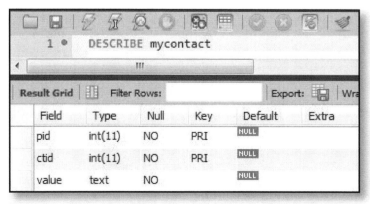

Figure 11-4: In *mycontact* both *pid* and *ctid* are primary keys.

Now that we have verified that our tables are defined as we intended, we can remove them. To demonstrate the key constraints between the two tables, first attempt to delete *myperson*. You will get the error displayed in figure 11-5.

Figure 11-5: You cannot remove *myperson* because a constraint exists.

A key from *myperson* is used as the foreign key in a table that still exists, so due to the constraint you cannot delete *myperson*. Instead, delete *mycontact* first and then delete *myperson*, as shown in figure 11-6.

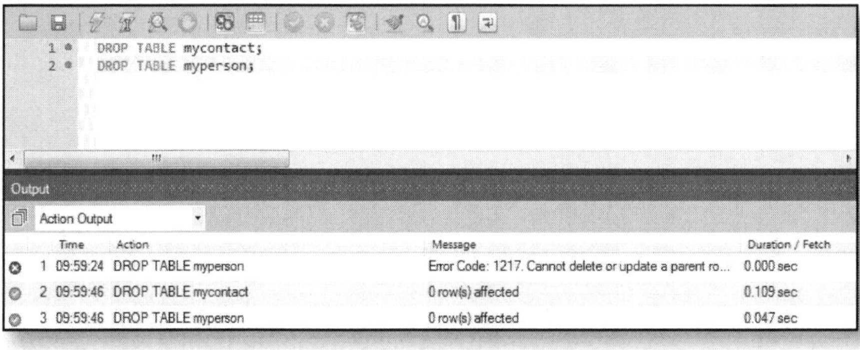

Figure 11-6: The table that uses the foreign key, *mycontact*, must be removed first.

Once you remove *mycontact* you have removed the foreign key constraint, so you can remove *myperson* without error.

Creating database schema is a large and complex topic that is beyond the scope of this book; however, the tools provided in this section will allow you to experiment with creating and linking tables.

QUESTIONS FOR REVIEW

1. What is the proper syntax for creating a table called *newtable*?
   a. CREATE newtable
   b. CREATE TABLE newtable
   c. CREATE NEW TABLE newtable
   d. CREATE newtable TABLE

2. Which of the following is the MySQL specific syntax for creating *newtable*?
   a. CREATE IF NOT EXISTS newtable
   b. CREATE newtable IF NOT EXISTS
   c. CREATE TABLE IF NOT EXISTS newtable
   d. IF NOT EXISTS CREATE TABLE newtable

3. What is the term for managing the value of a field in MSSQL?
   a. AUTO_INCREMENT
   b. IDENTITY
   c. AUTO_IDENTITY
   d. MANAGE

4. What is the keyword to delete a table?
   a. DELETE
   b. REMOVE
   c. EXTERMINATE
   d. DROP

LAB ACTIVITY

Create a table for employee's emergency contacts. The table should have fields for the emergency contact's first and last names, the value of the contact, a foreign key constraint that links to the employee they are a contact for, and a foreign key constraint that links to the type of contact it is. The primary key for this table should be a composite primary key consisting of the two foreign keys. The table should be named *emergencycontact* and it should be built for a MySQL database.

LAB SOLUTION

```sql
CREATE TABLE IF NOT EXISTS emergencycontact
(
    lastname VARCHAR(255) NOT NULL,
    firstname VARCHAR(255) NOT NULL,
    value VARCHAR(255) NOT NULL,
    pid INT(11) NOT NULL,
    ctid INT(11) NOT NULL,
    PRIMARY KEY (pid, ctid),
    KEY ctid(ctid)
) ENGINE=InnoDB DEFAULT CHARSET=latin1;

ALTER TABLE emergencycontact
    ADD CONSTRAINT emercontact_ibfk_1
FOREIGN KEY (pid) REFERENCES person(id),
    ADD CONSTRAINT emercontact_ibfk_2
FOREIGN KEY (ctid)
REFERENCES contacttype(id);
```

11.2 CREATING AND USING VIEWS

As we've been learning SQL the queries that we have been constructing have served specific purposes and have been designed towards a learning goal. In an actual production database the queries that you use will be designed to be as functional and efficient as possible. A complex SELECT statement that involves multiple table joins and that you will need to use often is not something that you will want to enter repeatedly. This is where views are needed.

Views are virtual tables that are the result of prepared queries that exist as part of your database schema. You use views as if they were tables.

Views

There are two main advantages of using views. First, the query that creates the view only needs to be developed once and it can be used as often as you like by simply referring to the view name as if it were a table. Second, and most importantly, the execution optimization of a view query is stored by the DBMS. When a normal query is run, the DBMS optimizes it at run time, every time. A view only needs to be optimized once and the optimized query is executed whenever you use the view. This can result in substantial performance gains.

A view is based on a SELECT statement, so in order to build a view you should first determine the data that you want the view to return and construct a query appropriately. There are two restrictions to keep in mind when using views. First, you cannot use ORDER BY and second, each view column needs a unique name.

To test views we will create a view that returns a table that includes every project, the project budget, every employee working on the project, and contact information for those employees. Enter and run the following code:

```
SELECT pr.label projectname, pr.budget,
p.firstname, p.lastname, ct.label
contacttype, c.value contactdetail
FROM project pr, projectperson pp, person
p, contact c, contacttype ct
```

```
WHERE pr.id = pp.prid
AND pp.pid = p.id
AND p.id = c.pid
AND c.ctid = ct.id;
```

There is nothing new in this query, but it is lengthy and it would be frustrating to type every time it needed to be run. Figure 11-7 shows the results of the query.

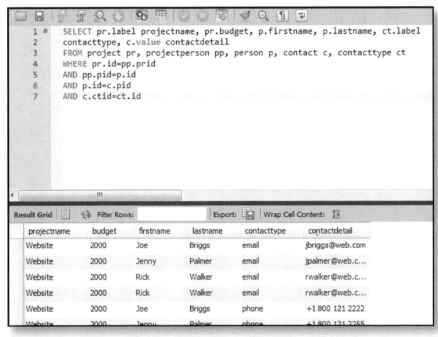

Figure 11-7: A lengthy joined query like this is an excellent candidate for a view.

Once you've verified that the query works as intended, you can use it as the basis for a view. Creating a view is simple. Above the code you've just written, enter the following:

```
CREATE VIEW projectteams AS
```

That's all you need to create a view. The AS keyword isn't required in every DBMS. Your code should look like figure 11-8.

CREATE VIEW

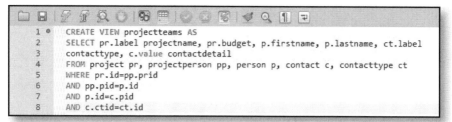

```
1 ●    CREATE VIEW projectteams AS
2      SELECT pr.label projectname, pr.budget, p.firstname, p.lastname, ct.label
3      contacttype, c.value contactdetail
4      FROM project pr, projectperson pp, person p, contact c, contacttype ct
5      WHERE pr.id=pp.prid
6      AND pp.pid=p.id
7      AND p.id=c.pid
8      AND c.ctid=ct.id
```

Figure 11-8: Creating a view from a properly structured query is easy.

Once you have created your view you can access it as though it were a table. Enter the following code to utilize your newly created view:

```
SELECT * FROM projectteams;
```

As you can see in figure 11-9, the view returns the same results as the length query from figure 11-7.

```
1 ●    SELECT * FROM projectteams
```

Result Grid | Filter Rows: | Export: | Wrap Cell Content:

projectname	budget	firstname	lastname	contacttype	contactdetail
Website	2000	Joe	Briggs	email	jbriggs@web.com
Website	2000	Jenny	Palmer	email	jpalmer@web.c...
Website	2000	Rick	Walker	email	rwalker@web.c...
Website	2000	Rick	Walker	email	rwalker@web.c...
Website	2000	Joe	Briggs	phone	+1 800 121 2222
Website	2000	Jenny	Palmer	phone	+1 800 121 2255
Website	2000	Rick	Walker	phone	+1 800 121 2200
Website	2000	Rick	Walker	phone	+1 800 121 2200
Website	2000	Rick	Walker	address	Web.com 425 ...
Website	2000	Rick	Walker	address	Web.com 425 ...
Facebook App	999.95	Paul	Miller	email	gener@yah.co.uk
Facebook App	999.95	Paul	Miller	email	gener@yah.co.uk
Facebook App	999.95	Jenny	James	email	jjames@facebo...
Facebook App	999.95	Jenny	James	email	jjames@facebo

Figure 11-9: Using a view is much more efficient for the developer and the database.

Deleting a view is done with the DROP VIEW command followed by the view's name.

DROP VIEW

Using a view is a simple way to improve database efficiency and to increase usability of your database for developers and end users.

QUESTIONS FOR REVIEW

1. What is the proper syntax to create a view named *myview*?
   a. CREATE VIEW myview
   b. CREATE myview VIEW AS
   c. CREATE VIEW myview AS
   d. CREATE myview AS

2. What is a view?
   a. A virtual table that is the result of a prepared query.
   b. The result of any query.
   c. The result of a complex JOIN.
   d. The output that is displayed in the results grid.

3. A view can be deleted with the DROP VIEW command.
   a. True.
   b. False.

4. A view, once created, can be used in much the same way as a table.
   a. True.
   b. False.

LAB ACTIVITY

Create a view to display employee's emergency contact information. It should include the first and last names of the employee, the first and last names of the employee's emergency contact, the type of contact, and the contact value.

LAB SOLUTION

```
CREATE VIEW emercontactlist AS
SELECT p.lastname "Last", p.firstname
"First", ec.lastname "EC Last", ec.firstname
"EC First", ct.label "Contact Type",
ec.value "Contact Info"
FROM person p, emergencycontact ec,
contacttype ct
WHERE p.id = ec.pid
AND p.id = ec.pid
AND ec.ctid = ct.id;
```

11.3 DEVELOPING AND CALLING STORED PROCEDURES

If you're familiar with procedural or functional programming then you'll quickly understand what stored procedures are and why they can be powerful. In their simplest form, **stored procedures** are groups of SQL statements that are stored in the database and that can be executed whenever necessary. They can be thought of as database functions.

Stored Procedures

Stored procedures are a massive topic and we won't cover them in their entirety here, but we will explain why they can be so useful and go over the syntax for creating and calling them.

First, like views, stored procedures are SQL statements that are saved as a part of the database schema and are pre-optimized. Unlike views, stored procedures can be passed arguments and return data based on processing those arguments. This makes them very powerful.

In a production environment, stored procedures allow you to minimize code repetition and increase efficiency. They also increase your control over your database by performing logical tasks in the database instead of in external application code. Users who do not have security access to modify a database can be granted access to a stored procedure that will modify the database for them, keeping the database safer. Finally, a call to a stored procedure is small, meaning that there is less network traffic when interacting with a remote database than there would be if a large group of SQL statements were sent.

To demonstrate stored procedures, we will slightly modify our view from the previous section. Enter the following code:

```
DELIMITER @@
CREATE PROCEDURE projectteam(p_projectname
text)
Begin
    SELECT p.firstname, p.lastname, ct.label
contacttype, c.value contactdetail
    FROM project pr, projectperson pp,
person p, contact c, contacttype ct
```

```
        WHERE pr.id=pp.prid
        AND pp.pid=p.id
        AND p.id=c.pid
        AND c.ctid=ct.id
        AND pr.label=p_projectname
        ORDER BY p.firstname asc;
end;
@@
DELIMITER ;
```

An important note: the instruction about stored procedures here is MySQL specific. Different DBMSs implement stored procedures in different ways. MySQL requires that stored procedures define a specific delimiter to define the body of the procedure. The default delimiter is the semicolon, but because we need to use semicolons to delimit statements within our procedure, we use the DELIMITER statement to set the global delimiter symbol to @@. Once we have finished our stored procedure we again use the defined delimiter, @@, to end the procedure and again use the DELIMITER command to set the global delimiter back to the semicolon.

DELIMITER

CREATE PROCEDURE

Within the delimiters, a stored procedure is defined by CREATE PROCEDURE and then it is given a name. The name declaration is followed by the definition of any arguments that the stored procedure might take. In our example we are using an argument named *p_projectname* that is a TEXT data type. We could include further parameters in a comma-separated list. After the declaration we create the stored procedure between **BEGIN** and **END** keywords.

BEGIN

END

The procedure itself is a set of SQL statements, all of which we have seen before. The important difference for our example is in the final AND clause. In that final AND clause we are using the argument that was passed to the stored procedure, *p_projectname*, as a condition in our output table. When called, the stored procedure will be passed a value for *p_projectname*. The AND clause is comparing it to pr.label, which we know from our time working on this database is the name of a project. The stored procedure will therefore only display records for projects whose name matches what we pass as an argument.

```
1    DELIMITER @@
2 ●  CREATE PROCEDURE projectteam (p_projectname text)
3  ┌ begin
4        SELECT p.firstname, p.lastname, ct.label contacttype, c.value contactdetail
5        FROM project pr, projectperson pp, person p, contact c, contacttype ct
6        WHERE pr.id=pp.prid
7        AND pp.pid=p.id
8        AND p.id=c.pid
9        AND c.ctid=ct.id
10       AND pr.label=p_projectname
11       ORDER BY p.firstname asc;
12 └ end;
13   @@
14   DELIMITER ;
```

Figure 11-10: The stored procedure syntax.

Once you run this code, the stored procedure will be created. In order to
call the stored procedure and execute the SQL statements that you've
created, you use the following code:

```
CALL projectteam('Facebook App')
```

To call a stored procedure in MySQL you use the CALL command
followed by the stored procedure's name and a comma-
separated list of arguments enclosed by parenthesis. The
example code has passed the TEXT value "Facebook App"
to our *projectteam* stored procedure. Execute this and
compare your result to figure 11-11.

CALL

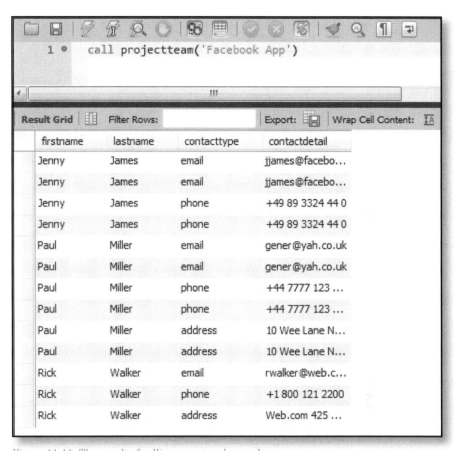

Figure 11-11: The result of calling our stored procedure.

Change the code to match the following, and then execute it:

```
CALL projectteam('Website')
```

Your output should match figure 11-12.

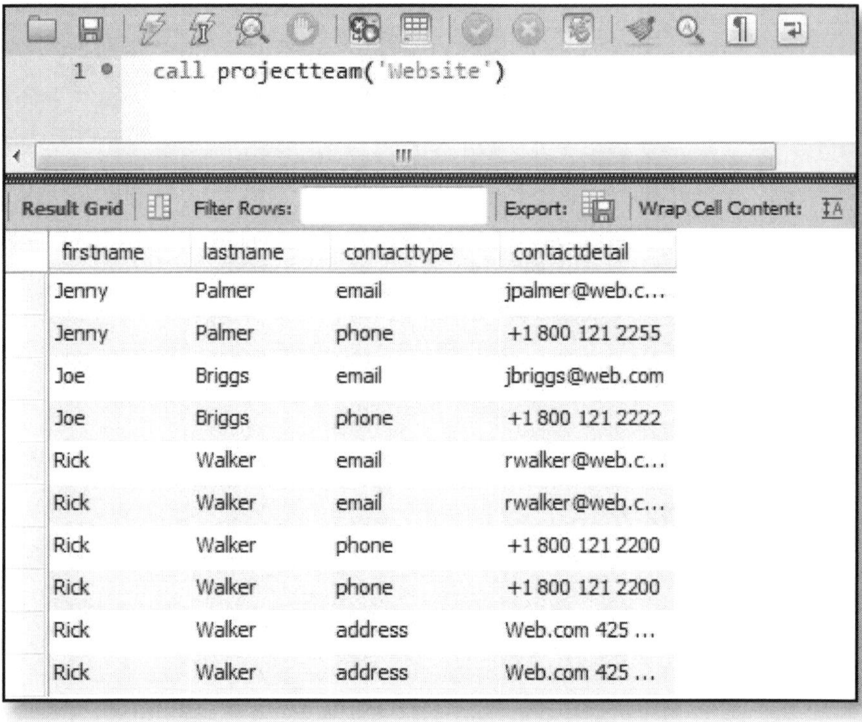
1 call projectteam('Website')
Result Grid
Filter Rows:
Export:
Wrap Cell Content:
firstname lastname contacttype contactdetail
Jenny Palmer email jpalmer@web.c...
Jenny Palmer phone +1 800 121 2255
Joe Briggs email jbriggs@web.com
Joe Briggs phone +1 800 121 2222
Rick Walker email rwalker@web.c...
Rick Walker email rwalker@web.c...
Rick Walker phone +1 800 121 2200
Rick Walker phone +1 800 121 2200
Rick Walker address Web.com 425 ...
Rick Walker address Web.com 425 ...

Figure 11-12: Using our stored procedure with a different argument.

You can see that our stored procedure returned a different table when passed a different argument.

Even with this simple example, it's possible to understand how powerful stored procedures can be. If there were hundreds of users attempting to access the employees on dozens of projects, they would each have to send many multiple lines of SQL code across the network in order to return the appropriate data. With stored procedures they would each only send one succinct line. If you did not want all of those users to be able to read from the table but you still needed them to be able to view a report about projects, then with this stored procedure they could safely retrieve the information needed.

QUESTIONS FOR REVIEW

1. What does a stored procedure allow you to do?
   a. Group SQL statements and call them with arguments as needed.
   b. Maintain database safety by limiting user access to database tables.
   c. Minimize network traffic through succinct SQL statements.
   d. All of the above.

2. A user who can access a stored procedure but who does not have permission to access the table that the stored procedure connects to will get an error when running the stored procedure.
   a. True.
   b. False.

3. The default delimiter in MySQL is the semicolon.
   a. True.
   b. False.

4. How are multiple parameters passed to the procedure *myProcedure*?
   a. myProcedure(param1, param2)
   b. myProcedure(param1 param2)
   c. myProcedure(param1; param2)
   d. myProcedure"param1, param2"

LAB ACTIVITY

Create a stored procedure that takes the last name of an employee as a parameter and returns the emergency contact information of any employees with that last name. You will use your view from the previous activity as the basis for this stored procedure.

LAB SOLUTION

```
DELIMITER @@
CREATE PROCEDURE getec(p_lastname
varchar(255))
BEGIN

SELECT p.lastname "Last", p.firstname
"First", ec.lastname "EC Last", ec.firstname
"EC First", ct.label "Contact Type",
ec.value "Contact Info"
FROM person p, emergencycontact ec,
contacttype ct
WHERE p.id = ec.pid
AND ec.ctid = ct.id
AND p.lastname = p_lastname;

END;
@@
DELIMITER ;
```

11.4 IMPLEMENTING TRIGGERS

In this chapter we will introduce triggers. Like stored procedures, a complete discussion of triggers in DBMS is beyond the scope of this book. Instead, we will introduce the idea of triggers and explain the basic syntax to utilize a trigger.

A **trigger** is a block of code that is automatically executed in response to a certain event in your database. A trigger can be executed on any kind of database activity. The idea of using triggers is to automate certain "housekeeping" activities so you can be confident that the information in your database is consistent.

Trigger

To demonstrate triggers, we will modify *person* to automatically update the value of *created* in a record any time that record is modified. Once this trigger is implemented, *created* will tell us how recently an employee's record was modified instead of just telling us when it was created.

Triggers define a delimiter similarly to stored procedures. Enter the following code into your query:

```
DELIMITER @@
CREATE TRIGGER setmodified BEFORE UPDATE ON
person
FOR EACH ROW BEGIN
    SET NEW.created=NOW();
END;
@@
DELIMITER ;
```

You create the trigger using the TRIGGER command. A trigger is a database object, so you name it and then instruct it when to operate and in what circumstance. A trigger can operate either before or after a DML command. In the example case we want our trigger to execute before an update command is performed. Finally, you define the database object you want the trigger to manipulate.

In MySQL there can only be a single trigger column in a table. This varies across other DBMS systems, so if you are not using MySQL ensure that you read the documentation for your DBMS platform.

Without going into too much detail, the body of the trigger has a FOR EACH loop that will iterate through every record that is modified by an update. In each of those records the value of *created* will be set to the current timestamp using **now()**. The NEW keyword instructs MySQL to create a new value to insert into the column. Finally, the loop code ends with the END command.

NEW

```
1      DELIMITER @@
2  •   CREATE TRIGGER setmodified BEFORE UPDATE ON person
3    ┌ FOR EACH ROW BEGIN
4    │      SET NEW.created=NOW();
5    └ END;
6      @@
7      DELIMITER ;
```

Figure 11-13: Setting up a trigger in MySQL.

Now that we have a trigger set up, we will modify a record to verify that it correctly updates the value of *created*. First, display the current records, shown in figure 11-14.

id	firstname	lastname	dob	managerid	notes	created
1	Joe	Briggs	1975-02-07	5	NULL	2014-09-17 09:01:13
2	Paul	Miller	1980-08-20	4	NULL	2014-09-17 09:01:13
3	Jenny	Palmer	1990-04-29	5	NULL	2014-09-17 09:01:13
4	Jenny	James	1970-11-03	5	NULL	2014-09-17 09:01:13
5	Rick	Walker	1960-10-10	NULL	Rick Wa...	2014-09-17 09:01:13
6	Susan	Baker	NULL	5	Rick Wa...	2014-09-17 09:01:13
7	Martin	Holzke	1990-01-01	5	xxx	2014-09-17 09:01:13
8	Martin	Holzke	1970-05-05	5	NULL	2014-09-17 09:01:13
*	NULL	NULL	NULL	NULL	NULL	NULL	NULL

Figure 11-14: The records from *person*. Note that the created dates are all the same.

The trigger is executed on a record update, so choose a record from *person* and update any of its values—except the *created* value, of course. In the example code that follows we updated the *firstname* value in the record with *id* 8.

```
UPDATE person SET firstname='Mike' WHERE
id=8;
```

You'll notice that nowhere in our UPDATE did we refer to *created*. Once you've run your update, look at the output and verify that *created* was changed for the record you updated. Figure 11-15 shows our result.

id	firstname	lastname	dob	managerid	notes	created
1	Joe	Briggs	1975-02-07	5	NULL	2014-09-17 09:01:13
2	Paul	Miller	1980-08-20	4	NULL	2014-09-17 09:01:13
3	Jenny	Palmer	1990-04-29	5	NULL	2014-09-17 09:01:13
4	Jenny	James	1970-11-03	5	NULL	2014-09-17 09:01:13
5	Rick	Walker	1960-10-10	NULL	Rick Wa...	2014-09-17 09:01:13
6	Susan	Baker	NULL	5	Rick Wa...	2014-09-17 09:01:13
7	Martin	Holzke	1990-01-01	5	xxx	2014-09-17 09:01:13
8	Mike	Holzke	1970-05-05	5	NULL	2014-09-22 10:21:29
*	NULL	NULL	NULL	NULL	NULL	NULL

Figure 11-15: The value of *created* was automatically updated due to the trigger we created.

Now we can be certain that anytime we modify any value in *person* the value of *created* will be set to the current timestamp. If we no longer want to use this trigger, we delete it using DROP TRIGGER followed by the trigger's name.

Triggers are often useful when implementing a cascading delete. As we know, the dependencies between tables ensure that we cannot delete an element that another element is dependent on, however with triggers we can have a delete command trigger the deletion of the dependent elements before the original command is executed. In this way any dependencies can be removed automatically and consistently, reducing incidences of errors and ensuring that your database does not contain junk data.

1. Multiple table columns can be trigger columns.
   a. True.
   b. False.

2. What is the proper syntax for building a trigger named *mytrigger*?
   a. CREATE TRIGGER mytrigger AFTER UPDATE ON mytable
   b. CREATE TRIGGER mytrigger
   c. CREATE mytrigger AS TRIGGER ON mytable
   d. TRIGGER mytrigger ON mytable AFTER UPDATE

3. Triggers are useful in which of the following scenarios? (Choose all that apply)
   a. Entering new data from a user-facing form.
   b. Ensuring that database "housekeeping" activities are performed.
   c. Performing a cascading delete that appropriately removes dependencies and cleanly deletes information.
   d. Creating temporary tables for later use.

4. A trigger requires a custom delimiter.
   a. True.
   b. False.

LAB ACTIVITY

Modify the emergency contact table and add a field to hold a "date modified" value. Once this is done, create a trigger that will automatically store the date that the record was modified.

LAB SOLUTION

First, create the new column in *emergencycontact*.

```
ALTER TABLE emergencycontact
ADD modified DATETIME;
```

Next, create the trigger.

```
DELIMITER @@
CREATE TRIGGER ecmodify BEFORE UPDATE ON
emergencycontact
FOR EACH ROW BEGIN
    SET NEW.modified=NOW();
END;
@@
DELIMITER ;
```

In this final exercise we are going to rebuild the emergency contact information that we have been working on so far in this chapter. First, remove the trigger, stored procedure, view, and table that you have created in previous exercises.

1. Create a new table that will hold the first and last name of the employees' emergency contacts and a link to the employee they are the emergency contact for. Include a date field to track when the information was added.

2. Create a table that duplicates the functionality of *contact*, but for emergency contacts. In general you do not want to duplicate functionality, however for the sake of the exercise we are doing so.

3. Add at least three records to the emergency contact table, ensuring that one record has a created date that is set at least one year prior to the current date.

4. Create a trigger that will automatically update the emergency contact's date field whenever a record is updated.

5. Create a view that will display an employee name, their emergency contact name, emergency contact type, emergency contact information, and emergency contact updated date.

6. Create a stored procedure that will take a date as an argument and will return a table with every emergency contact that has an updated date older then the argument date.

Chapter 11 Lab Solution

You have enough SQL knowledge now to introduce your own preferences into the lab, so use this solution as a guide to check against what you have created and not as an exact correct answer. The ultimate test is that your database functions properly and without errors.

1. First, we will create a table that will hold the emergency contact's vital information. We know that anyone who is an emergency contact must be linked to an employee, so we will create a table with a foreign key. We also know that we will need to refer to a record in this table later, so we will have a distinct primary key. We have chosen to call this table *ec_person*.

```
CREATE TABLE IF NOT EXISTS ec_person (
    id INT(11) AUTO_INCREMENT,
    lastname VARCHAR(255) NOT NULL,
    firstname VARCHAR(255) NOT NULL,
    updated DATETIME NOT NULL,
    PRIMARY KEY (id),
    KEY pid(pid)
) ENGINE=InnoDB DEFAULT CHARSET=latin1;

ALTER TABLE ec_person
    ADD CONSTRAINT ec_fk_1 FOREIGN KEY (pid)
REFERENCES person (id);
```

2. The functionality of our contact table will be identical to *contact*, so you can use that as a reference when creating *ec_contact*.

```
CREATE TABLE IF NOT EXISTS ec_contact (
    ecid INT(11) NOT NULL,
    ctid INT(11) NOT NULL,
    value TEXT NOT NULL,
    PRIMARY KEY (ecid,ctid),
    KEY ctid(ctid)
) ENGINE=InnoDB DEFAULT CHARSET=latin1;
```

```
ALTER TABLE ec_contact
   ADD CONSTRAINT ecct_fk_1 FOREIGN KEY
(ecid) REFERENCES ec_person(id),
   ADD CONSTRAINT ecct_fk_2 FOREIGN KEY
(ctid) REFERENCES contacttype(id);
```

3. When adding records, ensure that you keep the table constraints in mind. Each *ec_person* must link to a record of *person* and each *ec_contact* must link to both a record of *ec_person* and a record of *contacttype*.

```
INSERT INTO ec_person (lastname, firstname,
updated, pid) VALUES
("Briggs","Jane", now(), 1),
("Miller","Eric", "2014-01-05", 2),
("James","Brian", "2010-01-01", 4);

INSERT INTO ec_contact VALUES
(1, 1, "janebriggs@mail.com"),
(2, 2, "+1 800 123 1212"),
(3, 1, "bjames332@mail.com");
```

4. We want the trigger to update the value of *updated* in *ec_person* whenever any record in *ec_person* is updated. We want this update to occur before the trigger action occurs.

```
DELIMITER @@
CREATE TRIGGER ec_person_update BEFORE
UPDATE ON ec_person
FOR EACH ROW BEGIN
   SET NEW.updated=NOW();
END;
@@
DELIMITER ;
```

5. We want our view to output the name of the employee, the name of their emergency contact, the type of emergency contact, the value of that contact, and the date that it was last updated.

```
CREATE VIEW emergencycontact AS
SELECT
CONCAT_WS(", ",p.lastname, p.firstname)
"Employee Name",
CONCAT_WS(", ",ec.lastname, ec.firstname)
"Emergency Contact Name",
ct.label "Contact Type",
ect.value "Contact Information",
ec.updated "Last Updated"
FROM person p, ec_person ec, contacttype
ct, ec_contact ect
WHERE p.id = ec.pid
AND ect.ecid = ec.id
AND ct.id = ect.ctid;
```

6. Finally, we want to be able to test when an employee's emergency contact was last updated, so we can see if an update is required. This could be done a number of ways, but for our example we will assume that whoever is calling the stored procedure will manually input the date that they want to test against. We will use the same output format from our view, above.

```
DELIMITER @@
CREATE PROCEDURE getecinfo(ec_testdate
DATETIME)
BEGIN

SELECT * FROM emergencycontact
WHERE 'Last Updated' <= ec_testdate;
END;

@@
DELIMITER ;
```

Note that in this example we used the view that we created in step 5 within the stored procedure. In order to use the field name "Last Updated" we enclosed it in the grave symbol on the keyboard. This symbol, (`), is also known as the acute or back quote. We did not have to do this. In the select statement we could have recreated the body of *emergencycontact*.

CHAPTER SUMMARY

In this chapter you have learned how to create various database schema, including tables, views, stored procedures, and triggers. You have practiced by recreating tables that you have used throughout this book and then built upon the functionality that you have learned by creating stored procedures, views and triggers. Finally, you updated your database schema to include tables for employee emergency contact information and built some logic to support those tables.

This concludes our journey into SQL. SQL in particular and DBMSs in general are very powerful and integral parts of modern application, web, and business development. Learning how to use SQL and create effective, efficient and understandable databases is a skill that takes practice and perseverance to master, but you have completed the important first steps. Congratulations on your efforts and good luck in your future projects!

ANSWER KEY

Questions for Review: Chapter I

Section 1

1. What is the set of software tools called that lets authorized administrators and users define, manipulate, retrieve, and manage the data in a database?

     b. Database management system.

2. What are the structures used in organizing the data in a table of a relational database?

     b. Entities and relationships.

3. What are the three structural elements of an entity-relationship diagram?

     c. Entities, attributes, and relationships.

4. Which of the following is the most numerous object in a database?

     b. Tables.

Section 2

1. Why is it helpful to install WAMP before you install MySQL Workbench?

     b. WAMP contains the database server that MySQL Workbench will connect to.

2. MySQL Workbench is required to work with MySQL.

     b. False.

3. What is the purpose of the yellow lightning bolt icon in MySQL Workbench?

     a. It is the "Run Script" icon.

4. MySQL commands must be entered in uppercase.

    b. False.

Section 3

1. What is a data type of a field or column?

    d. The type of value the field or column will store.

2. What do the boxes in an entity-relationship diagram represent?

    d. Entities.

3. What is a constraint, as applied to a field of a table?

    d. The restrictions imposed on a field's values.

4. A table can only have one primary key.

    a. True.

Section 4

1. Which of the following are constraints used in database design?

    a. Primary Key Constraint

2. What concept or rule states that a foreign key's value must correspond to an existing value of a unique row in the referenced table?

    a. Referential integrity.

3. What relationship occurs when one entity is related to two or more entities?

    b. One-to-many.

4. What uniquely identifies a row in a table and distinguishes it from the other rows?

    b. Primary key.

Questions for Review: Chapter 2

Section 1:

1. Who was the DBMS vendor that came out with the first commercial DBMS?

      c. Relational Software, Inc.

2. Why do DBMS vendors persist in adding features to their implementations of SQL that do not comply with the ANSI/ISO standard?

      d. To fully exploit the unique features of their DBMS.

3. What DBMS product claimed to be a relational database system for desktops?

      d. Microsoft Access.

4. What event sparked the birth of the DBMS market?

      a. Codd's publication of his article, "A Relational Data Model..."

Section 2:

1. The three statements, MERGE, UPDATE, and DELETE, belong to what SQL component?

      a. Manipulation.

2. What is one purpose of grouping SQL statements into components?

      c. Access control.

3. The SELECT statement is sometimes bundled with the data manipulation language.

      a. True.

4. What would you use to create and modify database schema?

      a. DDL.

Section 3:

1. What type of SQL constants must be enclosed in single quotes?

    a. Strings.

2. Which of the following is an invalid numeric constant?

    d. 4,556.70

3. What format does MySQL use for its date data type?

    a. yyyy-mm-dd

4. The NULL value is equivalent to zero.

    b. False.

Questions for Review: Chapter 3

Section 1:

1. What clause in the SELECT statement lists the tables that will be the source of the query's data?

    b. FROM

2. What two terms are used to refer to the data generated by a query?

    b. Resultset, query result.

3. What two clauses in the SELECT statement are required?

    b. FROM, SELECT

4. What special character in the SELECT statement means "all?"

    d. *

Section 2:

1. How many column names can be listed in the SELECT clause of a query statement?

    d. None of the above.

2. Which of the following is correct to display *dob, firstname,* and *lastname,* in that order?

    d. SELECT dob, firstname, lastname FROM person

3. Which of the following will give compilation errors?

    c. SELECT person

4. Refer to figures 3-11 and 3-12. What are the differences between these two outputs? (Choose all that apply)

    a. There are five outputs in 3-11 and six in 3-12.
    b. The name "Jenny" is repeated twice in 3-12.
    c. The query used to produce the output in 3-11 used the DISTINCT keyword.

Section 3:

1. What function allows you to access portions of a string?

    b. substr()

2. Which of the following is not a SQL date function?

    d. round()

3. Which query cannot be executed because of a syntax error?

    c. SELECT firstname FROM person ORDER BY managerid ASC firstname DESC

4. Which of the following is not a function for text operations?

    d. round()

1. Which of the following queries will result in a compilation error?

    c. SELECT lastname last name FROM person;

2. What is the maximum number of columns that can be used in an ORDER BY clause?

    d. None of the above.

3. An alias must only be one word.

    b. False.

4. The AS keyword is optional.

    a. True.

Questions for Review: Chapter 4

Section 1:

1. In the WHERE clause of the SELECT statement, what should the keyword WHERE be followed by?

    b. An unlimited number of tests.

2. What operator uses the wildcard characters % and _?

    d. LIKE.

3. The logical operators AND and OR can be used to connect a maximum of four conditional expressions.

    b. False.

4. Which is a valid comparison operator?

    d. !=

Section 2:

1. What is the function of the predicate in the WHERE clause?

    d. It provides the search condition, which determines what records to retrieve.

2. What will "SELECT * FROM sometable" return?

    c. All of the fields and records from *sometable*.

3. What is the window or panel in MySQL Workbench called that displays status or error messages for every SQL statement that is executed?

    d. message window.

4. A conditional expression compared against a NULL value returns FALSE.

    b. False.

Section 3:

1. Which of the following is an invalid comparison operator?

    d. ==

2. The only time the OR operator returns FALSE is when the two conditional expressions it operates on are both FALSE.

    a. True.

3. Using parenthesis in a complex predicate is required.

    b. False.

4. What is the main focus of a truth table?

    b. It determines the Boolean result of a complex predicate.

Section 4:

1. What test operator would you use to determine if a 3 character code is one of a valid list of 3 character codes?

      d. IN

2. What test operator would you use to retrieve the records of a person that falls between the ages of 31 and 40?

      a. BETWEEN

3. What pattern string would retrieve names that start with an "A" and whose fifth character is "a?"

      d. A___a%

4. What pattern string would retrieve records that start with the character "A" and end with the character "z," with any number of characters in between?

      a. A%z

Section 5:

1. Why can't the equality operator (=) be used to test for NULL values?

      b. The NULL value is not a true data type.

2. Which conditional expression is valid for testing non NULL values in the field *managerid*?

      d. managerid IS NOT NULL

3. The NULL value can be considered to be the Boolean FALSE value in many cases.

      b. False

4. When an optional field does not have a value it is best practice to give that field the NULL value.

      a. True.

Questions for Review: Chapter 5

Section 2:

1. A query performs count() on a column which has 17 NULL values in a table that has 90 rows. What value will the count() function return?

    d. 83

2. A query performs the max() and min() function on an empty table. What values will be returned by the max() and min() functions, respectively?

    c. NULL and NULL

3. How will a query that performs count() on a column with NULL values treat those NULL values?

    c. They will not be included in the count() result value.

4. Using count() on a table will return the number of records in that table.

    b. True

Section 3:

1. Which of the following is not an aggregate function?

    b. round()

2. min() and max() select the smallest and largest values, respectively, in what data types?

    d. All of the above.

3. Using min() on a date will return the earliest date value of a set.

    a. True.

4. Which of the following is NOT a type of text encoding?

    c. UFO-16

1. What are the SELECT statement keywords that retain duplicates in the UNION of two queries?

d. UNION ALL

2. When should a sorting operation using the ORDER BY clause be carried out in a UNION operation?

d. After the queries have been merged.

3. A UNION operation does not require matching data types.

b. False

4. A UNION can be used to combine data from multiple tables.

a. True.

Questions for Review: Chapter 6

Section 1:

1. Which clause of the SELECT statement allows us to sort and retrieve data by groups?

d. GROUP BY clause

2. Which of the following aggregation functions can be used as a grouping column of the GROUP BY clause?

d. None of the above.

3. How does the GROUP BY clause differ from the DISTINCT keyword?

c. GROUP BY creates a group of records according to a grouping column, DISTINCT removes duplicate values.

4. Queries can be grouped according to more than one grouping column.

a. True.

Section 2:

1. Which pair of SELECT statement clauses accepts conditional expressions?

   a. WHERE, HAVING

2. Which SELECT statement clause applies conditional expressions to individual records?

   a. WHERE

3. Which SELECT statement clause applies conditional expressions to grouped records?

   b. HAVING

4. A HAVING clause in a statement with no GROUP BY clause will produce an error.

   b. False.

Questions for Review: Chapter 7

Section 1:

1. What do you call the process of linking two tables together on the basis of matching the value of a field in one table to the value of a field in the other table?

   d. Joining

2. What SQL tool or mechanism allows us to substitute a shorter label to replace a table's name in a query?

   b. Aliases.

3. What do you call a join that is based on an exact match between two columns?

   d. Equi-join.

4. What happens when three tables are joined in a single query?

a. The first two tables are joined into a set and the third table is joined to that set.

Section 2:

1. In which type of join is the query result unaffected by the listing order of the tables?

b. INNER

2. Why would you use a LEFT or RIGHT JOIN in a query that accesses two tables?

d. To find records in one table with no matching records in the other table.

3. A table with 20 records is linked by a LEFT JOIN with a table with 12 records. How many records will appear in the query result?

d. 20.

4. The functionality of a RIGHT JOIN can be replicated by using a LEFT JOIN and modifying the order of the joined tables.

a. True.

Section 3:

1. In a query, what type of join do you use to link a table to itself?

b. SELF JOIN

2. What SQL tool or mechanism lets SQL think that a self join on one table is a join between two tables?

c. Correlation name.

3. When joining a table to itself, you are restricted to using an INNER JOIN.

b. False.

4. Self joins can be done using the WHERE clause instead of a JOIN clause.

    a. True

Questions for Review: Chapter 8

Section 1:

1. What is a subquery?

    c. A second query that is built into the main query.

2. A subquery has to be a valid query in its own right.

    a. True.

3. What does the IN clause allow a user to check against?

    b. A range of values.

4. The WHERE clause expects a certain data type.

    a. True.

Section 2:

1. What is returned by the statement in a false EXISTS clause?

    c. A table that does not contain any rows.

2. An EXISTS clause can be modified with NOT.

    a. True.

3. What is the proper syntax for the EXISTS clause?

    c. SELECT * FROM persons WHERE EXISTS (subquery)

4. Each record from the SELECT statement's table is tested against the WHERE clause.

    a. True.

Section 3:

1. Joins are always more efficient than subqueries.

    b. False.

2. DBMS optimizations are always correct.

    b. False.

3. What is a difference between using a join and using a subquery?

    a. Joins will return all of the fields from multiple tables.

4. What is a good method of preparing your queries?

    d. Determine what works correctly and what you logically understand and optimize later as necessary.

Section 4:

1. A derived table is a permanent new table in your database.

    b. False.

2. You can use a subquery interchangeably with a derived table.

    b. False

3. What is the proper syntax to create a derived table?

    b. SELECT * FROM (derived table) tablename

4. A derived table requires a name.

    a. True.

Questions for Review: Chapter 9

Section 1:

1. When using an INSERT statement, which of the following fields is required?

      c. Any field with a NOT_NULL flag set.

2. The INSERT statement allows you to insert a new record at any point in the database.

      b. False.

3. INSERT statements must be explicit.

      b. False.

4. What is the correct syntax for INSERT?

      d. INSERT INTO table (field) VALUES (value)

Section 2:

1. Do we need to keep table constraints in mind when using UPDATE?

      a. Yes.

2. In order to safely use UPDATE, what should be your first step when building the query?

      d. Create a SELECT statement to verify that the WHERE clause of your UPDATE affects the correct values.

3. The UPDATE statement can only be used when its WHERE clause checks for a primary key.

      b. False.

4. It is possible to use UPDATE to modify multiple records at once.

      a. True.

Section 3:

1. DELETE statements can easily be reversed with an UNDO command.

    b. False.

2. What is the proper method to remove a value from an individual field?

    d. You cannot use DELETE for this, you must instead use UPDATE.

3. What is the proper syntax for the DELETE command?

    a. DELETE FROM table WHERE field=value

4. It is good to verify the WHERE clause of a DELETE statement before you execute your DELETE statement.

    a. True.

Questions for Review: Chapter 10

Section 1:

1. What is a good reason to use transactions?

    a. To ensure database reliability and consistency.

2. A transaction will only commit if every statement succeeds.

    a. True.

3. You cannot stop a transaction from changing values once it has been started.

    b. False.

4. What is a good way to mitigate performance issues in a multi-user database where transactions lock database records due to isolation levels?

    b. Keep transactions short and efficient.

Section 2:

1. What is the proper technique for making the transaction statement's changes permanent?

    a. COMMIT;

2. What is the proper technique for reversing the transaction statement's changes?

    d. ROLLBACK;

3. A second user will not see any changes a transaction will make until the COMMIT command is used.

    a. True.

4. ROLLBACK can be used after a COMMIT command has executed.

    b. False.

Questions for Review: Chapter 11

Section 1:

1. What is the proper syntax for creating a table called *newtable*?

    b. CREATE TABLE *newtable*

2. Which of the following is the MySQL specific syntax for creating *newtable*?

    c. CREATE TABLE IF NOT EXISTS newtable

3. What is the term for managing the value of a field in MSSQL?

    b. IDENTITY.

4. What is the keyword to delete a table?

    d. DROP.

Section 2:

1. What is the proper syntax to create a view named *myview*?

  c. CREATE VIEW myview AS

2. What is a view?

  a. A virtual table that is the result of a prepared query.

3. A view can be deleted with the DROP VIEW command.

  a. True.

4. A view, once created, can be used in much the same way as a table.

  a. True.

Section 3:

1. What does a stored procedure allow you to do?

  d. All of the above.

2. A user who can access a stored procedure but who does not have permission to access the table that the stored procedure connects to will get an error when running the stored procedure.

  b. False.

3. The default delimiter in MySQL is the semicolon.

  a. True.

4. How are multiple parameters passed to the procedure *myProcedure*?

  a. myProcedure(param1, param2)

Section 4:

1. Multiple table columns can be trigger columns.

  b. False.

2. What is the proper syntax for building a trigger named *mytrigger*?

    a. CREATE TRIGGER mytrigger AFTER UPDATE ON mytable

3. Triggers are useful in which of the following scenarios? (Choose all that apply.)

    b. Ensuring that database "housekeeping" activities are performed.
    c. Performing a cascading delete that appropriately removes dependencies and cleanly deletes information.

4. A trigger requires a custom delimiter.

    a. True.

SQL Database for Beginners

Appendix

Terms	Definitions and Descriptions
Aggregate function	A SQL function (for example, **avg()** and **sum()**) that computes values based on the data stored in one or more columns.
Attribute	In a relational database, a column in a relation.
Column	A set of data values of a particular type, one for each row.
Commit (a transaction)	Enact a transaction, making any changes. A committed transaction is never rolled back.
Composite foreign key	A foreign key composed of two or more fields that references a concatenated primary key.
Composite primary key	A primary key made up of the combination of two or more fields.
Concatenation	Combining two or more strings by placing one at the end of the other.
Constraint	In related tables, a rule that stored data must adhere to.
Database	A structure to store data in tables along with information about the relationships between the tables.
Database Management System, DBMS	Software which allows users to manipulate a database that isolates the user from the complexities of the inner workings of the database.
Entity	Something about which we store data in a database environment, such as a customer, an employee, an invoice, and so on.
Entity-relationship diagram (ERD)	A graphic method for depicting the relationships in a database environment.
Equi-join	A join that combines two tables based on matching (equivalent) data in rows in the two tables.
Field	A data structure for a single piece of data in a record.

Terms	Definitions and Descriptions
Foreign key	A key from another table that refers to a specific key, usually the primary key, in the table being used.
Function	A code block that performs a specific task and returns a value.
Hierarchy	A structure for data relationships where all relationships are one-to-many and no child entity may have more than one parent entity.
Indexes	Special tables that the database search engine can use to speed up data retrieval.
Inner join	A join that only joins records that are matched in both joined tables.
Join	An operation that combines two tables into an output table, combining the result set of both input tables.
NULL	A value distinct from zero, 0, or blank, that means "unknown," "not available at this time," or "not applicable."
Outer join	A join that preserves all rows from both joined tables.
Precedence	The order or sequence in which operators are evaluated in a predicate when multiple operators are present.
Precision	In a floating-point number, the number of digits to the right of the decimal point.
Predicate	A logical expression used to determine the rows that are affected by a data manipulation request.
Primary key	One or more columns whose values uniquely identify a row in a table.
Recursive query	A query that queries itself.
Referential integrity	A constraint on a relation that states that every non-NULL foreign key value must reference an existing primary key value.

Terms	Definitions and Descriptions
Relation	A two-dimensional database structure consisting of rows and columns.
Row	A single, structured data item from a table. Also called a record or tuple.
Rollback (a transaction)	Cancel a transaction, restoring the database to the state it was in before the transaction began.
Schema	The overall logical design of a database. A group of tables and supporting elements such as views and indexes.
Stored procedure	A subroutine available to applications that access a DBMS and stored in the database schema.
Subquery	A complete select statement that is part of another select statement.
Substring	A portion of a string.
Table	A collection of related data held in a structured format. Consists of column and rows.
Transaction	A unit of work assigned to a database that must be either committed or rolled back.
Trigger	Procedural code that automatically executes in response to certain events.
Tuple	An ordered list of elements.
Union	An operation that combines two tables by merging their rows into the same structure.
View	A stored SQL query from which a virtual table is created for use each time the view is invoked or executed.
Virtual table	A table that exists only in volatile memory. It may be created by the end user as a temporary table, or by a DBMS to hold the results of a query.

The Development Club

https://learntoprogram.tv/course/ultimate-monthly-bundle/?coupon=BOOK19

This comprehensive membership includes:

• Access to EVERY course in LearnToProgram's growing library--including our exciting lineup of new courses planned for the coming year. This alone is over a $3,000 value.

• Access to our Live Courses. Take any of our online instructor-led courses which normally cost up to $300. These courses will help you advance your professional skills and learn important techniques in web, mobile, and game development.

• Free certification exams. As you complete your courses, earn LearnToProgram's certifications by passing optional exams. All certification fees are waived for club members.

• Weekly instructor hangouts where you can ask questions about course material, your personal learning goals, or just chat!

• Free Personal Learning Plans. You'll never wonder what you should take next to achieve your goals!

• The LearnToProgram guarantee!

Our Guarantee:

THE LEARNTOPROGRAM GUARANTEE

If you watch the course videos and complete the lab exercises, **you will learn to program.** Guaranteed. If you don't, we will personally pay your membership fees for the next 90 days.

The Development Club

Use Coupon Code: **BOOK19**
and get $20 off your first month!

More Information at
https://LearnToProgram.tv